ALL POLITICS
IS LOCO

ALL POLITICS
IS LOCO

─────────────★─────────────

Musings from the Conservative
Next Door

TONY CORVO

iUniverse, Inc.

New York   Bloomington

ALL POLITICS IS LOCO
Musings from the Conservative Next Door

iUniverse books may be ordered through booksellers or by contacting:

iUniverse
1663 Liberty Drive
Bloomington, IN 47403
www.iuniverse.com
1-800-Authors (1-800-288-4677)

ISBN: 978-0-595-42651-5 (pbk)
ISBN: 978-0-595-68215-7 (cloth)
ISBN: 978-0-595-86979-4 (ebk)

Printed in the United States of America

To my wife Donna, a woman far better than I deserve,
and our daughters Julie and Sarah.
Though adults you may now be; our little girls you will always be.

Papà, la luna che splende sull' l'Italia
è la stessa luna che splende sugli Stati Uniti

Contents

Preface

As long as I can remember I have always been a political junkie at the national level, but being in the Air Force for most of my professional career prevented me from staying in one place long enough to care about local politics. However, in 1998 I retired from the Air Force and finally was able to settle down in one city long enough to consider it my new hometown. But having the opportunity to get involved is not the same as getting involved, so aside from judging a couple of my kids' science fairs and appearing in some school career days, I just continued to pay taxes and gripe.

Two factors motivated me to write this book. First, my involvement and subsequent observations in fighting inefficient or questionable local governmental initiatives, mostly through a political action committee that I and three others put together and operated from the spring of 2003 through the spring of 2007. What I learned from this effort is that as a country we're basically screwed from the top down or bottom up—take your pick. Smart people know this instinctively; some of us slower learners have to learn it the hard way.

The second motivating factor is that I love America, or at least what it could have been. Notice that I didn't say "at least how it used to be." America has always been a great country, but it had its faults, and these faults needed to be corrected. But whatever faults America had, they were not exclusive to America. However, the characteristics that made America great were unique to America; so unique that millions of past immigrants sought this country over others, including their own, and today's immigrants are continuing the tradition and the honor. Unfortunately, there are many, both foreign and domestic, that see America as fundamentally flawed or even fundamentally evil, and want to see a weakened or even a shattered America. Will they succeed? It looks grim, but I can't just let my country go down without a fight, or since the pen, or keyboard as the case may be, is mightier than the sword, I won't let it go down at least without a word or two.

Let there be no doubt that my political leanings are Conservative. If you think examples of Conservatives are Rev. Jerry Falwell, Senator Olympia Snowe (R-Maine), or even President George Bush (either one) then you are either a liberal or confused. If you're liberal, put down this book immediately! Your help is needed to stop George Bush and Dick Cheney from purposely leaving their Halliburton donated SUVs—with genuine cow hide leather—idling to increase global warming that will create more Category V hurricanes to slam into predominately Black cities to divert attention from Iraq. If you are just confused then please read on, hopefully you might benefit from reading this book, but if nothing else, you might nevertheless be entertained.

Although I cite references when I felt they were absolutely required to support some of my stronger statements and arguments, my story is meant to be informative and entertaining rather than a heady documentary. After all, in the age of the internet and near instant access to information, it is no longer a chore for one to further investigate topics of interest. It's not like you have to shower, shave (in any applicable area), put on clean clothes, make yourself presentable, drive down to the library, and use the Dewey Decimal System. All you need to do is stroll over to your computer, cup of coffee in hand, and make a few clicks.

Most of data I do use are readily available to the general public, including applicable government websites and records from local or national news sources. Unless otherwise specified, when I do use numerical examples I use rough figures so we won't get bogged down in number minutia. And I would like to apologize up front for making one of the greatest mistakes an author of general reading material can make: I have one equation in the book. But, it's really not too bad; only requiring a little multiplication and division on your part, and besides I do give you the option of skipping it all together.

In regards to website data; keep in mind that websites can be notoriously fluid and a return trip to a site may find changes from one day to the next. A process that would have made Winston Smith's job of rewriting history at the Ministry of Truth in George Orwell's *1984,* so much easier.

The first part of the book lays some ground work needed to put the remaining sections in context. The second and third parts deal mostly with education in America including a distinctive local twist. The fourth part deals predominantly with city and county issues. Finally, the last part sums it all up with a short treatise on the United States of *Flatland.*

Educational topics take up a big part of this book, not only because education in America is a trillion dollar industry, but also because every generation owes the next generation not only a set of facts, but also a principled set of time-tested values that will help guide them and subsequent generations to come. As societies have become more complex, the responsibility for this generational knowledge exchange has gone from parent-to-child to a government employee-to-child. And for many folks, the knowledge exchange process is broken.

Although I often use my hometown of Beavercreek, Ohio, as the catalyst for introducing discussion topics, I hopefully have broadened the dialogue enough to ensure that all readers, from Alabama to Wyoming, and from small to large cities, are able to identify with the issues and enjoy the discussions. Therefore, although the names of people and places may differ from your town, the dynamics and the occasional absurdity of the events are shared by all of us who may have taken the opportunity to remind our government officials of their responsibilities as our representatives.

I only included people's specific names when I thought it necessary for the story line. However, when names have been included it usually coincided with nationally known individuals or people quoted or referenced in public or national sources. Although most, if not all, of the information in this book is part of the public record, I felt it was more appropriate to proceed this way, since my intent is not to make individuals unknown to most readers the focus of my story, but rather in the human processes and institutions that these people exist in; processes and institutions we all helped create.

If I achieved this goal, then many of you will see that what I discuss in these pages are not peculiar to my community or state, but rather systemic in our country. How can it be any other way; after all, people are people, and the way we perform our public duties, as government officials or as private citizens, is influenced not only by our intrinsic individual qualities, but also through the sum of all external forces acting on us.

Of course, the opinions and views expressed in this book are entirely my own and do not necessarily reflect the opinions or views of anyone else. Although many of the topics I discuss in this book have been presented by others in ways far more eloquently than I have done here, I hope I have nevertheless added some freshness and uniqueness to the discussion.

Finally, as I was writing this book I knew that I would upset many of my friends and colleagues who may not see the world as I do. To them I only ask for their continued friendship and camaraderie.

I also knew that I would further upset many of my enemies, and possibly even create new ones. But there are two versions of history: the version you believe to be true versus the unbiased record. The former can easily be changed as required, and the latter doesn't exist. So, if any of you feel I have lied, distorted the truth, used extremes, or that I'm just plain nuts; I challenge you to write your own book with as many lies, half-truths, extreme anecdotes and nutty references as you see fit.

Tony Corvo
Beavercreek, Ohio

Acknowledgments

Isaac Newton captured the essence of giving credit where credit is due when he said [in more modern terminology]: "If I have seen further than other men, it is because I have stood on the shoulders of giants." What makes the quote interesting is that Newton was not known for his humility.

I therefore humbly submit to the fact that this book could not have been complete without the help of family and friends. Therefore, I would like to acknowledge the following for their general support, suggestions, and criticisms: Donna Corvo, Julie Corvo, Sarah Corvo, Dan Corvo, Nick Corvo, Matthew R. Byrne, Bruce Ronald Fiene, Major Mary F. Collier, USAF (Ret), Colonel William P. Murray IV, USAF (Ret), and Captain Dave Riley, USN (Ret).

PART I
Milieu

Whereas the curious reader is introduced to my hometown and provided some background information necessary to understand what follows in later chapters of my story.

1

Confucius says: Think Globally, Act Locally!

I can't remember if I cried when I read about his widowed bride, but something touched me deep inside, the day the music died.

—Don McLean, *American Pie*

P. J. O'Rourke's book *Parliament of Whores* is a satirical romp through the halls of our federal government. However, the book ends on a final note with a chapter on the author's hometown politics. Here we learn of a man referred to as the "Town Flake," a man who has made a name for himself by being a town pest for over thirty years. He is the first to point out inefficiencies in local governmental processes and is not shy to identify the myriad of stupid ideas that are common to politicians and bureaucrats everywhere. As the Town Flake he holds the record for being hushed by meeting moderators or shouted down by the townspeople.

Yet, as O'Rourke puts it, "He is always and invariably right on every issue."

There are many people who just shake their heads upon hearing of another useless $10 million federal study, but go nuts when their city council approves $1,000 for a few new plants to go in front of city hall. So it would be easy to say that local small town politics is often petty. Yet this label misses the mark.

Government in America is divided not only laterally in various branches in both federal and state governments, but also vertically. In the vertical direction, we are taught that federal and state constitutional laws are structured to ensure that federal, state, and local governments have distinct and clear responsibilities and a higher government level cannot easily encroach and abuse lower levels. Yet historically, we have seen an explosive growth in the federal government and its reach into the daily lives of all citizens. Increases at the state levels have followed suit, leaving taxpayers frustrated by their loss of control on one issue after another.

Therefore, although governments at all levels are inherently wasteful, the real issue is that to most folks their federal and state governments are for all practical purposes inaccessible, whereas for most small to medium size cities, their town halls are just down the street or around the corner. Politics becomes personal when it hits home and local politics always hits home.

While senators and representatives are modern versions of royalty, small town councilmen and school board members shop at the same grocery stores, look for the same sale items and squeeze the same melons as everyone else. Some of the local elected officials may even be your neighbors, sing in your church choir, or if brave enough to admit such a geekish act, be in your bowling league.

However, to add insult to injury, many times when citizens attempt to engage their local politicians and bureaucrats on various issues, they often get the response, "Our hands are tied by state and/or federal laws and regulations." Nothing brings this home more than the current fate of our community schools, where the word "community" is used here only to imply a location and tax base and has nothing to do with any local span of control. In fact, as we shall see local control of community schools totally and officially ended on May 4, 1980, which is the day that public education, after a long bout of pain and suffering, officially died in America, or to paraphrase Don Mclean in *American Pie*, it's *the day the learning died*.

So what's the average guy or gal supposed to do?

One thing is not to give up on the locals. Accessibility to local bureaucrats should be viewed from the following two perspectives:

1. It provides you the ability to have input to local issues to whatever extent state and federal laws allow.

2. It provides a leverage to get to your state and federal bureaucrats.

Thus, local accessibility should also be viewed and used in a more strategic sense, because the average person's link to his/her state capitol or to Washington D.C. is greatly amplified if leveraged using their local politicians and bureaucrats.

But this amplification is not made by going *through* your local politicians but rather by *acting on* your local politicians and forcing them to *act on* the next level. You do this by making the lives of your local politicians and bureaucrats politically miserable, and the quickest way to make politicians miserable is to deny them funding for those processes that are broken. And this is where the average schmoe can still exercise some influence: through the direct voting on levies and other local tax initiatives.

Even Confucius understood a linkage process between individual action and global results with his famous reasoning:

Only when things are investigated is knowledge extended
Only when knowledge is extended are thoughts sincere
Only when thoughts are sincere are minds rectified
Only when minds are rectified are the characters of persons cultivated
Only when character is cultivated are our families regulated
Only when families are regulated are states well governed
Only when states are well governed is there peace in the world.

This approach is summarized in the catchy Liberal *Think Globally, Act Locally* bumper sticker. (Liberals have better bumper stickers than Conservatives, although the post 2000 election sticker *Sore/Loserman* in place of *Gore/Lieberman* is pretty cute.) Therefore, following Confucius's example we might want to say:

Only when citizens assume responsibility can taxpayers take action
Only when taxpayers take action can bureaucrats be held accountable
Only when bureaucrats are held accountable can a levy be defeated
Only when a levy is defeated will local politicians panic
Only when local politicians panic will state reps feel the heat
Only when state reps feel the heat will the feds begin to listen
Only when the feds begin to listen will the problem be addressed.

In a nutshell, while many issues may or may not be controlled locally, eventually all actions occur locally. It must have been awareness of this fact, or at least partly so, that drove House Speaker Tip O'Neil (D-MA) to observe, "All politics is local." But what O'Neil left out is that it's also loco.

2

My Town

Change comes slowly to a small New Hampshire town in the early 20th century. People grow up, get married, live, and die. Milk and the newspaper get delivered every morning, and nobody locks their front doors.

—An IMDB.com plot summary of the 1940 movie version of
Thornton Wilder's *Our Town*

Beavercreek, Ohio may not be as idyllic as Thornton Wilder's Grover's Corners depicted above, but as towns go it is a pretty good place to live nevertheless. It is the largest city in Greene County, located just east of Dayton, Ohio. By official standards Beavercreek is a relatively young city, being incorporated in 1980, but its roots go back hundreds of years. The city's statistics for 2000 according to the U.S. Census Bureau are as follows:

- Population: 37,984

- Size: 26.4 square miles

- Median resident age: 40.5 years

- Median household income: $68,801

- Median house value: $143,300

- High school or higher: 92.4%

- Bachelor's degree or higher: 42.9%

- Graduate or professional degree: 20.8%

- Unemployed: 2.7%

- White: 93.4%

- Black: 1.4%

- American Indian: 0.2%

- Asian: 3.5%

- Hispanic: (1.1%)

Murder in Beavercreek is rare (0 in 2002 and 2001) and the overall crime rate is below the national average. There is no downtown in the classical sense. The unassuming city hall is located next to the modest city jail, and is several miles away from what might be considered the retail center of town. In fact, until the summer of 2004 you probably wouldn't be able to find the city hall or police station unless a local gave you directions (a new stonewall street entrance now points you in the right direction).

One of the area's larger malls, the Fairfield Commons, is located in northern Beavercreek, along with many smaller upscale satellite shopping "centres." As has become the custom, developers and retailers like using the snobbish looking British spelling of "centre" to give an upscale feel to shoppers. I don't really understand this since Europe still has yet to discover soft toilet paper, and in some places toilet paper period. But this is completely in line with modern Nobel-winning economic theories that say people will pay more for goods bought at shopping centres versus shopping centers, and at "shoppes" versus stores.

On the southern edge of the town is a new concept in shopping called the Greene. The Greene was built to resemble multiple blocks of a small town shopping district including a town central park. But instead of Mayberry's Bluebird Diner you will find upscale bistros and coffee shops, apartments, fitness centers, and upscale women's clothing stores. There is even one store that specializes in black and white clothes! Aunt Bee would be verklempted!

Some local shopping districts have built their own smaller versions of the Greene just to compete with the original. The Greene is very aesthetically pleasing, and if men are allowed to say that shopping is fun, then shopping at the Greene is fun. Nevertheless, the Greene has it own share of controversy that will be discussed in a later chapter.

In the same general area as the Fairfield Commons mall you will also find the city golf course, the local state college, Wright State University, and the area's biggest employer, Wright-Patterson Air Force Base. The rest of the city is a mix of small businesses, residential, and rural areas, where an occasional working farm can still be seen. In fact, from my home I often can hear the faint mooing from a nearby farm; although considering the pace of development, probably not for that much longer.

Any town near a major military base understands the pluses and minuses of having a base nearby. Clearly a benefit is the cash flow into the local area, care of Uncle Sam, through the creation of jobs and the subsequent boost to all the local businesses necessary to support the base.

Naturally, Beavercreek, as well as the general local area, has a high percentage of military retirees—and I'm one—who together bring a mix to the equation not necessarily seen in other communities. Unfortunately, a negative aspect of a nearby military base is the transient nature of many of the military personnel. I use the word transient here not in bad sense associated with vagrancy or crime, but to highlight the different perspectives between someone who has a long term stake in a community and those, after only 6 months on the job, already begin to wonder where their next assignment is going to be.

Just like Washington D.C., the Beavercreek area also has a "beltway." Interstate 675 and Colonel Glenn Boulevard (guess what Ohio son that street is named after) border east and south of the base and is home to many of the major contractors that support the base mission. The names of these companies are generally well known to those who work in the military establishment since these companies have similar satellite offices practically near every major military base.

Because of the mix discussed above, Beavercreek is schizophrenic. Its split personality stems from the fact that it is essentially a border town, as it sits on the western edge of largely rural Greene County but edges up against the more urban Montgomery County.

The split personality manifests itself in how citizens see the town and its future, and like any city, its future is tied to taxes and how they are spent. At the time of this writing the city has no income tax (the topic of a later chapter), thus property taxes form a large part of city revenue, with the remaining coming from various state, county, and other miscellaneous sources. Property taxes in Beavercreek are some of highest in the local area, and for comparable cities, possibly also ranks one of the highest across the state.

Approximately 15% of Beavercreek property taxes go to pay for city services such as street maintenance, parks and recreation, and police. Where does the remaining tax money go to? Various places, like Beavercreek Township, which operates the local Fire Department, and Greene County which operates the library system, county parks, the county hospital, and a host of other specialized services. But the 600 pound gorilla is the local school system.

For 2004, a little more than 60% of all property taxes went to the Beavercreek School System. These taxes in turn account for about 62% of the school district's total $51 million 2004 general fund, and about 47% of the district's $67 million total budget. The number of students in the 2004 School System was roughly 7,100, giving an annual cost per student of about $9,400. By the way, some of these numbers are hotly debated, because although you would think that "total budget" and "number of students" would be easy to define, it turns out that it depends on what your definition of "is" is.

There is no formal relationship between the school district and other local government bodies, since each run independently from one another, and are thus basically tax competitors. But together, our district, city, township, and county officials continuously remind us of how their needs far outstrip their revenues. And taxpayers are reminded nearly every six months, with at least one levy or another, on how expensive their government is. Although property taxes require annoying tax levy campaigns and public officials understandably hate the process, they do force government officials to periodically justify themselves to the voters.

However, life would be sweet for local bureaucrats if only they didn't have to periodically go to the taxpayers and beg for more money. Yes, life would be grand if only they had a continuous source of revenue. But they don't; at least not yet. But give them time. At the time of this writing the State of Ohio has already floated some options that would eliminate the need for school districts to go to voters and solicit new funds. One lobby group proposed a constitutional amendment that would take away the legislature's education budget oversight and give it to the State Board of Education!

This is just another disaster waiting to happen from a state that has gone from one of the lowest state/local tax rates in the country in the 1970s to one of the highest (3rd in 2006), during which companies are bailing out in droves, jobs are being lost by the hundreds of thousands, young people are leaving due to limited opportunities at home, and the education system has fallen nationally to the bottom 50% in several important categories. In general, as taxes have increased, almost all economic indicators have shown Ohio, as a whole, has regressed over the same time period. Yet the only solution offered by politicians is to increase taxes.

There are relative bright spots and even though I'm going to beat up the Beavercreek school district in later chapters for reasons that will be presented, truth be told, Beavercreek has a fairly decent school system when measured against certain limited state and national standards. The district also has many professional administrators, teachers, and staff members, many of which I have personally interacted with as my two daughters moved through the system. But relative educational performance and staff professionalism are not the reasons why I wrote this book.

The problem is much more global. The Beavercreek school district suffers from the same ailment that has infected public education throughout the country:

1. Much of the local control that property owners, taxpayers, or the community in general used to have has essentially been lost to federal and state regulations, teacher unions and a host of other special interests. This includes a distinctive and destructive politically correct culture that has swept nearly all districts in the country.

2. There is a disconnect between who uses the services and who pays for the services.

3. There is no clear proportionality between taxes, costs, programs offered, educational outcome, and the needs of society.

4. Any attempt to hold sensible discussions about public education is futile for a host of complex reasons that form the basis for much of later chapters of this book.

On the city side; city council governs, through a city manager, a fair sized and growing city with a budget that also relies heavily on property taxes. However, local tax-and-spend enthusiasts both in and out of the government often remind taxpayers that Beavercreek is one of the largest cities in Ohio without an income tax. The lack of an income tax, we are told, has tremendous negative impact not only to Beavercreek's potential growth but even in meeting its basic operations.

Basic operations are indeed very critical to the operations of the city. For example, in Beavercreek, basic city operations vital to the community also includes a city golf course described on the city website as:

A Fuzzy Zoeller signature golf course designed by golf course architect Brian Huntley. Beavercreek offers golfers of all levels the opportunity to combine golf with nature. The perfectly conditioned bent grass tees, greens, and fairways are interwoven through a rolling countryside. The sheer beauty makes Beavercreek an exceptional golfing experience.

Sounds impressive doesn't it? If you ever get a chance to play at the Beavercreek golf course and do have an exceptional golfing experience, thank the Beavercreek taxpayers, because the golf course has lost millions of dollars since its inception; and continues to do so at a rate of about $600,000 per year. A good question to ask now would be why are Beavercreek taxpayers supporting a financially draining golf course? The reason is not peculiar to Beavercreek and is replicated across the country, and is a topic we will discuss later.

Beavercreek may indeed need additional revenue, but fortunately, even income tax enthusiasts have to obey the law, and the city charter specifically prohibits an income tax without voter approval. That approval was sought in 1984 and 1994, and both times the initiatives went down in flaming defeat. Third and fourth attempts were made in 2004 and 2007, but never made it to the ballot because the city council backed down after sensing public discontent with the measures. Rack these up as victories for the little guy.

◆   ◆   ◆

These are just some of the issues that were simmering about when I and several others decided to organize a local political action committee (PAC) to fight what we considered arrogant and wasteful government spending. But there will be plenty of time later in the book to discuss our PAC adventures. For now, I can't leave this chapter on Beavercreek without a few words on our own Town Flake.

Our Town Flake, I'll call her Calamity Jane, has been a thorn in the sides of local elected officials for decades. She has arranged protests at shopping centers when she felt that the city gave special considerations to the developers. She has led recall petitions on several council members she thought abused their positions. She led a drive to derail a number of city income tax initiatives. She has written countless letters to local papers and organized several political action committees and informal citizens groups. One of her major victories came in November 1992, when she led a successful petition drive to place on the ballot an amendment to the city charter that put term limits on council members. Voters passed the initiative.

Calamity Jane is a short, maybe 5' 2" chain smoker with less energy now than she used to have. In 2004 she had a foot amputated due to circulatory problems which later led to a hip injury. Although her age and her health have slowed her down, she still has the occasional energy to stir the pot or poke the sleeping tiger.

I have personally met with Calamity on a number of occasions to discuss various local issues. I don't agree with all of Calamity's political positions, but if I really had to criticize her on any one thing, it would have to be on her inability to pick and choose her battles. To some people, Calamity Jane just cried wolf too many times to have been taken seriously more often than she should have been.

Every superhero has a nemesis. Flash Gordon has Emperor Ming, Underdog has Simon Bar Sinister, Superman has Lex Luther, Batman has the Joker, and Calamity Jane has Annie Oakley (not her real name; duh). Like Calamity, Annie has been a steady player in local politics for decades but on the government side of the fence, serving on various boards, councils and in other governmental positions. To some, Annie is a selfless public servant, to others she is someone who has never seen a government program or tax hike she didn't like.

Their battles reached their peak during the 1994 income tax campaign mentioned a few paragraphs above. Annie lodged formal charges with the Ohio Elections Commission against Calamity and her anti-tax political action committee for making false campaign statements. Annie had reason to be angry; she was one of the leaders of the pro-tax group that was crushed at the ballot box. But the Ohio Elections Commission found no violations with Calamity or her anti-tax group.

The clashes between Calamity Jane and Annie Oakley became so common that after Calamity lost her foot the following joke was circulated around town:

Q: "How did Calamity Jane lose her foot?"
A: "It got stuck up Annie Oakley's ass."

Now that's a Town Flake every town needs.

3

Constitution?
We Don't Need No Stinking
Constitution!

Host: The category is Government and the $1000 question is, "What group would you find the following: Scoundrels, Do-gooders, Busy-bodies, Regulists, Socialists and Communists?"

Joe: The Democratic Party.

Host: Sorry Joe, good guess though. Looks like Cassandra is going to give it the old college try.

Cassandra: The Hillary Clinton presidential campaign team.

Host: Oh, that's close but not quite it. And Tony just buzzed; Tony?

Tony: Government politicians.

Host: Can you be more specific?

Tony: The Government Class.

Host: Good show! You get $1000 and get to pick the next category.

Is the basic process of governing inheritably wasteful and corrupt? If you answered yes, then aren't we just all doomed? Wouldn't it be better to just go with the flow and work to get your own piece of the public pie while you can?

If you answered no, then you must believe some fix-it solution is possible. What is that solution? More regulations? More oversight?

Is the problem just one of elected officials continuing to seemingly mismanage public funds due to moral weaknesses or just plain incompetence? Is it then just a problem of electing more honest and competent politicians? How about if we all sit around in a big circle, discuss our differences, sing Kumbaya, and just try to get along?

The public should always hold a cynical view of politicians and government bureaucrats. However, it is wrong to automatically assume that people who hold government positions are inherently wasteful or dishonest, because politicians and other government officials have many complex motives for their actions. These motives range from the purely selfish to, believe it or not, the occasional good intention. The actions that derive from selfishness or self interest are often quite transparent and there are many processes that provide check and balances for cronyism, fraud, deception, or even incompetence.

But what do you do about good intentions? The public is much more forgiving when government claims to act on the public's behalf. But are good intentions sufficient reasons to warrant public funding of expensive nice-to-have services that either the government cannot handle efficiently, should not handle at all, or benefit the very few; especially if those programs can be handled by the private sector?

Keep in mind that government programs are funded by taxes and enforced by law. When government acts it always impacts personal freedom one way or another; if nothing more than taking a little bit more out your wallet. Some loss of personal freedom is necessary when we agree to live in an orderly society, and most reasonable people willingly make that tradeoff when properly warranted. Clear examples are traffic laws. But if you have traffic laws you must have police enforcement mechanisms. And police forces must get around and be housed somewhere, so you buy them cars and build them police stations. And all of this requires taxes, but you pay your taxes because providing a police service is a legitimate function of government. So far, so good.

Then you read that your local school district just decided to grade students on a pass/needs improvement system so as to not stigmatize the *academically challenged* kids. "Good," you say, "kids shouldn't be put under that much pressure."

Then you hear that your local state college dropped screening students based on grades. "Eureka," you shout, "finally equal opportunity for all!"

Then you find out that your state government just gave someone a $50,000 grant to pour bloody looking liquid on herself while dancing naked on stage, holding a knife in one hand and reading poetry that claims all men are rapists and should be castrated. "So what," you say, "sure it's a *little* extreme, but who am I to question what art is, and after all, isn't she just exercising her right of free speech?"

Then you read that the federal government just took over your health care system. You look up and say: "Thank you Lord, finally a *free* health care system."

Then twenty five years later you are told that you require immediate open heart surgery. After a 9 month wait, you are finally informed that your surgery will occur the next day and are given instructions to report to the Hillary Clinton

Memorial Hospital. When you report in you find yourself in the office of a government cardiologist who went to your school district, graduated from your local state college, and has pictures of herself covered in bloody looking liquid dancing naked on a stage, while holding a knife in one hand and looking like she was reading something.

Then two things pop in your mind: (1) she looked better 25 years ago, and (2) IN 24 HOURS SHE'S GOING TO HAVE YOU OPENED UP LIKE A PIECE OF MEAT! Something is wrong here, and it's not just that women dancing naked on stages covered in a bloody looking liquid and offering to make all men eunuchs may not be art.

Thomas Jefferson warned us of the slippery slope toward bigger government when he said, "The natural progress of things is for liberty to yield and government to gain ground." Of course, there are a number of historical examples during Jefferson's presidency as well as in his personal life—being a slave owner a big one—where Jefferson didn't always adhere to his own advice concerning liberty and government. Some call this hypocrisy, and I think in the case of slavery they have a strong argument. Maybe he was trying to solve one problem at a time. I don't know. I'll leave that argument to historians.

But what is clear to me is that Jefferson and the other founders set in motion a revolution that would move the country and the world toward a new concept of liberty and equality. And I think Jefferson was just making an observation on the never ending conflict between individual freedom and government encroachment. A conflict driven by the struggle within ourselves having to choose between liberty and security, having a respect for the rule of law versus the desire for personnel power, or, more often than not, just blowing it! The bottom line is that the concept of limited government our forefathers envisioned was under attack from the get-go.

However, some parts of the United States Constitution were easier to mangle than others. For example, although slowly at first, but more rapidly in the 20th century, some began interpreting the Constitution's "promote the general welfare" statement to mean that government was not just the means to an end but the preferred means to every end. This is essentially the current view of modern Liberalism. But in order to use the "general welfare" argument, you also have to assume that the Constitution's meaning is not fixed but fluid.

Thus, at the federal level it is now the norm to ignore Article 1, Section 8 of the U.S. Constitution that enumerates federal duties and also ignore the 10th amendment that limits federal authority relative to the states. Passing the 17th amendment in 1913 that provided for choosing senators by popular vote instead of being chosen by state legislatures hasn't helped the cause of liberty. This law has had the effect of weakening federalism and thus weakening the independence of the states. If you don't understand how this is so, then you have a lot of home-work on your hands.

Other instances are plentiful. For example, it is particularly noteworthy how we have decided to specifically butcher the definition of "commerce" so that the Commerce Clause, Article 1, Section 8, Clause 3, that governs federal regulation of commerce among states, can mean anything the federal government wants it to mean.

And it seems that many are more than happy to generate new laws based on the 14th Amendment's Equal Protection Clause to justify any cause or create any right beyond its original intent. (The 14th Amendment was enacted in 1868 to counteract "Black Codes" that were in-turn created to stifle the 13th Amendment that abolished Slavery.) This activist approach has helped maintain the govern-mental juggernaut that squanders tax dollars, inhibits innovation, and crushes liberties.

So where do Americans really stand on government's role in a free society? The school book answer is that Americans love freedom. However, the real answer in practice, as in most things in life, is much more complex, with many Americans too easily giving up freedom for security.

One method used to measure America's political pulse is to assess how people view certain hot-button issues of the day, for example, abortion, gay rights, gun control, social security, welfare, and so forth. Depending on how you answer pro or con to these questions supposedly determines your Liberal or Conservative politics, which in turn often implies your political party affiliation

But in practice, whether you are pro or con on a particular issue, sometimes has more to do with human emotions than defining your politics. The real test of your politics is how you view what the government's role (federal, state, or local) is in certain macroscopic processes. When individuals have a well defined concept of government, then addressing individual issues becomes one of assessing those issues against their conceptual template. Although this is understood by some, this concept is only given lip service and never really discussed in great detail or carried through a logical conclusion in the popular media or, more importantly, in the classroom. As a society, we never seem to be able to get past the sound bite.

In a nutshell, in regards to the federal government, if you are a Conservative then you must believe that the powers of the federal government are limited and enumerated by the constitution. If you understand what this means then you also understand why the Bill of Rights was an afterthought. After all, if the federal government could only do what is prescribed in the articles of the constitution, then there was no need to further delineate other federal limitations.

Although Liberals have mangled the Bill of Rights along with other parts of the constitution, the Bill of Rights remains a tremendous piece of work in the evolution of social thought. Whether amendments that covered the same issues as the Bill of Rights would have been eventually added in time is open to speculation, but at least maybe the later writers would have taken greater care in making them clearer. (If you want to know more about what the original thoughts were on the Constitution, start with the *Federalist Papers*, the *Anti-Federalist Papers*, or for a great overview see the *Heritage Guide to the Constitution*; Edwin Meese III, editor.)

Although an overwhelming number of Conservatives would agree with the points in the former paragraphs, how individual Conservatives approach state and local governmental responsibilities becomes a little bit fuzzier. But just saying a Conservative believes in "limited government" strikes me as a good sound bite but the devil is in the details.

For example, what does Conservatism say about a city funding a community recreation center? What if the private sector already provides a number of clubs offering similar services? And of course, as a taxpayer subsidized enterprise, the new public center would be in direct competition with the private clubs, who also pay taxes, of which some go to support their government competition. Is that fair?

If you answered no to a publicly funded center because your town has a private sector market, what about small towns that have no private commercial alternatives? Are they given a pass? What would your answer be if the recreation center was open to all city residents, but was to be funded by a limited subset of taxpayers? Even the most ardent conservatives at the national level soften their views at the local level. Some softening makes sense; after all, local governments have different responsibilities than state and federal governments.

Having a government template to gauge issues against doesn't automatically make decision making a simple process, or that two people starting from the same premise will always arrive at the same conclusion. But it does provide a formal starting point to counter the natural human tendency for knee-jerk emotional responses to political issues: pro or con. This tug of war between heart and brain helps explain the differences between Conservatism, Libertarianism, and modern Liberalism beyond the joke: "If you're not a liberal by the time you're 18, you have no heart, and if you're not a conservative by the time you're 40, you have no brain."

We have already defined Liberalism as being associated with big government. But Libertarianism is not well understood by most people. Sometimes you might hear Libertarianism referred to as *Classical Liberalism*, implying that what we now call "Liberalism" has been hijacked by the political left.

Nevertheless, Libertarians and Conservatives hold many of the same views toward the role of limited government especially in economic issues—in essence they begin in many cases from the same starting point. What makes them different is that as the two groups work through the myriad of political issues, they may end up at different conclusions, most notably in social issues because Libertarians tend to be socially liberal or indifferent. But differing on social issues or how one goes about conducting personal affairs shouldn't really matter under a limited government.

Conservatives should aspire to enforcing strong social morals by first limiting government and then by rebuilding the distinctive but separate responsibilities between government and society that have been jumbled together by the Left. This requires individuals to understand that government has a very limited role in a free society. And although some actions may be legal or not a matter for the law, society also has options for establishing varying degrees of acceptance of those actions and thus creating varying degrees of personal accountability.

However, there are some on the Right that tend to want government to go beyond providing a minimal legal system and correct all "immoralities" through law. This parallels those on the Left that desire government go beyond providing a minimal legal system and correct all "injustices" through law. But we need to note that what has corrupted society is the government's active advocacy and support of poor behavior through Liberal laws and policies. *Modern Liberalism cushions the affects of poor life style choices and prevents society from holding people accountable for their actions.*

It is said that you can't legislate morality. But you can legislate bad behavior, and when bad behavior is rewarded or protected, you get more bad behavior.

Those on the Right that seek a government solution to correct every "undesirable" social behavior are no better than their counterparts on the Left. Most undesirable *actions* will not be corrected by this type of government because all you end up with is different kinds of undesirable *reactions*. Keeping government small, but allowing society through direct and indirect economic and social processes to hold people accountable for their actions, will result in most people behaving according to what most often can be referred to as traditional social principles. However, if someone chooses to live outside the "norm" then so be it; just don't ask me or the rest of society to subsidize their behavior.

As a Conservative you have to believe the last paragraph or your convictions mean nothing. If some people decide to continue not to act in their own best interests; hey, it's their life. Basically, I'm telling Conservatives not to reject a good solution in order to seek what they may consider a perfect one that is doomed to fail.

All the stuff above is theory. How does it work in practice? Of course no single template can capture all of the diverse human behaviors and thus there will always be exceptions. Furthermore, in the real world, we are often forced to execute our various political philosophies through established political parties. (Libertarians won't like this but for the sake of brevity, I'm going to mostly exclude the Libertarian party from the discussion below. There just isn't enough data on how Libertarians would *actually* execute government functions to include them here. But they should take heart in the fact that I'm not going to be kind to either of the other two.)

It is important to note that although the strong general welfare group is mostly associated with Liberals and the Democratic Party, membership in this group is not completely restrictive to one political party and is thus not completely defined by party membership. The meaning of the general welfare statement can be morphed to mean anything to anyone when one is willing to ignore the rest of the original constitution and willing to trade freedom for security, individuality for collectivism, or just seek political power as an end to itself.

Members of both major parties have adapted the general welfare statement to serve their particular view of the world. Therefore, although Republicans do occasionally throw out a few tax cuts as political trinkets to its base, in reference to government growth and abuse, on average, the effective real-world differences *in the growth and execution of government* between the two parties are much less than the party apparatchik would want you to believe. And it was the fact that Republicans looked a lot like Democrats in 2006 that cost Republicans both houses of congress that year.

In practice, both parties working within current political dynamics on average exhibit macroscopic central tendencies, even if their respective end points are slightly on the left or right of center. But what is this "center" we keep hearing about? It's just more government. Thus, both parties have members holding offices that can be grouped as part of the *Government Class*. Although this term may have been used by others in different contexts, it is defined here as people, elected, appointed, or hired, holding any governmental office (including the judiciary) who when approaching a particular social or economic matter *instinctively* seek a government solution or *effectively* allow the same outcome.

Although the Government Class has a very high membership enrollment, it is important not to label every politician, judge, or government employee as a member of this group, because not everyone in the government always instinctively seeks a government solution; even though it too often appears that way. A member of the Government Class will spend a tremendous amount of energy to enact the government solution without caring or stopping to ask: "Does government even have a legitimate role in this issue?" A question true Conservatives would always first ask themselves (and ironically in some cases, classical Liberals as well.)

Keep in mind that as defined here, people not in government cannot be members of the Government Class, even if they also look to government as the solution for what ails them. That is because people in government have legal authority, whereas special interest groups, although powerful, have no direct control over you or your pocketbook. These people do have special roles that will be discussed separately.

What causes a politician or government bureaucrat to first seek a government solution goes to the core of what it means to be part of the Government Class? Wal-Mart executives may try to entice you to shop at their stores or even want to buy up your neighborhood to build new stores, but Wal-Mart cannot legally by force take away your property, your liberties, or your life. But members of the Government Class can. And it is your local Government Class that can give powerful corporations, special interest groups, or individuals what they want. And members of the Government Class know that by using the government's authority they can force a desired outcome or behavior whether across a broad spectrum of ideas or on a single particular issue.

Individual members of the Government Class are influenced by a mixture and variety of personal views-of-the-world but for the sake of our discussion can be identified under a number of distinct philosophical groups. Some of which are: Scoundrels, Do-gooders, Busy-bodies, Regulists, Socialists and Communists.

You may think of this list as elements, or ingredients, needed to build a member of the current American Government Class. In other words, if you broke down a member of the American Government Class you will see these basic components in various amounts just like water is one part oxygen and two parts hydrogen. Some members are fairly pure and can be defined by mostly a single element, but many members are made up of various combinations of the different elements. The list is not all inclusive, but it will provide a starting point for our discussion.

Scoundrels

Scoundrels are elected or appointed government officials who use an issue and their political power to expand government to directly or indirectly line their pockets with public funds or to further increase their political power. Scoundrels have a rich and time honored tradition and have been around since the first tribal council. Although often found in pure forms, there's a little bit of Scoundrel in most politicians and bureaucrats, because there is a little bit of Scoundrel in all of us: political power just does a great job in drawing it out of us.

Do-gooders

Do-gooders often represent issues that are immensely difficult for true Conservatives to oppose. A great example is smoking in public places, especially restaurants. In November 2006 Ohio had two state issues on the ballot. Essentially, one issue allowed smoking at the discretion of the business owner based on his clientele making consumer decisions, the other outlawed smoking in nearly all public places. Although I think smoking is a fairly disgusting habit, I voted for the free market, but the free market lost.

I voted for the free market because I believe that any inconvenience that I may experience due to inconsiderate smokers is nothing compared to the inconvenience I would experience under a nanny state. I also believe that with proper health education coupled with free-market economic and social pressures, smoking can be reduced to an occasional nuisance without resorting to a draconian government solution including the associated enforcement bureaucracy.

The argument that the law is also necessary to protect workers who have no choice is invalid because workers do have a choice not to work there. If the business owner can't find enough workers willing to put up with inside smoking, the owner would take appropriate action by either prohibiting smoking or paying workers more money and let the workers, as free individuals, decide their own fate. The free market works if it is allowed to work.

Another great example starting to really take form is the movement to get people to eat right. In this case, a Do-gooder is the politician or bureaucrat who says things like, "I am submitting the Americans Must Eat Right Act that will create a red meat excise tax and make it mandatory that everyone consume one pound of tofu daily." It is irrelevant that the individual is sincere in his or her concern for people's health, because this concern does not necessarily justify any mandatory governmental act of this caliber.

What makes this issue even more interesting than the smoking case is that this really gets to the heart of the nanny state, because what you eat affects only you. If humans fed their young like birds, then you might have an argument about the effects of *second hand regurgitation*. Of course, there is a wedge to violate the parent-child relationship here by also framing the issue in terms of what parents feed their children. The Government Class doesn't trust parents in making smart choices when given the right information.

The Government Class will also argue about the need to lower health care costs. But that's a red herring because the government shouldn't be in the health care business in the first place. However, most people don't realize that once government decides to pick up the tab for your health care, and this is unfortunately inevitable because of the various forces at play, and since what you eat may affect your heath, and whatever affects your health affects your health care costs, it will be only natural that the bursar (Uncle Sam) will limit what you may eat—by law.

If you don't believe me, New York City in September 2006 just proposed ordering its 25,000 restaurants to stop preparing foods with trans fat. Okay, so what, NYC isn't the federal government. Well, Rome wasn't built in day. As reported in various news services, Dr. Walter Willett, chairman of the Department of Nutrition at the Harvard University School of Public Health, praised the city health officials for bringing up a ban, which he said could save lives. "Artificial trans fats are very toxic, and they almost surely cause tens of thousands of premature deaths each year," he said. "*The federal government should have done this long ago*"; [emphasis added].

Did Dr. Willett understand the implications of his statement? What is amazing about demands like Dr. Willett's, is how easily like-statements roll off the tongues of many Americans.

If most well intended activists understood and believed in free enterprise, then they would understand how to get what they think is best for the country and still keep government at bay. Basically, government does have a role in funding health care research and providing general health related information to the public. If factual information is provided to consumers, most would ask the right questions and make the right decisions for themselves and their children. As consumers decide to buy less and less of a product, that product's price will go up, or the product may even stop being produced. In either case, the end result would be less trans fat in foods, and a slightly smaller nanny state. But the Government Class doesn't like that solution.

The other alternative is for government to charge you more based on your life style choices. But this isn't feasible. Can you imagine the reaction of civil rights lawyers if government decided to base your health care costs on the size of your butt? Of course, this won't prevent the government from charging your health care costs based on the size of your wallet. Which would be another example of government punishing success and rewarding failure.

Busy-bodies

Busy-bodies are often mistaken for Do-gooders. But Busy-bodies tend to be driven by idealist, moralist, or religious agendas, and confuse governmental, societal, and individual responsibilities.

At the local level, you can find some Busy-bodies directing your library not to carry the Bible, and others Huck Finn. And still others are more than willing to help state legislatures tell science teachers about the evils of teaching evolution.

A Busy-body is also someone who worries about what consenting adults do in their homes and wants the government to do something about it. Another example of a Busy-body is someone who wants anything consenting adults may do in their homes to be able to do it in the public streets, and wants government to do something about it. In both cases, there is confusion over the roles of government, society, and individuals.

Busy-bodies exist on both sides of the political fence and were active in the 2005 Terri Schiavo case. Terri was medically diagnosed as being in a permanent vegetative state and her husband wanted to discontinue life support. However, Terri's parents wanted to keep her on life support. This is an extremely emotional case and my heart goes out to Terri's parents. I can only imagine the pain they felt during this whole ordeal.

This case had many sub plots including a strong right-to-life component. But on the other hand, in an almost macabre sort of way, there were many rooting for the plug to be pulled just to trump the right-to-lifers. In any case, after dozens of legal challenges, and pronouncements from all over the Busy-body political spectrum, the courts sided with the husband.

Now you can argue on a personal level whether the husband should have given the daughter over to her parents who were willing to care for her, but even that was his decision to make. Why did his legal rights trump Terri's parent's legal rights (if that was even the issue)? I'll let the lawyers explain that. But I think it was the right decision if for no other reason than for thousands of years it has been recognized that when a man and a woman marry, they break their respective parent-child bonds to establish a new family where they are "one." Government may view marriage as a contract, but society must view marriage as an institution. Either that means something or it doesn't.

Another example of Busy-bodies is the current frenzy concerning sex offenders. Without well thought out definitions of what constitutes a sex offense, many new sex offender laws are in some cases nothing short of constitutional abuse; an abuse driven mostly by politicians pandering to hysteria.

When there isn't a desire to enforce existing laws or create actual tough laws then enforce those, politicians pass meaningless laws to give an appearance of caring about the applicable issues. For example, laws that make sex offenders move because they live within some given distance from schools or school bus stops give the appearance that the government is protecting children. But does it matter if a sex offender lives 1,000 feet away from a school or 1,001? I would think most of these people have cars. Some would argue that these laws make it easier to put these people away because they're easier to enforce. If true, what does this say about our legal system? When politicians propose these types of laws, what they really are saying is, "I'm a lazy coward and you're an idiot."

What is over-looked on purpose by the Government Class is the fact that: (1) Many sex offenders are relatives or good friends known to the victims and/or their families, but the responsible adults refuse to turn them in or take other appropriate actions. (2) Many sex-offenses are committed by repeat offenders that should have never been released from jail in the first place.

We do need better child sex offense protection laws in many states, but I can imagine that a great deal of sex offenses can be taken care of if individuals and government both do their basic jobs instead of trying to create meaningless new laws that do more harm than good; unless all you want to do is feel good or you're a politician and consider getting re-elected the success story. I don't want convicted sex-offenders to live near schools, but the best way to guarantee that is to turn 'em in, lock 'em up, leave 'em there, and make sure to tell the other inmates what they're there for. Provisions covered under Jessica's Law or similar laws should be the norm in every state.

Because Busy-bodies and Do-gooders lack feedback mechanisms to regulate their zeal, government will continue to meddle in the parent-child relationship beyond clear extreme physical or mental abuse. A fringe issue now, but one that will increase in tempo, will be the call to prohibit parents from teaching their children religion. If you think I'm nuts, do an internet search on "is teaching kids about religion abuse" or words to that effect and see what you get.

Busy-bodies and Do-gooders are at the front of the government ramming pole busting down your door in the name of proactively protecting "potential" victims. But that is not the purpose of government in a free society.

Regulists, Socialists, and Communists

Regulists, Socialists, and Communists are basically control freaks of varying degrees across all aspects of society and government. You probably have heard of Socialists and Communists, but not of Regulists.

A Regulist is a person who practices Regulism. To understand what Regulism is in the context used here, you first have to understand Fascism, Communism and Socialism. Fascism is the process where a dictatorial government allows private ownership at its discretion, but essentially is in control of everything, and when necessary can seize your property without justification. Communism and Socialism are processes where governments own and control everything.

Fascists are always depicted as brutes; and rightly so. But socialists and communists have better marketing teams thanks to the American Left. Thus, using canned statements like "worker's rights," "feed the hungry," or my favorite, "the greedy rich," these political ideologies tend to have softer connotations in our culture even though in practice they can be just as brutish as fascists.

Part of the marketing includes that nominally Socialists and Communists are people who believe in the noble goal of *from each according to their abilities, to each according to their needs.* But since they require state ownership and control of production to achieve this, you may interpret this philosophy as a license to *steal from those that produce and give to those that don't.*

With that in mind, I define Regulism as the process where the application of constitutional law gets in the way of direct government communist-like ownership, but fails for a number of reasons, to limit the government's indirect control through *excessive* regulations. The reasons for the constitutional failures primarily lie with either weakness in the law or just direct corruption by the Government Class (remember this includes the judiciary). Finally, Regulists differ from bureaucrats in that Regulists operate under the general strategic and philosophical umbrella of expanding government, whereas bureaucrats usually have much narrower and personal agendas dealing with operational aspects of their department, office, or corner of government.

Some might argue that Regulism could be the economic sweet spot between Communism and Capitalism. Except that they would be wrong. There is no sweet spot between Communism and anything. Communism mixes a warped state controlled economic philosophy with a governmental created and forced morality: the first commandment of which proclaims that the state knows what's best for you.

Capitalism does not mix economics with morality in the same sense as state controlled economies do. I think Dr. Edward Younkins, Professor of Accountancy and Business Administration at Wheeling Jesuit University in West Virginia and author of *Capitalism and Commerce*, said it best: "But some critics still contend that capitalism is not a moral system. Yet morality is impossible unless one is free to choose between alternatives without outside coercion. Since capitalism is based on freedom of choice, it provides the best environment for morality and character development."

Or more to the point: morality and freedom go hand-in-hand. Of course at this point of the conversation, there are always some that can't help themselves but bring up Enron. These people have such a blind allegiance to disastrous state controlled economic systems in a quest for unattainable "fairness," that they fixate on a few failures and ignore an economic system that has created countless ethical companies that in-turn have created an immense middle class. (Bill Gates has single handedly created more jobs than Bill Clinton and the whole Democratic party ever has or will.) What is often missed in their argument is that Enron executives *were* held accountable against existing laws by government executing one of its basic functions—law enforcement. (How ironic is it that these whiners could only be described with a word that starts with an "m" and rhymes with Enron.)

There is a popular system of definitions that define economic systems based on how a farmer is allowed to manage his cows. These have been added to over the years and are rather clever. I borrowed some of them and added some modifications of my own and included a new entry for Regulism. (There are many different versions of these lists, some differing from others by a few words or entries, but if you are interested just do an internet search on "two cows" or something similar and hunt around for the various lists.)

> **Fascism:** You have two cows. The government decides one day to take both of them from you but continues to make you care for them. If you complain, they shoot you.

> **Communism:** The state owns the two cows, but makes you care for them and milk them. The state collects the milk, skims off the cream for the party bosses, and redistributes the mostly spoiled remains to long lines of waiting consumers. If you complain, they send you to "re-education" gulags.

> **Socialism:** You have two cows. The government takes them and puts them in a barn with everyone else's cows. You have to take care of all the cows. A chicken farmer who knows nothing about cows is chosen to run the dairy

production plant. The government gives you milk and cheese based on governmental determined allocation levels that are far lower than what you used to get before the People's Democratic Socialist Labor Party won the last election. The only person to complain to is the chicken farmer, whose only comment is that, yes things are bad, but they are equally bad for everyone.

Regulism: You have two cows. The law allows you to sell a cow and buy a bull after applying and paying for the appropriate governmental permits. You won't be able to do any breeding until you attend the applicable mandatory cattle breeding training seminars; some even offered on line for your convenience. There are hundreds of laws and regulations telling you how to care for your cow and how and when to milk her. The government taxes you for every calf born but pays you for the milk it orders to be poured down the drain in order to regulate the milk supply. Snafus between the government's Animal Husbandry Division and Vegetable and Fruits Division prevents you from selling your manure in a timely manner adding costs to your operations and a smaller yield for the vegetable farmers. If you complain, the IRS suddenly discovers a minor mistake on your last year's 32 page tax statement and puts a lien on your farm. You get caught in IRS red tape, and end up spending all of your savings on tax attorneys and die broke.

Capitalism: You have two cows. You sell one and buy a bull and mate them. You complain to your wife about all of the manure piling up from all the little cows. She tells you to sell the manure to the vegetable farmers. Life is good.

Although Regulism is a political philosophy onto itself, in America many frustrated Communists and Socialists release their pent up frustrations as Regulists through the liberal creation of laws and governmental regulations. I don't really care if deep down inside some Communists and Socialists are pure in heart caring only for the equal distribution of resources, and the disasters in the Soviet Union and elsewhere were anomalies caused by corrupt individuals. Since Communists and Socialists believe in a comprehensive big government, and government is inherently wasteful, and only government has police powers, and power corrupts, and corrupted power leads to innocent people ending up shot or in gulags; forces me to the conclusion that Communists and Socialists are either evil, naïve, or incredibly dumb. You decide.

◆   ◆   ◆

In all cases, the various Government Class groups look at government, in one way or another, as a vehicle to force a social, moral, or economic agenda because the government has the police authority to make things happen. Because relying on government is the easy way out to force a desired outcome and emotionally appealing to many, it's easier to be a Liberal politician than a Conservative one. The reason is simple: the greatest failure of Republicans has always been buckling to the emotional cry to solve a problem through a government solution.

Appealing to emotion is one of the greatest weapons Liberals have, and as humans, it is a weapon that is difficult to defend against. Government programs have vocal constituency groups, and small organized vocal groups supporting a cause are almost always more powerful than larger unorganized groups hoping to keep a little bit more of their paychecks, and hold on to whatever independence they may have left.

Once a Liberal puts forth the thesis that we must stop hunger through more (failed) government programs, Conservatives are left with the image that they don't care about hunger or they even want to spread it. Of course, the real issue is what is the best way to end hunger (pssst, it's called the free market), including addressing the level of government involvement. But by the time the Conservative reply has been made, the Liberal sound bite has already made its round.

If we associate being a Republican to the color red and being a Democrat to the color blue, then under emotional pressure many Republican politicians and bureaucrats turn pink whereas their Democratic Party counterparts stay true blue. Thus, it seems that the hardest thing a sincere Republican politician can do is to practice what they preach and trust the free market or the ability of people to solve problems at the applicable societal level with proportional responses.

These solutions may not be esthetically pretty, but often are more effective than the government solutions, have less long term entanglements, and inevitably always cost less. I don't expect modern Liberals to trust the free market or believe in individual responsibility, so I'm not surprised by their words or actions. The nature of modern Liberalism is not to allow communities or individuals to vary from their view of the world. That is why it is imperative that modern Liberalism frequently seeks a federal-level course of action from agriculture to zoology.

It is often said that the reason why the media and educational and political organizations are populated with Liberals is because Conservatives tend toward other pursuits such as business. There may be something to that if you accept my

Government Class definition. This phenomenon is often wrongly confused with the observation that Liberals actively propose answers to problems whereas Conservatives are passive.

In reality, being part of the Government Class is not just a job, but a way of life. Members of the Government Class continuously seek new ways to get taxpayers to pay for questionable public projects, whereas for Conservatives *the solution is often not a government solution but rather the often more efficient free market*. Except for a well defined set of processes, true Conservatives do not see government as a means to an end. This applies also to the use of the judicial branch to correct all classes of social ills or individual wrongs at the micro level. Another way of looking at this is that when wronged, Conservatives don't look at themselves as victims.

Thus, Conservatives are not politically active in the same sense as Liberals are, or put another way, political activism is predominately a Liberal thing. That is why, even when Conservatives are the recipients of a private action, they tend not to react in the same victim-like behavior as a liberal might, i.e., seek a government solution. And when they do, doesn't it just seem a little *unnatural?*

The bottom line is our governments and other social and public institutions are, unsurprisingly, manned mostly by members of the Government Class defined by Blue Liberals and Pink Republicans: all seeking to either increase the role of government or for all intents and purposes enabling the same outcome. Since the Government Class is proactive in pursuing bigger government, this leaves true Conservatives in a constant reactive mode; but it doesn't have to be that way. Conservatives can also be politically active.

A recent example is the 1994 Republican congressional takeover of the House based on the Contract with America. The Contract with America if completely enacted would have been both a real and psychological conservative victory. But after the GOP victory, the Contract got mixed results because of Pink Conservatives and other members of the Government Class.

So why didn't Conservative Republicans continue to push for the remaining points of the Contract or create new ones, considering the GOP held power over at least two thirds of the government for a number of years? During the Cold War, Soviet Grand Pooh-Bah Leonid Ilyich Brezhnev announced a policy that later became known as the Brezhnev Doctrine. The Brezhnev Doctrine in essence said: *once a country went communist, it would remain communist.* Many in the West accepted that proclamation. Fortunately, President Reagan didn't. But many Republicans it seems have the same defeatist altitude about leftist politics: *once a liberal policy is in place, it shall remain in place.*

In the fall 2006 primaries, the national GOP backed moderate Republicans over conservative ones because of the fear that the conservative candidates couldn't win in the general election. Clearly the GOP just wanted to hold onto power and did not care about right or wrong. They didn't walk the talk; and they paid for it at the polls.

Democrats rightfully used the 2005 and 2006 U.S. Congressional lobbying and page scandals to label Republicans as corrupt. In reality, Republicans were corrupt because they: (1) were in power and money flows to those in power, and (2) they failed to adhere to Conservative principles of limiting government and thus limiting lobbying influences.

When Democrats get back into the swing of things they will become corrupt for two reasons: (1) they will be in power and money flows to those in power, and (2) they will expand government allowing even more lobbying influences.

At the state level, Ohio Republicans had been in power long enough to discount the argument that problems were inherited from previous Democratic administrations and legislatures. State Republicans had ample opportunity to enact a number of conservative political and economic initiatives, but they did not. Ohio's loss of competitiveness and the financial mess the state schools are in are just two examples of their failure.

The Republican Party as currently configured is not a conservative party. I recommend the Republican Party adopt a new motto: "Republicans, We're a lot like Democrats, but just not as committed."

◆   ◆   ◆

The Declaration of Independence declares that the "Creator" has endowed us with certain "unalienable rights" which include life, liberty and the pursuit of happiness. Ironically there are three pesky words in those unalienable rights that separate the Government Class from everyone else. Those words are "the pursuit of." Because the Government Class is not content in allowing us to pursue happiness as we see fit, but rather they see it as their duty to ensure happiness. Happiness of course defined by the Government Class, paid for by taxpayers, and enforced by government.

Sure, members of the Government Class pay taxes too, but taxes are just a fee to pay-to-play. The bottom line is that the Government Class has stoked the engine of government at all levels, with the result of consuming ever increasing resources but producing less and less meaningful output.

4

The Other Ten Commandments

Host: Welcome to our second round, where all dollar figures are doubled. Tony gets to go first. Tony?

Tony: I'll take Government Spending for $2000.

Host: The question is, "What major accomplishment can be attributed to the Government Class?" Joe buzzed first.

Joe: Increases in country club Republican membership applications.

Host: That's not what we were looking for. Cassandra? Tony?

Cassandra: Well, let's see … John Kerry got a D in his freshman government course at Yale.

Host: Well that may be true, but sorry that's not the type of "government class" we're referring to here.

Tony: A corrupt and bankrupt government.

Host: Tony, you get another $2000 added to your winnings. Go ahead and pick the next category.

Do any of the following sound familiar to you?

- A country's legislature working on a budget bursting with record deficits votes to approve over $200 million to build a "bridge-to-nowhere."

- A legislature in a state strapped for cash votes to support a privately-owned arts center to the tune of many tens of millions of dollars while many more essential programs go unfunded, education funding is in chaos, state taxes have risen to one of the highest in the country, and jobs are being lost at a phenomenal pace.

- A board of commissioners in a county strapped for cash votes to provide tax abatement for private retail development while at the same time floats the idea of a sales tax increase.

- A city council strapped for cash votes to build and operate a golf course at tax-payer's expense while bemoaning the lack of funds for more basic city services.

- A school board strapped for cash votes to fund unnecessary sports programs in a year when many students had no assigned textbooks and student overcrowding begins to appear as a problem.

The first case refers to a recent U.S. Senate budget item for construction of an Alaskan bridge that would have served only a few dozen residents; most of whom already get by just using their boats to visit the mainland. The other items can represent any state or community in America, because the shenanigans of the Government Class know no state or community boundaries. Across the country, in every city and state your tax money is being squandered by a Government Class out of control.

A great example is public funding of the arts and entertainment. In order to make the spending sound impressive, the Government Class sets up commissions that advertise themselves as Art Councils, Cultural Committees, Improvement Boards, and so on. As they spend your money, they have a great time at black tie affairs talking about future plans to further spend your money. In Ohio, some of this spending included $400,000 in 2006 to improve the Pro Football Hall of Fame in Canton, Ohio. Apparently professional sports organizations are too poor to afford improving monuments to themselves. And this was only chump change compared to the $430 million that the state has given out since 1988 for cultural facilities improvements, including over $100 million for Cleveland and Cincinnati sports stadiums. And that's just under one state commission.

Part of money also included $25 million for The Benjamin and Marian Schuster Performing Arts Center, a $120-130 million facility located in downtown Dayton. The center was named after Dr. Benjamin Schuster and his wife who generously donated $8 million to its construction. The remaining costs were covered by private donors, local business contributions, and other sources.

What is important is that a fairly large chunk of the construction costs was paid for by taxpayers. In this respect, there are at least two things that I have in common with millions of other Ohio taxpayers: (1) I have never attended a show at the Schuster Center and probably never will, and (2) I helped pay for it. (I came close to attending a concert in 2005. I'll pay $20 to see a show, which I recognize sounds unreasonable when compared to people who spend hundreds or even thousands on concert tickets, but tickets at $70, $80, $90 and higher, pretty much turn me into Mr. Cheapo.)

Members of the Government Class often justify the public financing of cultural and sports enterprises, as a means of providing "seed" money to enrich lives, help create jobs, and spur growth. The problem with this argument is that the government does a horrible job in choosing these projects, because its decision making process is politically driven not market driven. *When you look at the spending pattern what you often see is just pork barrel politics.* But even a blind squirrel finds a nut once in a while, and indeed in some cases this approach works.

Politicians made it a point when they visit communities to proudly proclaim how they helped fund this or that project. They make these claims while more fundamental government infrastructure needs go unfunded or are under funded. I have a suggestion for the Government Class if they really are interested in spurring growth, providing jobs, or increasing the quality of life: *cut taxes and get the hell out of the way.*

But the Government Class can't get out of the way. The Do-gooders of the Government Class press the argument that the arts enrich the lives of the great unwashed. They are convinced that large box store shoppers once exposed to incomprehensible German or Italian yodeling, would run out and peel the Dale Earnhart "3" off of their pick-up trucks and replace it with, "Ask Me About My Grandson the Opera Tenor."

Don't think that this is just a Dayton issue. There is a very good chance that your local Government Class has raided your pocket book for the sake of the "Arts."

One example is the *Dollar for Art* program in Naples, Florida. Under this local law, developers are forced to contribute $1 per square foot into an arts fund. The chairwoman of the Public Arts Advisory Committee and head artsy-fartsy activist said, "We're setting a standard for art, it is not a tax. It is a building standard."

Have you ever wondered why so many artists are called "starving artists?" It's because we have more artists than the market can bear. So we have created welfare programs for modern artists who by definition have no talent, because if they had talent, they wouldn't need to mooch off of taxpayers to make a living. To add insult to injury, these "starving artists" actually view funding for the arts as a right, thereby absolving themselves from having to at least say thank you. Again, don't make the mistake that this is a local Naples, Florida thing; the same program exists in other cities under various different names.

In general, spending money on the arts, including public broadcasting, is no different than when the jock lobby entices the Government Class to fund sports stadiums so that very rich team owners can use public money to get richer.

Remember all this happens as basic and legitimate state and local functions often go unfunded or under funded.

The education industry has one of the most active wings of the Government Class. Expanded pre-school programs, free breakfast and lunch programs, free condoms and abortion counseling, over-funded sports programs and numerous other programs never meant to fall under "public education" are all part of the mix. But don't dare criticize them. After all, regardless of the cost or the ethics, everything they do is *for the children.*

So what's wrong with the government providing day care? IT'S NOT THE GOVERNMENT'S JOB!!!!

Deciding what role the government has on a particular issue is complex but an attempt to arrive at a conclusion can be based on both human nature and history; and it's not like we don't know about human nature or that we are short on historical lessons of governmental failures and abuse. We will return to this particular discussion later in the book. For now let's remember that only government has police authority and can deprive people of their rights, or take away from people the results of their blood, sweat and tears. Therefore, on gray issues everyone should be on the "no government involvement side" of the fence, but more often than not, most of us aren't even paying attention.

It is hard to imagine any other institution besides government that would be able to build roads, construct and maintain sewers, create public parks, protect our borders (ahem), provide fire and police services, print currency and mint coins, establish weights and measures, and in a limited sense provide for a general education. Clearly government does have many legitimate and meaningful roles, even if it often does these inefficiently. (Historically, some of these functions were originally private enterprises, so I would imagine there are people who would even argue the validity of these functions.)

On the flip side of the issue, can anyone imagine private enterprises singularly involved in creating and operating entertainment complexes, radio and TV stations, golf courses, pre-schools, schools, airlines, taxis, malls and countless other enterprises? Yes of course, because it happens all the time. And when these enterprises are successful it is because there was a market need. That's why there isn't a commercial passenger train system in the United States; because there is no market for one. However, there is a public train system because there is a Government Class need for one. And how well does the Government Class operate our trains? They run the trains into recurring annual bankruptcy.

How did we get here? Earlier I defined Regulism as the process where the application of constitutional law gets in the way of direct government ownership but fails to limit the government's indirect control through *excessive* regulations. I also asked the question in the previous chapter on where Americans stood on government's role in a free society. Let's further address both of those issues now. Read the following statements and consider how you feel about the government carrying out the actions in each subject area.

1. Abolish private property and apply land use to the public good

2. Establish a heavy progressive or graduated income tax

3. Abolish rights of inheritance

4. Confiscate the property of all criminals

5. Centralize all credit in state banks by means of a national bank under an exclusive government monopoly

6. Establish state control of communication and transportation systems

7. Establish state control of factory production and farming

8. Enforce an equal liability of all to work and establish government controlled industries such as agriculture

9. Gradually abolish the distinction between town and country by a more equable distribution of the populace over the country

10. Provide free education for all children in public schools

The ten commandments above are gifts from Karl Marx (with some rewording to put the statements in an applicable modern context). So if you answered yes or had an inclination to answer yes to all or most of the questions above; congratulations comrade, you earn the Red Star and you have Government Class potential.

Ironically, a large number of Americas would answer NO or be inclined to answer NO to most of the 10 questions. So given the popular perception that Americans are independent freedom loving people, let's take a quick look at the actual status of these ten items in America today.

Item 1: Abolish private property and apply land use to the public good

Phase I is complete, the government is no longer just an arbitrator of land disputes. Just consider the excessive limitations put on property owners by ever increasing environmental and other laws. This establishes the concept that one only rents land from the government but never really owns it.

Then consider how eminent domain cases are now handled, where you must give up the land you thought you owned to make room for important public projects like putt-putt golf courses. We are now in Phase II where the government is re-educating us to understand that the term "private property" is an oxymoron. What is amazing is that it was the respect of property rights that propelled western culture ahead of the rest of the world in science and technology, because "property" was more than land, but also included intellectual property.

Item 2: Establish a heavy progressive or graduated income tax

Today the highest marginal federal tax rate is 35% and is sadly, for a lot of reasons, one of few Conservative victories. (For some, adding state and local income taxes could bring their total marginal income tax burden to the 45% to 50% range or higher.) Although the current federal rate is down from 90%+ during the 1940s and the 70% rate in the 1980s it is still too high. It would still be too high even if it were half of what it is today because an income tax is a fundamentally corrupt process. But Liberals can take heart because the current federal upper limit is unstable. When the Left retakes the government, the marginal rates will more than likely increase again.

The Government Class would like to see the upper brackets get back up to the 70-90% range again, even though every sound economic theory and real world results show that the tax versus revenue sweet spot is at the lower end of the tax rate scale as described by the Laffer Curve and related economic theories. In other words, although increasing taxes raises revenues, there is a point where people stop being productive, become tax cheaters, or develop an underground bartering system for the sole purpose of avoiding paying excessive taxes.

This concept was even known in ancient Egypt as recorded by Ibn Khaldūn, a 14th century Islamic all-around-smart guy. It is also known but conveniently ignored by the 21st century Government Class because *it's all about control, not revenue.*

If the government were only concerned about revenue, it would adopt a tax similar to the Fair Tax as discussed in *The Fair Tax Book* by talk show host Neal Boortz and Congressman John Linder, and presented in House and Senate bills. One immediate benefit would be the reduction of tax codes from 50,000 pages to a few hundred, followed by an explosion of business development and growth.

You should note how once your income is taxed, it is taxed again when you make profits on your investments; investments that you took all the risk on, and the government gets a share. To add insult to injury, the IRS calls many of these types of income "unearned," as if you're not worthy of receiving the returns on your investments.

Item 3: Abolish rights of inheritance

Done already for the "greedy rich," only a matter of time for everyone else since the center of gravity for this argument is no longer whether inheritance taxes are immoral, but merely what the government considers "rich." This is related to property rights of Item 1, i.e., what is property and do you own the fruits of your labor to dispense with as you see fit?

Item 4: Confiscate the property of all criminals

Actually, Marx used the terms "emigrants and rebels." I changed it to criminals for a variety of reasons. One being I have no idea what Marx meant by emigrants and rebels. I read Marx's *Communist Manifesto* many years ago and would rather read the 2000 page Federal Acquisition Regulation (FAR) then read Marx again. (The FAR is over 16 megabytes if you care to download it.)

The second reason has to do with the popular statement that the current income tax system makes criminals out of every taxpayer. So "criminals" could include people with legitimate disputes with the IRS, as well as people that decide to fight questionable eminent domain motions trying to hold on to their homes. The government needs a bully agency like the IRS to be able to execute bad tax law.

Item 5: Centralize all credit in state banks by means of a national bank under an exclusive government monopoly

Our banking industry is privately owned but regulated. Some regulations are necessary; however some of the more socialistic regulations led to the mortgage meltdown and the subsequent 2008 government takeover and bailout of a number of banking and related services. Government overreach, corruption, and incompetence caused the meltdown and the solution was more government. The solution should have been the repeal of the bad laws and holding applicable government officials accountable.

Item 6: Establish state control of communication and transportation systems

Light to heavily regulated with some limited government ownership. However, in almost all cases where the government owns these processes, the industries are losing money, such as AmTrak.

At the local level, one might even make quasi-legitimate arguments for tax supported regional transit systems. But it would be nice if the local governments would run these systems in good faith. Instead, in many cases, they are rife with inefficiencies and corruption.

If communication systems also include entertainment media then there is of course the Corporation for Public Broadcasting (CPB). The CPB is a front organization to allow the federal government to meddle in affairs that can be handled by the private sector.

Item 7: Establish state control of factory production and farming

Light to heavily regulated depending on the specific industry (some warranted) with more than enough insane farming regulations managed by a bloated Department of Agriculture that manages farm land as if we lived in a permanent 1930s depression. I wish the government would pay me not to grow crops in my 12' x 12' garden.

This topic allows us to go back to the abuse of the Commerce Cause. Under the New Deal, the government set quotas on a number of crops. A farmer, Roscoe Filburn, decided to produce more wheat than allowed under the government's quota. He claimed that the excess was to be used for personal consumption and thus did not fall under commerce regulations (however the amount in excess was rather large).

In 1942, the Supreme Court in Wickard v. Filburn, ruled that Filburn's wheat competed with wheat sold in interstate commerce, reasoning that if Filburn had not used home-grown wheat, he would have had to buy wheat on the open market. In effect the court ruled that not only can congress regulate commerce on the supply side but can also regulate demand. Furthermore, congress can do all this regulating even if individual effects are small as long as it determines the overall affect from numerous individual violations is substantial.

Item 8: Enforce an equal liability of all to work and establish government controlled industries such as agriculture

If I understand this statement correctly, this is the only item where the federal and state governments have flipped Marx's meaning, which probably was meant to ensure that the bourgeois did their fair share of work. Currently, the federal and state governments actually reward people for not working. As to the second part of the item, see Item 7.

Item 9: Gradually abolish the distinction between town and country by a more equable distribution of the populace over the country

I doubt a forced mass migration of people will literary happen under the context assumed here. Of course, there have been times in America's past where forced migrations have occurred by law, such as the Indian Removal Act of 1830, the Japanese camps during World War II, and of course African Slavery.

However, what will more likely occur is the federal government's increasing power over local and state governmental authorities. Thus, what is being abolished is the real distinction between levels of city, state, and federal governments.

Item 10: Provide free education for all children in public schools

This is a biggie. First of all, of course, nothing is free, the government has managed to force a taxpayer supported education monopoly on the country whether you use the service or not, and like many other services that should have limited or no government involvement depending on the specifics, the system is bankrupt both financially and intellectually. If you wish to use a private school, you are still liable to pay education taxes. Occasional "rebels" pop up to fight for charter schools and/or vouchers and some silly parents still think they have parental rights over their children. Public education is a big part of this book and will be discussed in more detail as we proceed.

◆   ◆   ◆

So as the Left fights hard to destroy the Commandants of Moses. They are fighting equally as hard to establish the Commandants of Marx. The only thing missing is putting in the proper "Thou shalts" and "Thou shalt nots" as applicable.

How did we get to where we are today? We got to this state because a number of very vocal Americans really don't want freedom; they want security and are willing to sell their souls for it. A significant portion of the rest of the country is more worried about who the next Hollywood couple is going to be than about the politician rummaging in their purse or wallet.

Although the majority of Americans philosophically hold mostly conservative principles when it comes to government spending, there aren't enough true conservative leaders in government to combat one-for-one the activism of the Government Class. When a member of the Government Class puts forth an issue, the vocal emotional pressure to compromise is intense.

Pink Republicans help the spiraling-down process through compromise with the Left with what is often called "bipartisanship." Some bipartisanship is okay when you are talking about nuances in NASA's budget but not in compromising your principles.

But regardless of what the politicians say about win-win compromises, they are usually always victories for the Government Class. They are more often victories because of the Hegel, Marx, Engels and Lenin use of the *thesis, antithesis and synthesis* triad. The compromise becomes the basis for the next thesis sometime in the future, which in a continuous fashion leads to the government offering programs it cannot afford and shouldn't even offer.

So what do we make of the conclusions above? Basically, governments are broke because we have allowed them to take on basic processes that governments were not designed to do. Thus, although governments will always be inefficient, limiting government to a set of legitimate but well defined functions ensures both economic stability as well as personal freedoms.

Out-right fraud in government is controlled by laws and check and balance processes, but legal over zealous and ill-conceived actions of the Government Class can only be controlled by active taxpayers knowledgeable in the proper role of government, at all levels, in a free society. However, that also requires a competent education system.

Taxes are the life blood of government and to the Government Class. Our founders envisioned a republic not a democracy. But they envisioned a republic where the people and their representatives understood the difference. As an eerie follow up to Jefferson's statement noted earlier, Marx had this to say: "Democracy is the road to socialism."

Part II
For the Children?

Whereas the now better informed reader having been introduced to the Government Class is guided through a somewhat different discussion of education in America.

5

The Education Industrial Complex

I would promise the whole amount were I not afraid that someday my gift might be abused for someone's selfish purposes, as I see happen in many places where teachers' salaries are paid from public funds.

—Gaius Plinius Caecilius Secundus (63-113 AD)

Historically, it would be difficult to pinpoint the birth of public education. In the United States, public education, as we think we currently understand it, evolved to where it is today from a vague beginning along a somewhat disjointed process. Central to this is that early in our history there *really* were 13 independent and sovereign states united primarily for their common good and defense. The design was for each of these states to act largely independently when it came to internal affairs.

The States' interest in keeping their independence and sovereignty combined with their fear of a powerful federal government permeates throughout the constitution and specifically in the 10th amendment, which basically further emphasizes and delineates the limitations of federal power, or in simple terms, "If it ain't said here, then it ain't gonna happen." Public education, being one of those things not mentioned in the constitution, meant that in whatever form it took, public education was a state and local function and thus could vary greatly from one state to the next.

Pinpointing the exact time of death of public education is much easier. A close call came in 1867, when President Andrew Johnson signed legislation creating the first Department of Education. The Department's main purpose was to collect information and statistics about the country's schools. This could have been the death of public education, however, many people feared the Department would exercise too much control over local schools and called for its abolition. Thus, the new Department was demoted to an Office of Education in 1868.

(Boy weren't they silly; imagine a federal department exercising too much control at the local level; what's that all about?)

Public education took a series of mortal hits in the 1960s with President Johnson's War on Poverty which increased federal educational "assistance" (ahem) at the local level. This "assistance" (ahem) continued through the 1970s, and finally public education received the fatal wound and died on May 4, 1980. That's the day the learning died, because that's the day the Department of Education Organization Act (Public Law 96-88 of October 1979) took effect and the modern federal Department of Education was formed.

At the time of this writing the Department's website lists a handful or so of seemingly innocuous objectives to improve this, promote that, blah, blah, blah. But as of 2002, meeting these goals required 4,800 employees and a $54.4 billion budget. The 1867 department had four employees and a budget of $15,000.

It is understandable but unfortunate that the term *public education* is still used to denote that process that uses public money for public educational purposes. The use of the term *public education* is often directly and indirectly coupled with the concept of public education being locally paid for and controlled. However, a more appropriate term following the use of the term Government Class would be *government schools* (this term is also used heavily by Neal Boortz, but I'm not sure if he originated it).

Here I use the word "government" in its libertarian contemptuous sense, because although much of public education is paid for locally or at the state level, in reality the paying public has lost control over the style and substance of their community school systems. Public schools are now government schools run under the umbrella of politicians, bureaucrats, lawyers and several other groups to be discussed later. At the local level, PTOs, booster clubs and parents in general are told they are part of the education team, but in reality their participation is usually limited to buying classroom crayons or helping to organize proms.

The education industry would balk at the use of the term government schools as used here, after all, the Department of Education's website in 2006 describing the federal role in education shows them boasting the following facts:

- Education is primarily a State and local responsibility in the United States.

- Of an estimated $852 billion being spent nationwide on education at all levels for school year 2003-2004, about 90 percent comes from State, local, and private sources.

- The remaining 10 percent includes educational expenditures from other Federal agencies, such as the Department of Health and Human Services' Head Start program and the Department of Agriculture's School Lunch program.

- The department's $63.3 billion appropriation is only about 2.7 percent of the Federal Government's nearly $2.3 trillion budget in fiscal year 2004.

- The department targets its funds where they can do the most good. This targeting reflects the historical development of the Federal role in education as a kind of "emergency response system," filling gaps in State and local support for education when critical national needs arise.

Sounds like a great deal, doesn't it? But why does a department that has little to do have 5,000 employees? In reality the Department doesn't need a great deal of money to carry through with an agenda. The agenda is carried out by either bureaucratic fiat by its nearly 5,000 employees or through the procedural actions of congress and the administration through it or other related government agencies. Thus, although its *direct* budget may be under 3% of the federal budget, through *federal* governmental dictates, the Department of Education and other agencies related to the education industry have direct and indirect access or influence to the full $852 billion national educational budget regardless of what level those funds are raised.

Now, I'm going to go out on a limb and raise that number to $1 trillion. Not only because that's a nice round number, but surely the amount of indirect money that goes into education, especially at the local district level, has to be worth about another measly $148 billion.

This includes the revenue from the countless local nickel and dime contributions, volunteer time, and various fund raisers. But it also includes the support from businesses that contribute time or resources as part of their community good neighbor obligations.

For the record, I'm not saying that individuals or corporations shouldn't volunteer or help local school districts. However, the help should *complement* the educational program not *supplement* it. But that is not what is happening in many districts. Government schools are so inefficient and wasteful that many districts across the country rely on outside help just to stay alive. Occasionally you hear of a local news media story about how some parents and neighborhoods have banded together to save their schools. Well, good for them, but how long can they keep piling on sand bags in a permanent storm? Why isn't anyone asking where the education tax revenues are going to? Why aren't people in charge being held accountable?

One trillion dollars is a lot of money to control, and when the feds speak, states and communities are forced to listen. One method the feds use to spread their power and influence is through *unfunded mandates*. This approach epitomizes the most cowardly form of federal leadership, one that dictates actions and outcomes without regard to the problems faced at the local level including the difficulty in raising the funds necessary to carry out the mandates. It is as naïve or arrogant as Marie Antoinette's "Let them eat cake"; only it takes the form, "Let them raise levies."

W's *No Child Left Behind Act* is a prime example of a lousy federal mandate on so many levels; it is an emotional appealing law that sets impossible goals. However, all three branches of government are guilty of unfunded mandates, including activist judges when they mandate specific solutions or programs from the bench whose details are left to be worked out by others; including finding the funds to pay for the subsequent chaos.

When a district superintendent makes a controversial decision within his or her control, parents have direct access to that person. But what options do you have with an unfunded government mandate? In practical terms, you have absolutely none. But the problem with the Department of Education is more than its arrogance and inefficiencies.

In 1961, President Eisenhower warned Americans of the military industrial complex, a vague conglomerate of industries ostensibly supplying military goods and services. The concern was that as a collective sub-culture individual members of the military industrial complex were and are often just looking out for their own self-interest, and the usefulness of a weapon system not measured by its need, but its value in congressional pork. Central to Eisenhower's speech was the warning that because of the natural lure of the immenseness of the public treasury, we must always strive for a "balance between the clearly necessary and the comfortably desirable."

Although the term "industrial complex" is often used only in conjunction with the military (thanks to the Left), the expansion of government has given rise to a number of industrial complexes. The military was naturally identified first since defense is one of the oldest of governmental functions and one with an immense public purse.

What makes an industrial complex? This question can be answered by identifying two key attributes and one common effect. First, the process or enterprise must have a large federal department-level or equivalent agency or set of similar agencies ripe for looting. The second attribute is the looters must be able to hide behind and effectively use emotional arguments when logical ones fail. Finally, all industrial complexes have the same effect: *they all destroy, corrupt, or greatly weaken the legitimate purpose of the applicable government agency's mission.*

A department level agency guarantees a large budget and/or federal power, and ensures nearly all applicable issues become national issues thereby destroying any chance of local control and the development of a system of best practices. Emotional arguments allow dropping any semblance of civility or proportionality when discussing relevant issues. This is why when logical arguments about the benefits of this or that weapon system fail, lobbyists whisper the magical four letter word, P-O-R-K, in politicians' ears; while simultaneously waving the American Flag for consumption by the general public. (I am not necessarily making statements about particular calls to support military actions to defend America or our interests. I'm talking about the corruption in the political and funding process.)

As government agencies such as the Environmental Protection Agency, Department of Energy, and Department of Education and others, were created, so followed their respective industrial complexes. Each of these agencies now must both fulfill the legitimate aspects of their mission (if any) as well as appease the looters ready to steal from the public purse.

Eisenhower called on the "councils of government" to counterbalance this attack on the public treasury. Although Eisenhower was referring mostly to military issues, his words could be used against many of the problems we see today across society including education.

However, Eisenhower made the same mistake as our founders did when they thought that elected representatives understood their responsibilities under the new republic. Thus, the problem with Eisenhower's councils of government theory is that either he didn't know or overlooked that these councils of government were manned by mostly members of the Government Class. He might as well have said that in order for our country to protect our chicken farms we would have to rely on a council of wolves. Therefore, the creation of the Department of Education has merely led to the *Education Industrial Complex*. (In September 2004, I published an article in a local paper that used the term *Educational* Industrial Complex. However, variations of these terms have also been used by others as a quick internet search would show.)

Some members of the Education Industrial Complex are quite obvious, such as teachers unions. In fact, the gusto that teachers unions have for using public money to expand their powers is legendary. As one transitions from local unions to their state and national organizations, one finds the unions going beyond just employment issues but shaping much of what is taught inside government schools as well as controlling their basic operations, thereby ensuring a steady stream of questionable education funding. Teachers unions have become so powerful that they contribute to political causes and candidates that have little if anything to do directly with education.

Another group includes the nation's Colleges of Education, where professors, and associated intellectuals, who have more book learning than common sense, are always more than happy to spew out the educational theory du jour. These studies are often paid for by either publicly funded educational grants or sometimes by teachers union grants.

These same Colleges of Education are ensured a steady stream of business through laws and regulations that require would-be teachers to obtain certification for the right to teach. If the mob did this, we would call it extortion.

To make matters worse, a whispered but well circulated rumor is that education training programs are not known for their academic rigor. Therefore, acquiring the coveted certificate is mostly based on whether the student teacher has mastered a long list of academically questionable courses. Furthermore, the constant shifting of teaching or learning practices to fit "today's theory," coupled with changing political pressure, as well as corrupted political processes including political correctness, has made most formal teacher training indistinguishable from babble. This is unfortunate.

Then there is the university/college industry in general that directly or indirectly promulgates the notion that you can actually get a job by graduating with any one of a plethora of useless degrees. Thus, when a Medieval Welsh Art History major graduates and can't get a job in her field, she accuses the capitalist system for not appreciating the contributions that she and thousands of other Medieval Welsh Art History graduates that graduated that year can make.

Our funding of higher education promotes wasteful spending on courses and disciplines that serve no useful societal purpose *in the numbers that are graduating*. Meanwhile American companies are left to hire foreign Software Engineers because Americans are studying Medieval Welsh Art History. America needs artists, but it needs more engineers to design bridges than artists who can paint them on a canvass.

Let's not also forget the tendency of many universities that have just outright abandoned education as their primary mission, opting instead to pursue grant writing as their primary end goal. The "publish or perish" operating philosophy, if checked, has some benefit as a forcing function to new discoveries, especially in technology areas and some non-technical fields, but how many more modern interpretations of Beowulf do we need?

The Education Industrial Complex also includes the countless cottage industries bombarding parents with the next "need to have" book, software, or tutoring service that will make the difference between State U and Harvard for precious little Ariel. This includes those companies that offer $1000 courses to get your future Einsteins to pass the SAT or ACT. This bombardment process starts the moment your child is born and whose only function is to create a crises environment. This cottage industry also includes the colleges themselves who have created expensive procedures whose only purpose is to "help" parents and potential students guide themselves through the chaotic application and entrance process.

This may sound all conspiratorial, and although some of it is in limited ways, overall many actions within an industrial complex are independent of each other. It is not necessary to have a secret board or single person pulling the strings, after all, the superintendent in New York does not have to coordinate with the superintendent in Peoria. It is enough that they serve the same cultural master that ensures the end result is the same, i.e., a tremendous amount of money spent on a process that more often than not, does not serve the people it purports to serve. This type of nonsense is costing us individually and collectively as a nation. And I'm not just talking money.

Let me make an analogy here. In the 1970s the American car companies were making horrible cars; mechanically dysfunctional cars that Americans didn't want or need. If you lived through those years, then you know what I mean. A 2x4 to the head by the Arab oil exporting countries, followed by a kick in the groin by the Japanese, got the American car companies' attention and had the affect in producing the needed improvements. In the 21st century, the American educational system is in the same state of affairs as our automobile industry was in the 1970s, but this time we are talking about crop after crop of dysfunctional graduates.

An education system must fit the needs of the society it purports to serve. America capitalized on the industrial revolution and became an industrial giant.

It is not a coincidence that our education system was patterned after a factory assembly line, where instead of moving toasters from one station or worker to the next station or worker, we move kids from one grade or subject to the next grade or subject. The model that worked for making toasters and increasing our standard of living, also worked for educating kids: it got us through many difficult times in our history and produced the finest minds in the world.

The problem is we are no longer a manufacturing society, but our education system is still set up as if we were. And there is a tremendous resistance to change that.

In every community across the country the Education Industrial Complex hammers the point that no matter how much we are spending on education, we must spend more. We must spend more ... *for the children.* In reality, the self-serving Education Industrial Complex is wasting dollars and wasting lives, and in the mean time, we are going financially and ideologically bankrupt. Even districts that earn high marks are in reality barely keeping their heads above water in terms of supplying the educated adults our society needs. How frustrating must it be for committed professionals to be suffocating in the Education Industrial Complex?

A newspaper headline reads, "Students can't find Iraq on map." Another headline may read, "Nearly half of population reads below average." Or another may cite a study that concludes, "Many adult high school graduates can't do 9th grade math." (Believe it or not, as I wrote this paragraph, a commercial came on the radio and rattled off geography statistics claiming 20% of students couldn't identify the Pacific Ocean. The commercial's purpose of course was to solicit more money for geography studies.)

The responses to these headlines are always the same: more funding for *special programs* for geography; more funding for *special programs* for reading; more funding for *special programs* for math; ad infinitum.

There are of course a few souls that raise some interesting questions like isn't geography, reading, and math part of the basic curriculum already? Or, if districts are spending up to $20,000 or higher per student per year, isn't the process broken? Or how about a more direct approach like by definition half the population is below average intelligence and some of these will never achieve the academic success of the general population, so what's the problem? In terms of the 20% in the radio ad that couldn't tell the difference between the Pacific Ocean and their bath tub, what are the chances that a great number of the 20% was the bottom academic 20%?

I hate to be so blunt, but how much money will be spent on losing propositions, while America sinks further behind the rest of the world? Some people will never be able to find the Pacific Ocean, even if you told them they were swimming in it. And 20% is probably right. But that doesn't mean they can't be educated. It means the education system has to be smarter and more agile to serve our society's modern needs. *It has to be equal access, not equal outcome.* The system will have to be able to—dare I say it—discriminate based on abilities, and formulate polices and programs as appropriate. But will the current interpretation of the 14th Amendment allow that? No.

Of course people asking these questions are troublemakers, anti-children zealots, or even worse, *Moronaphobic.* (I made that one up to describe people who are afraid of, and thus discriminate against, people on a basis of their intelligence. See, Conservatives can make up stupid labels too.)

The real problem is these studies presuppose that everyone is trainable to the same level. But most honest teachers will tell you after a few beers that this is not the case. In reality, when a student cannot meet a standard due to inherent inabilities, tremendous resources are spent on an often losing cause. School districts often get hammered for offering expensive one-on-one or remedial training for "less gifted" students, but frequently they do so because of federal or state laws. In the mean time, above average and brighter students are shortchanged; you know, the ones that will grow up to be doctors, engineers, and hopefully not lawyers.

Another fallacy with these studies is that people should be able to do 9th grade math their whole lives, or using the assembly line analogy again, people should behave like trustworthy toasters who just have to know when to pop out bread as designed. In reality, the only ones who need to know 9th grade math in the context that is implied in these studies are 9th graders.

A great part of the population does not think, or need to think, like the academics who conduct these studies. In fact, I wouldn't be surprised at the number of the academics who conduct these type of studies couldn't do 9th grade math themselves.

I'm not saying 9th grade math and other equivalent level subjects should not be widely available, but using knowledge of 9th grade math or similar metrics for measuring broad post graduation educational success serves no useful purpose except to instill a false sense of needed expensive fixes. In Ohio, as in many other states, students are given numerous chances to pass a mandatory but useless graduation test whose only purpose is to make politicians feel good. In the mean time, teachers are told to *teach to the test* as more money and time are wasted. (Ironically the state also has a list of exceptions that allow students who fail the tests to still graduate. So these tests are mandatory for some but not-quite-so-mandatory for others.)

An engineer will always be able to do 9th grade math because he or she needs that skill level to be able to do even higher mathematics. A cable installer does not need those same skills. I can go into any professional office or work place and amuse myself by asking people a range of academic-like math, science, history, geography, or other questions and sit back and enjoy watching the panic on many of their faces. People will retain what is necessary for them to succeed in life as they see fit, based on personal variables as well as external ones. In fact, we make these decisions very early in our lives.

Reading, riting, and rithmetic are abstract concepts that are difficult to learn and even more difficult to maintain a set skill level. So what does it really mean when we see that 40% of a state's college students can't find their home state on the map? Well, the Education Industrial Complex wants you to believe that it's an education funding issue and to spend more on the "Students Can't Find Their Home State" crisis. What if it's a matter of just admitting that there are a lot of (ahem) academically challenged people out there and/or many college entrance requirements in their current form mean nothing?

Because politicians are lousy at solving problems but good at raising taxes that temporarily mask the problems; politicians support bloating by continuing to look for politically convenient solutions and associated tax gimmicks to pay for them. Sometimes they find temporary relief in lotteries, sin taxes, or miscellaneous impact fees. With each new gimmick comes the promise that education standards have been raised and education funding has been solved for generations to come. Unfortunately, the results are always the same; more feeding of an ever bigger industrial complex that continues to produce inferior human toasters. *If Politicians really wanted to help, they would get out of the way and let people who know what they're doing solve the problem.*

Some people say the answer is that we need to teach our kids how to think, not what to think. I have absolutely no idea how to do that. But if it is possible, there are probably a lot of talented teachers and administrators in the current education system that could make it happen, if given the chance. And teachers should not look at my diatribe above as a slap at them. This is not about teachers, it's about policies, and policies are made at the highest levels.

I don't have the answers, but I do know how to get the answers, and I will share my idea with you in a later chapter. It's really quite simple.

In the mean time, all I can offer is a few humble tidbits of my own. Instead of worrying whether every high school graduate knows 9th grade math, I would rather have the general portion of the population master and retain at least the following facts:

Math: Know enough math to calculate their car's mpg, figure square footage so they can order carpet, calculate their gross and net pay, balance their check book, calculate sales tax, and how to look up interest payments off of a table.

Economics: Understand how supply and demand determines prices and wages, not the President, congress, or some judge. In fact, you don't want to live in a country where one person or the government has enough power to set prices and wages.

Government: Understand that the Constitution was a limitation on government put there by the people and thus the constitution does not speak to people-to-people interactions. Use examples like it's not a freedom of speech issue when the Dixie Chicks can't fill stadiums because their fans disagree with their anti-Bush speeches. It's a freedom of speech issue only if Bush stopped them from filling those stadiums. Finally, popular perceptions aside, there is no federal constitutional right to welfare, or protection from stupidity or bad luck.

History: America is the greatest country in the world and historical human rights struggles should be put not in terms of when slavery ended, but as Thomas Sowell put it, when did freedom begin.

Physical and Biological Sciences: For the most part scientists know very little, and what they do know, they know with only great uncertainty. Also when one hears about some new scientific finding, always find out who paid for the study. This especially applies to global warming, most medical research on rats, many of the health and diet studies, and any study that says marijuana cures something.

Sociology and Psychology: It all sounds scientific and stuff, but it's really mostly babble.

Geography: The world is round. There are seven continents. The Arctic is an ice sheet and the Antarctic actually is a land mass.

Our education system is not designed to prepare students with the skills they need and society requires. Rather it is designed to perpetuate itself.

The pin heads that go about creating useless graduation tests and worry whether the general adult population knows high school math, won't like the list above. The problem with the list is it doesn't require the general adult toaster population to know that: "If two sides and the included angle of one triangle are equal to two sides and the included angle of another triangle, the triangles are congruent." But then again, in a nation where the majority of people don't understand the meaning of the Bill of Rights, or think that the government should control wages and prices; does it really even matter?

6

Le Public Institute de Artiste de Knoxville

Question: *What do liberal arts graduates say on the job?*
Answer: *Do you want fries to go with that?*

—An old joke mostly told by engineers to each other

The approach the Education Industrial Complex uses to make college more affordable is to pressure governments to make more public money available in the form of grants, scholarships, or low cost loans. This is the Education Industrial Complex's version of supply and demand: *as the public money supply increases, they demand more tuition.*

Tuition goes up because as the supply of public assistance money increases so does the cost of the service or product. I know this doesn't seem to make sense, but think of it this way. The price of cars would skyrocket if sellers knew that consumers had a large supply of cash or access to low interest loans. In addition to increasing basic prices, as the money flowed in, car manufacturers would add fluff that further increases the costs. In colleges, the fluff is the endless amount of questionable courses, mostly politically correct, that have no useful educational value and generally operate under no academic standards. If the money supply would decrease, would colleges cut "useless" courses like *Microprocessor Theory*, or "important" ones like *United Nations Policy Successes in Eradicating Third World Hunger?*

This phenomenon in turn inhibits innovation and efficient operations, which further drives up costs. So education is like any other supply and demand commodity. If Americans chose colleges and fields of study like they choose common consumer goods, a college education would cost much less than it typically does today.

One of the biggest misconceptions is that only an "out of town" or "out of state" college can provide the necessary quality education for your darling little Damien. (This argument doesn't apply to parents who would pay anything to get rid of their demon seed Damiens.) The other misconception (and sometimes scam) is that a liberal arts degree can actually land darling little Damien a job. If a set of parents never went to college, you can excuse their ignorance, but many parents who should know better—don't. (Technically, I really should be using the term "humanities" instead of liberal arts, but it's not worth distinguishing between the two for our purposes.)

The liberal arts are a great source of human knowledge and skill sets, and I'm glad I took as many liberal art classes as I did, but I also knew that I would have to eventually feed the wife and kids, even before I had wife or kids (in that order). Of course, that was when men actually had such silly responsibilities as providing for their families. Fortunately, the government provides that service now, freeing men to be boys, and freeing women to be single mothers.

Ironically, the term "liberal arts" in its original usage really meant those skills (arts) needed by free men (liberalis), which many years ago were restricted to society's elites. If you weren't elite then you learned the "servilis arts," like the skills necessary to clean out the royal chamber pot. Thus, the problem with liberal arts as an end to themselves, is that they were really originally designed for the nobility; kings, queens, and the like, who could afford to spend time learning to read the Iliad in classical Greek, because they didn't have to worry about getting jobs.

Therefore, parents and students, as consumers, have decision making responsibilities and those responsibilities shouldn't be underestimated. By making poor decisions, we hurt ourselves and contribute to high education costs. Unfortunately, here is how college decisions are often currently made.

Daughter: Hi mom and dad, I wanted to talk to you about my college choice and major.

Father: Well that's great honey, what are they?

Daughter: The college is called Le Public Institute de Artiste de Knoxville and I want to study Feminist Art.

Mother: I never heard of that college sweetheart, and what is Feminist Art?

Daughter: Le Public Institute de Artiste de Knoxville is one of the most prestigious arts schools in the country and they just hired Madame Garçonette de La Pew, the world famous French feminist artist. Students take whatever courses they want and don't have to follow rigid class schedules.

Father: Oh yes, I think I heard of her, isn't she the one whose student came

up with the bloody naked skit reading poetry about killing men or something like that? What kind of job can you get with a degree in Feminist Art?
Daughter: Dad, don't be so closed minded. Jobs and money aren't everything. This is a once in a lifetime chance.
Father: Yes, but how much?
Daughter: There you go again worrying about money instead of what I
want. Okay, if you have to know, about $50,000 a year, but that includes art
supplies and a trip to Paris to get a first hand look at the cultural center of
the world!
Mother: Oh my dear, that's $200,000 for four years, and isn't Paris where
labor unions, college students, and disenchanted Muslim youths take turns
rioting?
Daughter: Well, it may be longer than four years, you graduate only when
Madame La Pew thinks you're ready to graduate. But please, please, please;
this is my life we are talking about.
Mother: Okay dear if that's what you want, your father and I don't want to
stop you from pursuing your dream. I guess we can take out a third mortgage.

Results: Daughter graduates in 6 years and lands a $15,000 a year job as a
substitute art teacher teaching kids to express their dislike for meat through
art. Years later, parents celebrate their 50th wedding anniversary with their
first steak dinner in five years.

The way it should have happened:

Daughter: Hi mom and dad, I wanted to talk to you about my college
choice and major.
Father: Well that's great honey, what are they?
Daughter: The College is called Le Public Institute de Artiste de Knoxville
and I want to study Feminist Art.
Mother: I never heard of that college sweetheart, and what is Feminist Art?
Father: I don't give le manure about Le Public Institute de Artiste de Knoxville or Feminist Art. It sounds like the brain fairy that took your brain away
at 13 hasn't returned yet, so here is what your mother and I will support. On
Monday, you will go down and enroll to the local community college and
for $4,000 a year you can take general courses that you will need for 90% of
any major. In a year or two if you still want to study Art, you can transfer to
the local state college. Who knows, you may take a class in another subject

and change your major. During this time you can stay at home for free and your mother and I will help you financially as much as we can, but you still may have to get a part-time job. If you don't like that plan and still insist on Le Institute then au revoir mon chéri et bonne chance.

Result: The daughter attends a community college, switches to graphical design in her second year, and later studies to be an architect at a four year college. She starts out with a $50,000 a year job and no school loans. She tells her parents on graduation day: "Thank you for being my parents not my friends."

Here's another version:

Daughter: Hi mom and dad, I wanted to talk to you about my college choice and major.
Father: Well that's great honey, what are they?
Daughter: Well I've been accepted to MIT's engineering program.
Mother: That's fantastic! Did you get a scholarship?
Daughter: I got a partial one; it will only pay for about half of the total cost.
Father: I don't care how much it costs. You have our full cooperation. We will find a way to pay for this. You don't turn down an MIT offer.

Result: The daughter graduates with a mechanical engineering degree and lands a $70,000 a year job as a robotics engineer and the company agrees to pay a sign-up bonus that makes a pretty good dent in her student loans. The parents turn to each other and agree that it was one of the best investments they have ever made.

The MIT example above leads to another related topic. I have worked my whole professional adult life in heavily technical areas. The engineering industry has been moaning for some time that it can't get enough engineers and one reason cited is that American kids aren't going into technical fields. Some companies have proactive out-reach programs at the secondary and college levels, but many do not.

I was at a technical conference where at the lunch table, a government senior engineer was bemoaning an often cited fact that today's kids aren't going into engineering in enough numbers to satisfy demand. I was also told by a friend, who works at a very large well known high tech corporation, that his CEO gave grim statistics regarding the number of engineers his company will need versus the engineering graduation rates. The numbers he used were in agreement with a presentation given at yet another technical conference I attended where the graduation rate was given at around 65,000 per year. Do these two complaints have validity? I don't really know for sure, but the solution often cited is to spend more public money on science and engineering programs to increase the number of graduates in those fields. Can that work?

Let's use a little estimating. Let's use math aptitude as a benchmark and assume that math aptitude follows a normal distribution curve. That means half (50%) of the high school senior student population has an average or above average math capability. Let's also assume that the desire to go into science or engineering as a profession also follows the same distribution. That means that only about 25% of seniors (50% x 50%) might have an average or above average ability *and* desire to pursue a science or engineering degree. (I know this last assumption is a little shaky, and this tendency may not follow a normal distribution curve, but remember, many high school students who take advance math and science courses in high school are in college prep programs, and have no desire to go into technical fields. Besides, my overall message is more important than the exact numbers.)

I examined the National Center for Education Statistics website for some insight into this problem. According to the site data, in 2000, about 53% of high school graduates took a calculus or some other post algebra II/trigonometry class such as pre-calculus or statistics. The number of graduates that took physics or some other advanced technical course such as engineering or advanced placement chemistry was about 46%. Therefore, the number of students who are prospective candidates for a possible college technical major is right around 50%, exactly what you would expect from the normal distribution curve.

According to the same website, the number of high school graduates in 2003 was about 2.7 million. Out of these, about 44% went on to a four year college and 23% went on to a two year college. So a total of 67% of high school graduates went on to some type of post secondary education. That's not bad, although of course not all of these completed college. I suppose some would like to see the enrollment number much higher, but if you assume that the 67% roughly correlates to the top 67% in intelligence and/or drive, then I don't know what it means if 95% went on to college in terms of the quality of students and the quality of the available education. Of course, there are some students who might academically do well in college but just decide not to go. Some of these may just be too talented to waste time in college and end up in various important trades.

The number of students enrolled in college science or engineering programs in 2004 was 5.6 million or about 25% of the total number of 21.9 million. Furthermore, the number of technical Bachelor degrees conferred in 2004 was 321,200, or about 24% of the total number of 1.35 million. These percentages agree with what was concluded from the simple 50% x 50% analysis a few paragraphs above. (Approximately 43,000 degrees were awarded to nonresident aliens of which 14,000 were technical degrees. And I'm defining technical degrees by all degrees that fall into engineering, agriculture, mathematics, the life and physical sciences, and health related fields. I'm assuming that the students in these fields would have a better chance of successfully switching to a specific engineering discipline than the general population.)

Out of the 321,200 technical degrees, it is true that there may have been only about 65,000 that fell under the generic engineering category, but another 57,000 fell under computer sciences, 18,000 under physical sciences, and 12,000 under mathematics. The rest were in the biological, biomedical, health, and mis-cellaneous technology fields. (I find the 65,000 figure for engineering degrees often quoted by speakers rather strange. Statistics tend to have a life of their own, and many times a number is borrowed and repeated so often that it becomes a fact. But whoever began this thread of using the 65,000 number for some reason left out the 57,000 computer science degrees. Some purists would frown at me lumping the two together but it is more wrong to leave them separated. Lumping computer science degrees in with the rest, nearly doubles our engineering gradua-tion rate.)

Sometimes statistics citing the large number of engineers graduating from other countries are used to stress our domestic problem. But without context these statistics mean nothing. Many countries have limited options for many stu-dents in choosing other career fields. This is a fancy way of saying that most countries can't afford to teach nice to have courses, like the impact of comic books on culture and society, as we do in this country. More importantly, many countries have centralized planning programs that dictate the number of butch-ers, bakers, and candlestick makers that are produced each year. What this does is force those 25% of students who have the math aptitude into technical fields that would rather pursue other disciplines if given the chance.

I know there are a lot of smart people out there who studied this problem and understand it better than me. But I get nervous when I hear of another crisis in education and we need to spend more money to solve the problem.

What if the problem in supply is not fixable to the extent we think it is? In other words, if America requires a higher density of technical skills than the rest of the world, what if the "natural supply" of domestic technical talent has nearly peaked? If this is true then the problem requires a different approach than brute force recruitment of more engineering majors from non-technical fields of study or from the general population. Remember, I'm defining technical talent as people who can do "the math" as well as who "want to do the math." With the understanding that the latter category is somewhat less defined, but the constraint cannot be dismissed outright if quality means anything.

If I'm right about the supply issue then increases we wish to see in student engineering recruitment may be in the few percents instead of many percents. Figuring this out is important in order to formulate correct educational policies. In any case, there a number of approaches that can be used to at least marginally increase our engineering graduation rates. One is to entice potential candidates from other technical fields, especially if those fields are overpopulated. This approach will result in some increases to the engineering pool. For example, I've known a number of scientists and mathematicians who later regretted that they didn't go into an engineering field, if for no other reason than job market potential. If we need to shift numbers from one group to the other, there are various ways to do so ($$$$$$).

Another avenue is to look at groups that may be underrepresented in classical engineering, such as women and minorities, who have members that are not even looking at technical professions as options but would do well in them. College students with undecided majors are not included in the statistics above and may be another source of candidates.

Let's also not forget that we have to do a better job at math and science training, if for no other reason than to make those that will become our future geeks, better geeks. Improvements to the style of math and science education need to be made also. How many reading this book have had the pleasure of having to drop a ball 50 times in their physics class, measure its acceleration each time, then compute some average number that may be within 100% error of the accepted acceleration of gravity? Mainstream math and science education is horrible. Geeks who like the stuff will bear with it, but how many are we losing due to sheer boredom that might make the difference in our engineering manpower requirements.

According to a February 8, 2007, Dayton Daily News article, Wright State University's engineering program claims 60% of first year engineering students drop out of the program. A major reason given was difficulty in passing first year calculus. To remedy this, the school started a program where students were trained in enough math to start them going into upper engineering course work with the hope that they will catch up in their math requirements later. A number of other colleges are considering a similar approach.

Back in the old days when I was in school, we looked upon first year classes such as calculus and physics as weeding out courses. If you couldn't pass these classes you didn't deserve to belong to the geek club. So part of me looks upon this program with skepticism—will the students just drop out in their third year instead of their first? Will this approach affect post graduation job quality? On the other hand, this sort of thinking outside the box is necessary in order to radically change (all) our education programs to meet current and future demands across all disciplines.

But industry also has responsibility. Some of the most successful companies in terms of recruitment are those that identify college students for future employment and hire them early as interns or part-time help. These programs include steering potential engineering, science, and math students into specialties and disciplines that the company can use. If a company lacks this type of program, but it is within their financial capabilities, then they have no room to whine. In fact, for many companies, recruitment problems can be summed up with two letters: HR.

My relationship with human resource departments throughout my professional career, as both a rank-and-file employee and as a manager and supervisor of engineers and scientists, has nearly always been adversarial. Before you say it just might be me, consider that Scott Adams' depiction of the evil HR director in his *Dilbert* comic strip is a hit because it is recognized as at least partially factual by most people.

On a serious note, this HR image problem is also recognized by many who study business processes, as can be verified by an internet search on problems with HR departments. There are some outstanding HR people out there, but it also seems that many companies operate under a national HR hiring culture that badly needs overhauling. This most often applies to large companies where HR departments, like other service departments, operate like fiefdoms instead of internal service organizations (this applies to government personnel offices especially). Many of these departments have forgotten that companies aren't in business to support them, but they exist to support the company's primary service or product.

This leads to another point for organizations to consider in how they use their engineering talent, and this is especially true for government. The federal government sucks up a tremendous amount of the nation's engineering talent, but for the most part, the federal government doesn't use its engineers and scientists in any real technical capacity. They mostly do program management where their technical talents are often wasted answering weekly budget cut drills, feeding the government's endless calls for program restructuring, and providing weekly data updates to feed the "Earned Value" monster (program managers know what I mean.) What makes it even worse is that many of the programs they manage are questionable in the first place.

Then there is the tendency for private and public organizations to cut support staff to save money, thereby shifting miscellaneous office duties to the remaining technical staff. The end result is saving $15 per hour by shifting the jobs over to people who make $50 per hour. Part of this has to do with the advances in office software and equipment; but part of it is short sighted accountants.

The most important point I'm trying to make here is that I do not believe one can simply spend money to take and educate bodies from an art department and assume that they would make adequate engineers, anymore than one can borrow from the business school to get more artists (real artists, not the modern kind). At least not necessarily in the numbers we think we can. Maybe with God and money, all things are possible. I don't know.

If all this tweaking doesn't work, or is too expensive, the second option of course is (controlled) immigration. It's a classical supply and demand problem.

As in all cases when you try to summarize a complex problem in a few paragraphs, someone can always find holes in the argument, but I do know that I'm not wrong in questioning the ability of the Education Industrial Complex to fix itself. *All I'm saying is to use a little common sense. Let's spend our education money wisely. The Government Class loves to hear people say that there is a crisis, because it empowers them. But let's think and define the problem before going off and spending billions and billions of dollars. And let's also make sure that the ones that are whining the loudest in the private sector aren't just shirking their responsibilities in addressing their own hiring, retention, and other problems.*

◆   ◆   ◆

The majority of teachers, principals, school staffs, district administrators, and others in the Education Industrial Complex are not looters; many are hard working people just as you would find in other walks of life; mostly trying to make an insane system work. However, it's clear that many politicians and government administrators are the worst kind of looters, because they have failed as our councils of government to strike a balance between the necessary and the desirable. But, the Government Class needs an army to carry off the heist.

The people populating this army fall into several characteristic groups. Some work mostly at the local level, some at the state or federal levels, some have counterparts at all levels, some fall into formal membership categories that are fully aware of what they are doing, and some are just regular parents and citizens with much narrower goals. Individually, any one of these groups would warrant no more attention than any other special interest group, but together they provide a formidable force. In the following chapters we will look at both what can be described as army regulars, as well as their associated guerilla units.

7

Psychosocial-babblers

A mix of red and blue, the color purple embodies red's sense of authority but also blue's association with serenity, making it a less negative and more constructive color for correcting student papers.

—Recommendations by "color psychologists", as reported in the August 23, 2004, Boston Globe

The term *Psychobabblers* is often used to describe psychologists that display an intuitive knack for making ridiculous pseudoscientific pronouncements. I added the "social" part to include the field of sociology, because although the fields of psychology and sociology clearly encompass many specialized areas of study, the two linked fields have had a related disastrous effect on education and social policies in general.

Basically, the term *Psychosocial-babblers* refers to the myriad of behavioral and social "scientists" that seem to spew a tremendous amount of crap du jour and call it science. This junk science has evolved into a key pop cultural tool used not only by the Government Class to expand the nanny state, but also in general by a lazy society always looking for the next snake oil remedy.

Psychosocial-babblers are the same bunch in 2006 that proclaimed people losing their temper while driving are really displaying *Intermittent Explosive Disorder.* You won't get government funding or peer prestige if you call people losing their tempers on the highway just a bunch of idiots. Additionally, calling every messy behavior a "disorder" implies a medical condition and thus instills a certain scientific respectability, and a certain sense of caregiver dependency. (In researching this topic, I was amazed at the number of "disorders" that have been identified. But to be fair, not all of them have been officially recognized by the applicable professional groups.)

Psychosocial-babblers are the ones that are called in to give their expert opinions on whether a criminal with name-the-disorder is "cured" and should be set free. After much consternation accompanied by big words, the esteemed scientists proclaim the patient cured, setting in motion his/her freedom and the subsequent crimes that person will likely commit again. Can you say sex offenders?

This process should be viewed as similar to witch doctors shaking bags of bones and proclaiming some poor wretch cured. Okay, Okay, maybe a step above that.

You run into Psychosocial-babblers across many facets of society and across many different industrial complexes. In the Education Industrial Complex, they work for the research and development department where their task is to generate new theories based on junk science that will expand government education programs. The quote at the beginning of this chapter, the ever increasing use of therapy for every minor politically incorrect action and the fabrication of a plethora of questionable behavioral disorders, such as Attention Deficit Disorder (ADD), or Attention Deficit/Hyperactivity Disorder (ADHD), or whatever they are calling it now, are further examples of Psychosocial-babbling.

The issue is not that these behaviors don't exist; the issue is whether they are "disorders." The difference is profound.

ADD and ADHD are particularly relevant to our discussion and are worth a word or two here. ADD and ADHD are generally associated with inappropriate levels of inattention and/or hyperactive-impulsive behavior. The operative word here is "inappropriate," which of course can be modified to fit any occasion of convenience, and the modern classroom is one of those occasions.

Let's take Little Johnny who is sitting in his desk at about 30 minutes before lunch. Johnny is known to day dream which gives his teacher fits. The teacher pulls out the grammar book and begins to show the class how to diagram the sentence: *Sally was seen running to the store to boldly buy her mother 5 pounds of beef tongue and cow ruminants.* The teacher asks the class if anyone can identify the subject, the verb, any adjectives, the past, present, perfect, and imperfect participles where applicable, any prepositional phases, simple and/or compound predicates, and her favorite, any split infinitives.

The teacher notices Johnny once again looking out the window, followed by Johnny bothering Heather sitting next to him. This time the teacher immediately recognizes this behavior, because she just attended a district workshop by the district's Psychosocial-babblers on what to do with little boys that fidget. The teacher can't legally diagnose the problem, but calls Johnny's parents in to discuss Johnny's behavior and hints at chemical castration.

Chemical castration? Ironically, boys are more often tagged for politically incorrect or other "bad" behavior and doped to treat ADD/ADHD at a rate of about 2 to 3 times more than girls. Considering that the vast majority of teachers in government school systems are female (about 75%-80%), some say that this is just female led chemical castration. But I want to put this to rest once and for all. The fact that the vast majority of teachers are female has nothing to do with the subsequent growth in the chemical castration process, because everyone knows that women don't discriminate (throat clearing noises go here). Of course, a related topic is how boys are drastically falling academically behind girls from primary school through college, thanks to modern cultural and legal policies that favor girls over boys. But that's a subject for another day.

Is it possible that inattention and/or hyperactive-impulsive behavior is due to the fact that sitting in a classroom diagramming sentences is boring and would be chosen second to having your nails ripped out? Who has the greater abnormal emotional disorder, the boy fidgeting to go to recess or the girl actually worried about where to put the split infinitive in the sentence diagram?

On his October 9, 2006, Imus in the Morning broadcast, Don Imus was bemoaning the national lack of attention (my pun intended) on the ADD "epidemic." Imus was just repeating what the Psychosocial-babblers want you to believe. But, did a meteor fall from the sky in the 1980s with a virus picked up from the Pleiades star cluster in the constellation Taurus that all of a sudden caused our children to display never heard-of-before unchild-like behavior. *Rare* behavior like failing to pay attention, losing school supplies, avoiding tasks that require work, difficulty keeping quiet or, God forbid, having mood swings?

Did ADD/ADHD exist prior to the meteor strike? Would a little boy or girl diagnosed with ADD/ADHD today have been diagnosed with inattention and/or hyperactive-impulsive behavior when fidgeting while milking a cow or dipping string into hot wax to make candles 400 hundred years ago? What do you think was the preventive measure used even only 40 years ago when a kid refused to do his or her chores?

The following is a possible conversation between a modern third grade teacher speaking to three of her district's behavioral experts (DBE).

Teacher: I have here, the first three report cards of this student. Notice the past teachers' comments.

Kindergarten: His attitude is one of the "smarty types" … he gets noisy and naughty sometimes.

First Grade: He often disturbs his neighbors and wastes time by talking when he should be working.

Second Grade: If (he) learned to work a little better at his seat he might be able to improve his poor skill grades. He spends too much time playing and talking to his neighbors.

Teacher: Ladies and gentlemen what we have here is a consistent behavior of failing to pay attention. I'm afraid that he might disrupt my third grade class. What do you think we should do with him?
DBE 1: Seems like he has ADD. He may need to be tested and medicated. Call his parents in.
DBE 2: No, he seems to have ADHD. He may need to be tested and medicated. Call his parents in.
DBE 3: They're going to rename the behavior again but it doesn't matter. He definitely needs to be medicated. Call his parents in.

In some cases the behavior specialists are just doing their job as dictated by law or policy. It's the law itself as well as the ones that religiously push the process that worry me since being diagnosed by behavioral analysts is often depicted in popular culture as a frustrating affair, because no matter what you say or do "NUTJOB" always gets stamped on your records. So excuse me if it seems that I take great umbrage at today's cavalier attitude toward fidgeting boys (or kids in general). You see those report card comments were real and the boy was me.

My two brothers and I attended both private and government schools and were trouble makers and poor students throughout our K-12 academic careers. I'm convinced that if we were students today, we would be chemically castrated.

I know that many child behavioral specialists are very professional in their approach, and that often their hands are tied. I also know that many of them are doing the best they can within the environment they operate in. But my point is that the system is out of control.

Let's answer that question about the preventive measure used 40 years ago to control fidgeting. You see my brothers and I didn't have ADD or ADHD, it was SAD, otherwise known as *Smart Ass Disorder*. What kept us under any semblance of control was respect for authority, an absolute fear of the Sisters of Charities, *and the fact that our parents backed* whatever Sister Mary This or Sister Margaret That or any other teacher, public or private, did to us to instill discipline in the classroom. Our parents backed the teachers because they knew that 95% of the time we probably deserved whatever we got, so they were just playing the odds.

No it wasn't a strange outer space virus that hit us years ago. It wasn't even "better diagnostic" methods. It was the man-made mutated virus technically called Liberaloviridae. Chemical castration is used today because given the nature of the classical classroom learning environment, we have taken away the moral and real authority that teachers and other adults once enjoyed over children through a complex pseudo-intellectual change in our societal and legal approach to child rearing and education.

Although there are individual voices in the behavioral and social sciences that have objected to ADD/ADHD as currently diagnosed, these objections have been nearly universally rejected by the professional national or international associations. In other words, an ADD/ADHD culture has been officially blessed, forcing many rank and file workers to tow the line.

Part of the problem is that besides the need for government funding, Psychosocial-babblers at the theoretical level work from an inferiority complex and are always trying to compensate for something they are lacking. No, not that; all of you Freudians get your minds out of the gutter; I'm talking about scientific rigor.

When Isaac Newton developed his mathematical formulation of the laws of planetary motion he solidified the underpinnings of a growing philosophical movement that viewed the universe as a mechanical system. The earth didn't go around the sun being pushed by angels, but rather the Earth revolved around the sun under the force of gravity and this motion could be described by very precise and concise mathematical expressions. Thus, the motions of the planets were nothing more than the motions of a mechanical clock: different in degree, but not in kind.

Psychosocial-babblers see their counterparts in science making great progress in quantitatively understanding the physical world and in some limited aspects, biological systems. They want to emulate this success by also assuming a Newtonian view of human behavior; in essence, human behavior is a distinct, discoverable and understandable cause and effect system.

Although some may have a philosophical problem with this approach, seeking a mechanical view of human behavior is probably a reasonable methodology for a variety of technical and practical reasons. *The real problem lies in their inability, as professional disciplines, to set better control over the workers in those disciplines including research expectations, conclusions, and pronouncements.*

Since the relative simplicity of many physical systems allows mathematical analyses or straight-forward experimental investigations, results are readily quantifiable and verifiable. But the complexity of human behavior increases the possibilities of errors and premature scientific bravado without proper controls and safeguards, because it is too difficult to prove or disprove a finding.

For example, in the 1980s two cold fusion researchers were receiving standing ovations at technical conferences for their recent experimental results that if correct would have revolutionized energy production. However, the physical science community was able to debunk their experimental results in a matter of months. This put a damper on state and federal politicians who were trying to capitalize on their claims. The end result was a few bruised egos but also the savings of many millions of tax dollars that was about to be blown on a Utah Cold Fusion Center of Excellence or other such nonsense that the Government Class was pushing for.

One example out of many psychosocial-babble generated by one of our higher institutions of learning was published in a psychology trade journal and reported by various news services in July 2006. Basically a female psychology student and her professors studied the correlation between handling a gun and the rise in men's testosterone levels as measured through saliva samples. The men were told they'd be taking part in a study of the effect of attention to detail on taste sensitivity. She led each man into a room where he sat at a table with an object on it. The man had to take apart the object and put it back together according to instructions. For half the men, the object was a photo of a pellet gun. The other half of the men worked with the child's game called Mouse Trap.

Some minutes later, another saliva sample was taken. The men were asked to taste a lidded 3-ounce cup of water with a drop of hot sauce in it. They then were given a 3-ounce cup of water and a bottle of the hot sauce. They were told the water would be given to the next man in the study, and that they could anonymously put as much hot sauce in the water as they liked. The idea is that the more aggressive a man is feeling, the more hot sauce he would put in the next guy's drink.

Testosterone levels were found to go up about 100 times more in the men who handled the gun than in the men who handled the toy. And the gun handlers on average put three times more hot sauce in the water than the toy handlers.

The student and her professors concluded that, "Such findings raise many of the usual questions about whether the presence of guns in modern society contributes to violent behavior." They then went on to claim, "Although our study is clearly far from definitive, its results suggest that guns may indeed increase aggressiveness partially via changes in the hormone testosterone."

In my view, the study and its conclusions shouldn't have even made it past the department's monthly newsletter. I'm not questioning their data or specific results. What troubles me are their conclusions, because Government Class policy makers don't read details, they only care about using sound bites in order to push their agendas. And quite frankly, I don't want to give the Government Class any more unfounded ammo to mess around with the Second Amendment.

All scientists struggle with personal prejudices in dealing with forming hypotheses and interpreting data. After all, we all want the world to fit our model of reality not the other way around. With that in mind, dare I go on a limb? Sure, why not.

If I had been given the chance, here's what I would have liked to have asked the student and her research advisors. Why do you hate men? Why are you against the Second Amendment? Does the fact that you hate men and the Second Amendment affect your research? What did you expect the men to say? "Gun good. Me like gun. Gun go boom. Boom good." What about a test on women? How about men raised only by women? Men raised only by men? Men raised by wolves? And the scariest group of all: men that sport mullets?

A gun is just a special type of weapon. Does the handling of knives also raise testosterone levels? Does a butter knife raise testosterone levels only half as much as a steak knife? And what's up with sporks, those plastic half spoon/half fork abominations? Since the spork was introduced in America's finer fast food restaurants, has there been a correlation between men losing their tempers when the sporks break and increases in family violence?

We had knives before we had guns and clubs before we had knives. You had to use something to bring that woolly mammoth steak back to the cave wife and cave kids. So you can't blame men can you? It all started over competing for cave babes and satisfying their endless demands—no saber tooth tiger teeth necklace for cave wife, no zug-zug for you (as the natives would say in the movie *Caveman*). And as every guy knows 100,000 years later and the fundamental process hasn't changed, except diamonds have replaced tiger teeth.

The statement referring to the study as being far from definitive is an understatement. But that's okay, that's what research is all about. However, let's have some restraint on what we may imply in our conclusions; after all, the Government Class is listening.

The researchers want to lead you to believe that the presence of guns in modern society may contribute to violent behavior and that males are inherently violent or prone to be because they are awash in the inferior testosterone hormone. This is the same underlining philosophy that put forth the statement that wife beatings go up during the Superbowl. A statement that made the rounds for months before it was debunked with a just a little research. Yet, I bet it is still being taught as fact at many colleges across the country. But that's the state of the behavioral and social sciences today.

Maybe I have been too pre-judgmental. I'm sure this research team's next project will be an experiment where 25 randomly selected females are subjected to pictures of shoe sales and another 25 randomly selected females to pictures of flowers. Then they give the women directions to the store holding the shoe sale and instruct them to pass the instructions to the other women in the study group. The researchers record how many women in each group give the wrong instructions to the next woman to limit the competition at the shoe sale. The research goal is to study whether when it comes to shoes women can be …, well, let's just say it rhymes with witchy.

The nature of Psychosocial-babbling gives rise to many related theories. According to Ted Nugent's official website, the following story further highlights the insanity of modern Liberal thought:

> Ted Nugent, a heavy metal guitar legend and devoted (bow) hunter, was being interviewed by a French journalist. Eventually, the conversation turned to his love of outdoor pursuits. The journalist asked, "What do you think the last thought is in the head of a deer before you shoot it? Is it, "Are you my friend?" or maybe "Are you the one who killed my brother?"
>
> Nugent replied, "They aren't capable of that kind of thinking. All they care about is, What am I going to eat next? Who am I going to screw next? and, Can I run fast enough to get away? They are very much like the French in that way."

(Okay, maybe the Ted Nugent story is a little out of context here, but it's funny, mildly related to the story line and makes fun of the French, so it's all good.) The problem with many aspects of modern Psychosocial-babble theory is it forgets one of Freud's most famous lines, or at least attributed to him, referring to the symbolism behind men who smoke cigars: "Sometimes a cigar is just a cigar." Think about it.

◆   ◆   ◆

In the early part of the 20th century Psychosocial-babblers expanded their Newtonian view of the universe and began to erroneously borrow another physics theory. This time it was Einstein's theory of relativity. Somehow Psychosocial-babblers took Einstein's postulate, "All inertial frames are equivalent with respect to all the laws of physics," to mean, "Whatever turns you on baby."

What Einstein meant by his postulate is too complicated to go into here, but he didn't mean that everything was relative, or more to the point, as interpreted by modern social thought, that there is no right or wrong, just different views of the world. Considering that Einstein was also known to occasionally exhibit Smart Ass Disorder, it didn't help when he reportedly explained relativity with the statement: "Put your hand on a hot stove for a minute, and it seems like an hour. Sit with a pretty girl for an hour, and it seems like a minute. That's relativity."

Take any Introduction to Sociology course at your local community college and you will soon understand why our national social infrastructure is decaying. There is a plethora of Sociological theories: Feminism, Conflict Theory, Marxism, Rational Choice/Exchange Theory, Phenomenology, Social Construction Theory, Post-Structuralism and Postmodernism, Structure Functionalism, and Symbolic Interactionism just to name a few. What do these mean? Since Sociology as a discipline has been hijacked by the Left, they almost always are used to support the notion that American society, the West, capitalism, and all males are inherently corrupt, evil, or just basic failures.

Sociology as a field of knowledge tends to deny the very grounds on which Western cultures have based their truths and the very basis of our historical and social progress: a large part of which rests on the concept of individuality and individual responsibility. We have gotten to a point where we are incapable of blaming individuals for poor life-style choices. For example, poverty is always addressed macroscopically and always blamed entirely on the *system*, completely absolving individuals for their decisions. In fact, maybe its time to replace the term "sociology" with the term "victimology."

Here's the problem: some claims have real components. In the case of Black poverty, Blacks did suffer tremendously because of slavery.

But the difference between a true academic discipline and one that has been politically hijacked is one of standards. That's why we can't establish successful public economic development programs without operating under the absurd politically correct conclusion that parents and kids, of any background, can be excused for their behavior because they haven't been *taught* that going to jail, getting pregnant before you marry, and dropping out of school are generally bad career moves. Or equally disturbing, that society shouldn't be judgmental in addressing bad or harmful behavior.

My immigrant parents didn't speak English and had little if any formal education when we arrived here, but they knew these pearls of wisdom. They even stressed that my older brother and I spoke English at home! How dare they? Who gave them the cheat sheet? Who told them that English was the key to prosperity? Who whispered in their ears, "Tell your kids not to go to jail?" Well my kindergarten teacher for one, she wrote in my first report card that I needed to practice speaking English at home. Can you imagine a teacher writing that today? No, today we make no such demands on students.

I was flipping the TV channels one late Sunday night and came across one of the Cartoon Channel's Adult Swim programs; which are basically cartoons for adults. I had no idea what was going on but it had something to do about stereotyping various minority groups. In one scene a Chinese father was yelling at his son for only scoring a 1580 on his SAT. The father kept asking in a heavy Chinese accent: "Why you so lazy?" His son tried to explain to him that 1580 was a very good score just below the perfect 1600. His father wouldn't hear any of it. He just kept asking: "Why you so lazy?" The father then told the boy: "You play piano now." When the boy started to play, the father slammed the key cover on the boy's fingers and kept yelling: "Why you so lazy?"

The point of course is that the Asian culture has a reputation of setting high standards for its children resulting in them typically outperforming all other groups, including Whites. Who gave them the cheat sheet?

In her book, *Uncle Sam's Plantation: How Big Government Enslaves America's Poor and What We Can Do About It,* Star Parker explains how we got to where we are today. In the parlance of this book, the Government Class continues to hold down America's poor and the Psychosocial-babblers provide the supporting self-serving pseudo-science.

◆   ◆   ◆

What's sad about all this is that public policy has been created on poorly formulated and inconclusive studies or ideas because the Government Class is always looking for any justification for their policy initiatives, and there are many Psychosocial-babblers more than happy to oblige them.

The Busy-bodies and Do-gooders of the Government Class especially like Psychosocial-babblers because the latter provide the fuel to support the legislation or court decisions that are helping unravel, for example, the parent-child relationship I mentioned in an earlier chapter. As I hinted to before, the next great venture will be parental "emotional" abuse that only the state can prevent. What's that you say? Emotional abuse is too difficult to define? Exactly.

The underlining principle behind all this is that the simpler the system, the easier it is to show that the emperor has no clothes. The more complex the system, the more care that must be applied before making conclusions, creating laws, spending public money, making judicial decisions, applying theories, or teaching these ideas in our schools as if it were gospel (ahem).

I want to make sure everyone understands that I recognize there exists legitimate human behavioral and social research and that there are many reputable researchers in these areas who understand the limitations and the meaning of their results. I have even come across some during my professional career and personal life. There are even some within the system who are outspoken on the problems these professions face. For example, Nobel Laureate for psychiatry, Dr. Eric Kandel made the following comment in regards to therapy: "I think it's going to go down the tubes if the psychoanalytic community doesn't make a serious effort to verify its concepts and show which aspects of therapy work, under what conditions, for what patients and with which therapists."

Although psychology and sociology as professions may have some noble goals, the lack of discipline in these fields has made many of their conclusions scientifically worthless as well as legally and culturally dangerous. This lack of adult supervision has put the behavioral and social fields in a very exclusive club comprised of academic fields of study where the amount of useful information has actually decreased over time as a percentage of the total.

Real army units specialize in various weapons and tactics, and have strengths and weaknesses. It is helpful to summarize Educational Industrial Complex army units in the same way. For Psychosocial-babblers:

Weapons: The ability to re-label undesirable but common human behavior as complex sounding disorders, and thereby completely absolving individuals from any personal responsibility.
Strengths: They quack like real scientists but ...
Weaknesses: ... they often just look like turkeys.

8

Educationologists

All of the feel-good stuff in the Educator's Book of Education won't work if the patient is already dead.

—A teacher responding to the psychologists' comment at the beginning of the previous chapter

Educationologist is a silly word to describe certain academics who work in the Educational Industrial Complex's implementation and training departments, otherwise known as Colleges of Education, or as I will refer to them here, Colleges of Educationology. Do not confuse Educationologist with "educators" or other similar words. And Educationologists are definitely not most rank and file teachers who are too busy trying to teach your kids to worry about using purple versus red ink to grade papers.

I guess the best way to help define the term is to say that Educationologists are to education as Psychosocial-babblers are to social science. In fact, Educationologists and Psychosocial-babblers are hard to distinguish from each other except by trained professionals. When they mate they produce virile offspring indicating they may be members of the same species. With the advances in DNA science, this issue may be answered in the near future.

Unfortunately, many Colleges of Educationology, as currently constructed, are enormous wastes of time and money and are excellent examples of "plausible deniability." Plausible deniability refers to the process wherein you have to come up with a plausible alternative to cover up what you really are doing. People in the intelligence community do this all the time to hide their true mission, much like when Napoleon Solo and Illya Kuryakin entered Del Floria's Tailor Shop to hide their jobs as agents of U.N.C.L.E.

Nominally, Colleges of Educationology will claim they prepare teachers for teaching, provide a certification process for teachers, and conduct education research. Their importance has been heightened by legal requirements in many states that in order to teach you have to be certified.

In reality, Colleges of Educationology are part indoctrination centers for the Education Industrial Complex and part scapegoats for the Government Class "concerned" about the failed education system. As the nation's education system worsens, the more attention is given to teacher performance and the more pressure is put on the certification process. As more regulations are passed and more money is spent on the certification process, the sillier the process becomes. Blaming teachers or claiming that better training will fix education problems is just the easy way out. But it's not the teachers; it's the Government Class, stupid!

Colleges of Educationology are where students pay enormous amounts of money to study impressive sounding but often academically questionable topics. Many of these topics are courtesy of the Psychosocial-babblers. Since education is an art and not a science, the emphasis in Colleges of Educationology is the politically correct topic du jour. So courses like *Early Childhood Education in a Multicultural and Pluralistic Society* become the norm. In these and other courses, student teachers learn to teach with sensitively, how no answer is wrong (even in math), that everyone finishes in first place, and not to pre-judge except when identifying candidates for chemical castration and elementary school age boys with tendencies toward sexual harassment.

This is where student teachers still take courses in American History but now learn that George Washington and Osama bin Laden are "morally equivalent" men (the Psychosocial-babbler's theory of relativity) who just happen to have led resistance movements against oppressive regimes. This is where student teachers are encouraged to do senior papers like: *The benefits of alternate music technologies for middle and high school students dealing with post Vietnam/Iraqi shock syndrome and its affect on gay/lesbian, transgender, transracial and transcultural musical expression vis a vis the noncognitive use of master/slave hard drives as an example of white male misogynism.*

Colleges of Educationology receive grants to publish impressive sounding education theories in esoteric journals about what this or that program will do to improve your little Tyler's education. Sometimes members of boards of education may even attend a college's School of Educationology sponsored seminar or workshop to learn the newest in educational theories, like the benefits of eliminating standards as a means of instilling self-esteem.

Let's also not forget the studies that recommend the student/teacher ratio should be 25 to 1. Followed in a few years by a better study that took into consideration the *subconscious cognitive biopsies of prepubertal children in a post-modern society* that concluded the ratio should be 20 to 1. Followed in a few years … well you get the point. These studies, of course, are conducted *for the children*, and any increase in the number of teachers in the union ranks that would result along with any new power the union may attain is purely coincidental.

Besides their role in teacher certification, Colleges of Educationology are always ready to help teachers in the field acquire further training. In 2004, Wright State University was given a $150,000 state grant to teach teachers how to use Palm Pilots. That's right, Palm Pilots! Apparently, some teachers can't read the instruction manuals like millions of other people have done and since the state is always willing to blow taxpayer money; it's a winning combo.

What we have here are trained teachers either incapable of learning how to use a modern business tool or too lazy to do so on their own, and an over funded College of Educationology that is part of an over funded Education Industrial Complex. You may think $150,000 is peanuts, but this happens every day across the country in countless programs.

Back to teacher certification …, do all teachers come out of the certification process as robots? Of course not. Like any political machine, the Education Industrial Complex doesn't necessarily care what you think, as long as you speak and tow the party line. But the intelligent teachers learn to separate the wheat from the chaff. One example is the quote at the beginning of this chapter. Here are some more comments from different teachers stemming from the purple versus red ink theory at the beginning of the previous chapter, as published in the Dayton Daily News during September 2004.

Could someone please tell me when education is going to get over itself?

Once again teachers are being battered with the "expert" opinions of those whose backsides haven't touched a teacher's chair in decades.

Band-Aids! We keep slapping Band-Aids on the seeping arteries of education when what we need is major surgery.

I loved the part about red ink for correction. We have become so concerned with damaging their psyche and self-esteem that we have lost sight of the child.

Just like giving trophies to the last place Little League team, more and more students at all levels are deemed successful simply by participating and not by tangible accomplishments and measured results.

This is not the philosophic foundation this country's great achievements came from …

And as we say in France, *le pièce de résistance*:

Over the last 15 years, I have personally worked with several young women who were taking college-course study to become teachers. Everyone of these women defaulted to an "education major" because the curriculum was among the least demanding scholastic paths of choice.

The importance of these words should not be overlooked. They come from the front line soldiers in the education foxholes. Like generals who ignore the advice of the troops on the front line experiencing the combat conditions first hand, leaders in the Education Industrial Complex continue on giving each other medals for empty achievements while telling the education grunts to advance forward.

When attacked, the powerful always blames the powerless, knowing there will always be a receptive ear seeking the easiest solution. In Vietnam they vilified and blamed our soldiers and many believed it. For education, they vilify and blame our teachers, and many believe it. But it all has to do with leadership, so it's unfortunate that teachers, as a group, are often blamed for our failing government school system, because teachers as individuals are no more to blame for that, than individual soldiers were to blame for Vietnam.

Within the first few years of teaching, the poor teachers have continued to preach the party line. The good teachers have recognized the difference between fantasy and reality and occasionally break the rules even at the risk or ruining their professional careers. The great teachers have left. Meanwhile, the Educationologists tinker with turning our kids into better toasters.

Like in the social sciences, there are many people in colleges of education that do not fit what I wrote in this chapter. But like in the social sciences, the industry is in bad need of discipline. This is unfortunate, considering the importance of a sound educational system.

Weapons: Teacher certification authority
Strengths: State backed job security
Weaknesses: You can identify Educationologists by using the George Orwell test. Orwell, author of *1984* and *Animal Farm,* reportedly once stated that some ideas are so stupid that even intellectuals would embrace them. So at a dinner party you can throw out something incredibly stupid and see who bites. Here's a

good one to try: "Dolphins and whales are just as intelligent as humans and should have the right to a free taxpayer provided aqua-centered education."

9

Peeps in da Hood

The most fundamental fact about the ideas of the political left is that they do not work. Therefore, we should not be surprised to find the left concentrated in institutions where ideas do not have to work in order to survive.

—Thomas Sowell

David Horowitz, author of *The Professors: The 101 Most Dangerous Academics in America*, has made a career investigating the deception on American colleges that we call post-secondary education. I have not read his book yet, but from what I know of him and the subject matter, and from what I have seen in snippets, I look forward to reading it. Along with Horowitz's book, Bernie Goldberg's *100 People Who Are Screwing Up America (and Al Franken is #37)*, Bill O'Reilly's *Culture Warrior*, and a number of other books have documented so well the political correctness (PC) on our college campuses, that the biggest challenge for me in writing this section was to come up with something original. Hopefully, I succeeded.

◆　　◆　　◆

Some college graduation gowns have varying sizes and styles of hoods that usually lie flat on the back. Many colleges still undergo a "hooding" ceremony for certain degree levels such as doctorate and law school graduates, where the hood is actually lifted over the head of the candidate symbolizing the official awarding of the degree.

There are a number of people that have gone through this ceremony that run around putting "Doctor" in front of their names or "Esquire" after it, and are busy running our colleges, teaching our kids, writing our text books, and generally serving as society's experts on all imaginable subjects. Historically, these highly educated experts have often been at the forefront in developing new philosophical "schools-of-thought." Some of these schools-of-thought have ushered in ages of enlightenment; others brought dark ages. The latest Dark Age is brought to you by the Leftist School of Political Correctness (PC).

Since the PC philosophy is beaten into students by academic "thugs," it is only natural that I refer to the people that have been recognized by the hooding ceremony and live in the PC neighborhood by the gangsta rap title, "Peeps in da Hood" or "Peeps" for short. Peeps have two things in common: (1) regardless of their academic field of study, they all adhere to the PC template; and (2) they are responsible for a great deal of the academic rot that has spread throughout our education system and subsequently spilled over into society in general. The second condition follows naturally from the first. Of course, not all college professors and administrators are Peeps in da Hood, but the ones who are not, usually have their offices in the basement next to the boiler room.

At the risk of becoming too academic myself, let me just say that Political Correctness is what you get when you mix socialistic utopian zeal with the natural human tendency for the acquisition of power and the subsequent corruption that follows. When organized religions do it under the pretense of religious dogma, it's called persecution with one of the most famous being the Inquisition.

Even though the Left denies the need for religion or a god, basic human nature seems to require those beliefs. Thus, the above analogy to religion is not by accident. We have already seen in an earlier chapter the Left's Ten Commandants handed to us by Marx. But each PC discipline, or denomination if you wish, also has its gods, priests, sins, guilts, sacraments, repentances, and punishments. Although modern laws prevent burning at the stake, a political inquisition that destroys property, reputations, careers, and lives for those who challenge the PC orthodoxy is alive and well on American college campuses, and also in general society.

The PC modus operandi is as follows: *take subjective opinions and force society and individuals, through laws, regulations, policies, or intimidation to accept them as objective reality;* also known as brainwashing or indoctrination. I talked about this somewhat in the Psychosocial-babbler and Educationlogist sections, but this same phenomenon is also exhibited by their fellow Peeps in the departments of Political Science, Art, Music, History, Philosophy, Journalism, Law, and other related subject areas.

However, I want to make it clear that the problem is not that there are PC schools-of-thought on college campuses; the problem is that the Peeps make sure it is the only allowed school-of-thought. Thus, the key word in the definition in the previous paragraph is the word "force." You can change people's minds by the force of persuasion through application of reason and proven facts or by brute coercive force. Unfortunately, liberal arts are supposed to teach you skills like the universal ability to question and reason, but questioning and reasoning is the last thing the PC community wants you to do. The PC movement uses brute coercive force. That's one, of two reasons, why Political Correctness is at its heart a socialist movement. Socialism (or communism) by definition requires a strong central government, or central authority, operating under a single philosophy that permeates, by force, all aspects of society or the organization.

For Peeps, the rival philosophy that must be eliminated is the concept we call "America," and western civilization in general. It is America, and what it represents, that defines the Peep psyche. Don't be fooled by the constant barrage of accusations about American poverty, greed, racism, sexism and all of the other "isms." America has had its share of failings, but these accusations are intentionally taken out of context from the *great historical facts about the global evolution of human societies, economic systems, and individual rights.*

With regard to their views on America, Peeps fall under two different categories. The first Peep category includes professors who basically consider America a fundamentally flawed experiment. But if America was just flawed, then there would be room to talk, because everything is flawed and can be improved. However, being fundamentally flawed means it cannot be fixed; in fact, it means something even stronger: that America must be replaced because its free-market economy and western Judeo-Christian belief system are unjust failures. Of course, the replacement system is humanistic socialism. Yeah, that will work.

The Peeps in the second category have a pathologic hatred for America, the West, or males in general. America to them is not just fundamentally flawed, but fundamentally evil. This group is most likely to use an "ism" label at every opportunity. Their hatred results in "lying for justice" as a valid rationalization for any wrong statement they may make, whether for the war on terror, homelessness, race issues, marriage, feminism and so on.

Furthermore, believing that a legal or social system is fundamentally evil absolves them from facing the consequences of any civil disobedience. Thus, not only is permissible to break the law, but they also excuse themselves from having to face any legal consequence for their actions because in their view the system is unjust.

This radical view is a basic tenet of political correctness as long as it's applied to politically correct protected causes, but it is an extreme departure from Martin Luther King's position as expressed in his April 16, 1963, *Letter from Birmingham*

Jail: "One who breaks an unjust law must do so openly, lovingly, and with a willingness to accept the penalty."

If one of your professors uses words like "bringing truth to power," he or she is probably a Peep of the Second Type, and if you can you should consider dropping the class or at least get ready to digest a tremendous amount of America bashing. If you are a white male, you will learn that you are nothing more than a Hitler or a (George) Bush, as the case may be, and males in general will find out that you are nothing more than a "potential" rapist.

This brings us to the second reason why PC is coupled to socialism. Socialism does not recognize and openly discourages individual achievements, thus elevating the lowest common denominator as the social norm. This has the side effect of destroying any standards that might be held up as a measure of merit; this applies to much of modern scholarly work especially in the "soft" fields of study.

We can see both the hatred and disrespect for America and the lack of objective peer standards by comparing the following quotes:

> "As a Ph.D. Islamologist and Arabist I really hate to say this, but I'll say it anyway: 9/11 had nothing to do with Islam. The war on terror is as phony as the latest Osama bin Laden tape." Other purported terrorist attacks, including the July 7, 2005, London bombing, and the March 11, 2004, Madrid bombing, were the actions of a "special wing of, probably, U.S. or western military intelligence," and not Islamic terrorists.

Professor Kevin Barrett
University of Wisconsin at Madison

> As a Ph.D. scientist and researcher, I really hate to say this, but I'll say it anyway: the Periodic Table of Elements has nothing to do with chemistry. Oxygen is as phony as the latest Nobel Prize in Chemistry. Other research in quantum physics and chemistry represents the actions of a special wing of, probably, the U.S. or western scientific establishment and not true scientists.

Tony Corvo
Conservative Next Door

The major difference between the two statements is that 99.99% of the applicable academic subject matter experts (physicists, chemists, etc.) would recognize and label my statement as nonsense. But, 99.99% of the applicable academic subject matter experts (historians, sociologists, poli-sci folks, etc.) at our colleges and universities would label Barrett's statement as "interesting," "insightful," "plausible," or my favorites, "courageous" or even "heroic," with quite a number even saying "factual."

Let's not pick on Barrett. He is just one of a long list of other esteemed members of academia, another being Ward Churchill from the University of Colorado, that took their turn at the national spotlight making like-minded statements about 9/11, as well as a host of outlandish PC statements about many other subject matters. Of course, they all have full support of their respective institutions.

In real gangs, you prove your worth and increase your status by committing certain gang sanctioned acts; mostly criminal. To increase your status as a Peep in da Hood and have any chance in reaching the envied status of a tenured Peep, you have to bash America. Again, not just on the war on terror, but every facet of American politics, culture or history. Once tenure is reached, the Peep can even further dispense with any remaining standards he or she may have had left.

You can get a good feel for how pervasive the PC dogma is in public colleges by looking at private schools, especially many religious affiliated universities. Whatever you may think of abortion, one thing for sure is that the official position of the Catholic Church is anti-abortion. Yet many Catholic colleges often take a sympathetic view or even outright blanket support for abortion rights, far above any possibly legitimate pragmatic reason. Their excuse is that they want to expose the students to all viewpoints. But what does having a religious affiliation mean if it doesn't mean you live and teach it? This would be like animal rights groups reserving office space for baby seal fur trappers because they want both sides of the issue represented.

But it's not just about abortion. Religious affiliated colleges have a very large share of PC professors across all disciplines, and offer loony courses that can rival the best that any public college can provide. I can imagine a number of reasons for this, three of which are competition for students, legal strings tied to federal or state funds that the private school may be receiving, and finally, many of the private school professors received their education at public colleges, and *nuts* don't fall too far from the tree.

A fourth reason is the influence of what used to be called "Liberation Theology." Liberation Theology is just basically a fancy name for a Frankenstein monster cobbled together with parts from various Christian and "social justice" (i.e., Marxist) ideologies. Although Liberation Theology, under various names, is currently practiced by many American Christian churches, both Catholic and Protestant, it took an early foothold primarily in Latin America. In fact, some of you may recall a scene when Pope John Paul II stepped off his plane when visiting Nicaragua in the 1983 and began wagging a scolding finger at the kneeling Rev. Ernesto Cardenal. Cardenal was the minister of culture in Nicaragua's then-new Sandinista government and a devoted Liberation Theologian.

◆   ◆   ◆

To understand how the Type I and II Peeps train students to be PC, it's important to look into the classroom and distinguish three types of PC classes. The first type consists of introductory courses. These are the classes almost everyone has to take from one department or another as part of their graduation requirements. Intro to Psychology, Intro to Sociology, History 101, English 101, Art Appreciation, and so on, are first level opportunities for the Peeps to reach almost all students.

Classes of the second type are specifically titled and designed to be overtly anti-American, anti-white, anti-west, anti-capitalist, and anti-male. Most of these classes are taken by the most extreme students as well as many in the general student body who are forced to take them again due to graduation requirements. The instructors in these classes tend to be wackos.

Finally, there are the advanced upper level courses specifically designed for the students majoring in the applicable field. Since I have never taken a PC course of the third type, I will restrict my observations to the first two types, leaving you to extrapolate to the third, if you so desire.

Most type I and II courses taught by Peeps are academically light. When I took my introductory Sociology class way back when, the course was taught in modules where students could take the exams at their own pace. I completed the course in three weeks, and most of that time was waiting for the proctors to grade individual module tests. And so on for Psychology, Anthropology, Education courses, etc.

During my undergraduate career I was also forced to take several indoctrination courses. One was called *Contemporary Social Welfare*, taught by a Communist (really). He wasn't just an ideological communist; he was actually a Soviet apologist.

When a young lady in the class told him that she and her family escaped from Czechoslovakia and that basically he was full of BS (the B stands for Bolshevik), his only response was that the reason why Eastern Europe hadn't become a socialist worker's paradise is because of American interference. You could tell he didn't read any of the student essays or tests. I argued with him all the time, but since he was prevented by law to send me to the re-education gulag he gave me a B instead. Since Comrade Teacher didn't really grade anything, I think he gave everybody a B thereby demonstrating true communism.

Another indoctrination class was a senior level Political Science class called *Dissent and Disobedience*. Although it was a senior level course it was designed for the general student population who needed to take an indoctrination course and needed senior level hours to fulfill graduation requirements.

One paper we had to write was defining "power." I knew the teacher wanted to hear the classical liberal spew about race and power or gender and power, but I wasn't going to play her game. So I decided to provide my own spew and used the physics definition of power. My paper said something like: energy is the ability to do work and power is the time rate of change of energy, therefore the more power you have the faster you can get work done. It was a little longer than that and I tied it to democracy, voting, blah blah blah, but basically that's it. It was mostly "mierda del toro." I got a B in the class, clearly demonstrating who had power over whom.

The sole purpose of these courses is to shock you. To make you read pornography as literature or appreciate phallic symbols as art. To sum it up, you can think of the PC curriculum as an ideological boot camp. This is where you take young people and strip away their individualism and make them question their God, their country, and even their parents: but not their professors—the new priests. The goal is to recast them into a cohesive unthinking ant colony willing to bring *truth* to power, lie for *justice, and* fight against *the American way*.

At this point of my writing on the material for this chapter, I was reminded of what Bill O'Reilly said in *The Culture Warrior*. O'Reilly *opined* something to the effect that he had so much to say, that he went nuts thinking about it. But a few examples are necessary

White Devils

There are two great tragedies in American history regarding race and civil rights. The first is slavery in all of its various ugly pre and post civil war phases. The second is our inability to discuss race issues openly and honestly.

First, we must define two important words that are often used incorrectly: racism and bigotry. Racism is when someone from one race views another race as inferior. Bigotry is when someone from one group obstinately treats members of another group with hated or intolerance particularly after facts have been presented to prove his/her opinions in error. In America, we have pretty much adopted "racism" as a catch-all word when bigotry, boorish, or other lesser applicable words are more appropriate to describe a particular behavior. This is not by chance. The accusation of "racism" has certain legal connotations and its *liberal* use is meant to stifle dialogue.

It is often taught and believed that America had Black slaves because of White racism. That's true, but not in that simple context. White opportunists took Black slaves for the same reason that people, since the dawn of time, took other people outside of their group as slaves: because they wanted to exploit them and they militarily could.

For this type of exploitation to work, it always helps for the vanquished group to be "different," even if these differences are almost non-existent. Just look at today's religious wars between sects within religions, let alone between religions, or conflicts between tribes whose only difference is that they live on opposite sides of the same river. You have to be one hell of a salesman to convince the river eastsiders to die in order to defeat those inferior or evil river westsiders.

Jonathan Swift captured this craziness in *Gulliver's Travels*, where Little Endian and Big Endian political factions in the kingdoms of Littliput and Blefuscu started wars over which end of the egg to crack. Doesn't it make you wonder how we have survived as a species?

History is ripe with cultures, races, and religions that have butchered, raped, conquered, and enslaved others. Yet, it is common in today's history courses to ignore brutality as a human trait, and instead concentrate only on the shortcomings of Western culture. This view is expressed in current events in how America is often presented as the root of the world's problems. Thus, today's students get an earful about the widespread killing of North American Indians by Europeans, but little if any information on the barbarity of these same Indian civilizations or tribes to each other. These tribes were more like city-states than the innocent simple communes typically depicted in modern history books. And like most city-states they waged wars against each other and reaped the spoils of their wars including stealing land belonging to other tribes.

The Aztec pyramids were more than religious altars with cute astronomical symbols. As described by Larry Schweikart and Michael Allen in *A Patriot's History of the United States*, "A four day sacrifice in 1487 by the Aztec king Ahuitzotl involved the butchery of 80,400 prisoners by shifts of priests working four at a time at convex killing tables who kicked lifeless, heartless bodies down the side of the pyramid temple." The priests would cut out the hearts while the victims were alive. This worked out to a rate of about 14 victims a minute over 96 hours. The prisoners were mostly from other villages.

Racism is the justification given by those that can exploit slavery or brutality to justify their actions to themselves and to the general public in order to get their support and cooperation. Ironically, more often than not, the average person has little if anything directly to financially gain from the exploitation. Their support comes mostly from fear and ignorance, generated by those that benefit from the exploitation.

Many Americans who owned slaves were typically rich and powerful, so the general public was forced to pronounce and act out the belief of Black racial inferiority. As generations came and went, many believed it, but others didn't. Those Whites that didn't tow the line were also punished. *Racism and bigotry may still exist in America, but racism and bigotry were not invented here, nor are they a creation of White culture.* As Thomas Sowell put it:

> What "multiculturalism" boils down to is that you can praise any culture in the world except Western culture—and you cannot blame any culture in the world except Western culture

> Slavery was just not an issue, not even among intellectuals, much less among political leaders, until the 18th century—and then only in Western civilization. Among those who turned against slavery in the 18th century were George Washington, Thomas Jefferson, Patrick Henry and other American leaders. You could research all of 18th century Africa or Asia or the Middle East without finding any comparable rejection of slavery there. But who is singled out for scathing criticism today? American leaders of the 18th century.

I think what Sowell was saying was that even though some of the Founders owned slaves; they set in motion a political process to eradicate slavery.

Racism and bigotry, in various forms, unfortunately still exist in the world *on every continent.* But distorting history, preventing open dialogue, calling Whites "devils," or calling for killing white people, and being awarded academic honors and appointments for doing so, as some radical professors have done, may make some people feel good, but it won't solve the race problems for those of us who need to work and live together. The choice is ours to make.

Gyrls Gone Wyld

Many feminists prefer the spelling "wymyn" to "women" as a small but symbolic step in their liberation from men. This may seem just a minor thing, but when coupled to all of the other feminist zaniness on college campuses, led me to the title for this section.

The women's rights movement was not the problem. Women, as with other groups, had legitimate societal wrongs that needed to be addressed (but so did men, but that's another story). But as in all other civil rights issues, common sense and the rule of law has been hijacked. This leads to the next Peep example: *Pathological Feminism*. What is Pathological Feminism? Instead of trying to define the term, let me offer this. You can tell a normal woman from a Pathological Feminist by how she answers the following question: *How many sexes are there?* Here are the possible answers you would get:

Normal Woman: There are two sexes, male and female, and my boyfriend is a slob.

Confused Woman: Well, when I was growing up, I thought there were only two, but in my *Introduction to Sociology*, *Introduction to Psychology*, and *Introduction to Elementary Education*, I was told there weren't any sexes, only genders such as female, male and transgender. To tell you the truth, I sort of can imagine what a transgender is, if it's what I think it is, but I still really don't know what the difference is between "sex" and "gender." In my *Introduction to Sex and Power* course, the instructor, Dr. Ima Manhater, said that men's inferiority stems from the incomplete XY chromosome which produces incomplete humans. Also, although my mother says that all men are pigs, my boyfriend does buy me flowers.

Pathological Feminist: First of all, it's more appropriate to talk about gender rather than "sex". Gender is essentially a social construct and as such encompasses the total behavioral, cultural, psychological, as well as physiological traits typically associated with one's "sex." Since sexual intercourse by its nature is a violation of a woman's body, as long as we live in a misogynistic world where males dominate sexual relationships, there are at least three genders: female, transgender, and rapist.

Pathological Feminists see everything around them as phallic symbols, which based on their statements and actions, is defined as anything longer than it is wide, including many buildings. If you think I'm joking, do an internet search on any number of the key words above such as "phallic symbols, feminists," and so on. You may also wish to search "are all men rapists" or "is all sex rape" and see what you get. As you read the material, just remember that this is what is being taught at your tax supported colleges.

Further lunacy is evident by the Feminist's use of the word "herstory" in place of "history" even though the latter's origins in Latin and Greek have nothing to do with a perceived male-centered "his story." I can appreciate a cute turn of a word as well as the next nonspecific gender life form, but I think this is just another example of misdirected bitterness. Do we also need to replace the word "dictionary?"

Feminist Peeps thus see the world in a warped sexual way. I don't have the skills of a Psychosocial-babbler so I don't know the right words but offer *vaginal retentive* as an option. Men see the world in a warped sexual way also, but men's sexual view of the world is rather simple: it's basically that of a 14 year old. But Feminist Peeps have taken all aspects of male/female sexuality and converted them to pseudo-intellectual hate filled diatribes.

In the course of my research for this topic, I came across two other terms I had never heard of before that may also apply here: *Gender Narcissism* and *Sexual Narcissism*, which you may also wish to read up on. Like most descriptions of human behaviors, the writings are all over the place and you can read almost anything you want in them, so you can make you own conclusions. But whatever their mental state may be, these wymyn "scholars" are indoctrinating our young men and women to hate each other (I found one reference that referred to this as a subset of *heterophobia*).

The question I have for Feminist Peeps is, "What do caves and mountains remind you of?" Again, going back to Freud, sometimes a cigar is just a cigar.

How many piano tuners are there in New York City?

A typical topic in some freshman physics courses is training to make rough estimates based on common sense with little if any other information. This is a useful skill that often can help you determine if someone is blowing smoke up your tailpipe.

One such problem, originally posed by physicist Enrico Fermi who liked doing this sort of thing when he wasn't busy working on nuclear reactions, is determining how many piano tuners are in New York City. That's it; no other information is given. The answer, *of course*, is about 100. (No, I'm not going to show you how that number is derived, because that would require equations and in the preface I promised there was only going to be one in the book.)

The reason why I bring this up is because Peeps use statistics that often just don't pass the sniff test. But lying for justice is often the only way for wacko professors to support their opinions, and frequently this involves using unsupportable statistics or ill defined words. The only thing between the statistics and the government reaching into your wallet is your common sense.

A good example is statistics on homelessness. In its generic form homelessness is caused by a variety of conditions, some of which are mental illness, domestic violence, bad luck, personal life choices, and just deciding to be a bum. Distinguishing between the various forms of homelessness and their origins is important if public policy is to be formulated correctly because some causes of homelessness may or may not be of a nature that government can or should solve i.e., bumitis. But in order to get government involved you have to create a crisis of immense proportions.

My quick internet search on homelessness found that the number of homeless people in America is estimated to be somewhere from 150,000 to 3,000,000 (other searches may show other numbers). An honest professor would lead the class into a discussion about what is meant by homelessness, its causes, what the numbers mean, how the different numbers were arrived at, and what are the best social policies needed to fix the various sources of the problem if applicable.

A Peep would just use the higher number, assign it to the worst definition possible, and blame capitalism. The problem with the higher number is that it means 1 out of every 100 Americans is homeless.

If that ridiculous ratio isn't enough to convince you that the higher number is questionable; how about this. I was listening to a New York City homeless advocate being interviewed on TV where she claimed that 35,000 homeless people are in the city. Again let's use a little math. Let's put the New York City population at about 10 million people. If you spread the homeless population of New York City to the entire 300 million Americans, then the national homeless population is at about 1 million, or about 1 out of every 300 people.

But I don't believe this is correct either, because many of the homeless tend to live in places where they can get free services such as large urban areas; in fact, San Francisco has made it official policy to welcome the homeless into the city. So even if the New York City number is correct, it doesn't proportionally represent the homeless picture across the country. Just based on this analysis, I would tend to believe the actual number is probably closer to 500,000. If you throw in the requirement of using strict guidelines in defining homelessness, and assume that some of the 35,000 in New York are just bums (and this includes many drug addicts), then the national number might drop to 250,000 or less. But hey I could be wrong. Anyway, I don't need to say anything else, because either you have a feel for how ludicrous the 1 out 100 ratio is or you don't.

Chances are that you might also hear a Peep say, "In America, thousands of homeless people die everyday." The Government Class loves hearing stats like these because it justifies more money for programs that usually don't work, and let's face it, most students, and people in general, don't think pass the numbers. But if you did, you would realize that this means about 500,000 homeless people are dying in the streets of major cities every year!

From the previous analysis, at this death rate homelessness would vanish in 6 to 24 months, or you have to believe that as many homeless people are added to the count at the same rate to keep the status quo. Trust me, if either of those were true, you wouldn't need a college education to know it. The real lesson is that for any subject it is important to first determine how words are being defined and numbers generated, or anything can be concluded.

Is it getting warm in here, or is it just me?

This section has nothing to do with menopause, but it does have to do with how even a physical science can be hijacked. This should not be surprising; after all, the Catholic Church forced Galileo to recant his views on planetary motion, not because the Church leaders thought his views were wrong, but because it was all about information control and political power. (Galileo was reported to have said after his mea culpa, "It moves nevertheless," or something to that effect.)

As in all cases where a subject has become politicized, all pronouncements coming out of that field of study should be suspect, as we have discussed in relation to the social disciplines. So keep in mind that physical scientists are not saints. There are PC wackos in university science and engineering departments, but the root cause of homelessness (i.e., Ronald Reagan) doesn't typically come up in the classroom when you are discussing thermodynamics. But environmental science and global warming in particular, are two examples of physical sciences that have been hijacked by the left. (In fact, Environmentalism is closer to being a religion than any other PC discipline. Besides adhering to Marx's Ten Commandants, Pope Al Gore I serves as its spiritual leader, and Mother Earth as its deity.)

Remember what I said about how the less quantitative or more complex a subject is, the greater care we have to exercise before making conclusions? Remember how I also said that the Government Class doesn't wait around for real science when pseudoscience would do if it fits the PC template? Just ask Senators Olympia Snowe (R-ME) and Jay Rockefeller (D-WV). They teamed up and sent a letter to ExxonMobil browbeating them to no longer fund climate change skeptics. In their infinite understanding of physics, the senators already know enough and are not interested in hearing opposing arguments. Of course, blaming global warming on mankind expands government, which is their real goal.

As in the psychology experiment on hot sauce and guns discussed earlier, I have no problem with any particular result or opinion as part of a scientific process. But I do have a problem when someone claims we have to "fix" the Second Amendment or destroy the American industrial machine because some experiment or model tells them so. The purpose of peer review in science is to provide a mechanism to reach a conclusion between competing theories based on rigorous analysis and debate. That peer review and debate cannot occur if some political or governmental authority predetermines the outcome, and that is exactly what is happening in global warming studies, where both funding and political pressure are working to kill voices of opposition.

The life blood of college tenure is the ability to win grant money. With the federal government now in cahoots with the global warming Left, there is a tremendous amount of pressure for researchers to make sure that whatever conclusions they come to in their global warming research, they better make sure it always spells doomsday. And there are many professors who are more than happy to oblige or are forced to oblige in order to keep their jobs.

There is an old joke that I think sometimes is attributed to Benjamin Franklin that I'm going to modify for the discussion here. In the following joke, replace "government rep" with "diplomat," "professor" with "lady," and "publish a pro global warming paper" with "having sex," and you will generally get the main thrust of the original joke.

> A government rep at a dinner party turned to the professor sitting next to him and asked, "Would you publish a pro global warming paper if I awarded you a million dollar grant?" The professor thinks for a minute and replies, "Why, I do believe that I would." The government rep then asks, "Would you publish a pro global warming paper for a $10 grant?" Furious, the professor responds, "Absolutely not, what type of person do you think I am?" To this, the government rep replies, "We have already established what type of person you are; now we are negotiating a price."

Global warming arguments require determining changes in average temperatures and the causes of those changes, which in turn currently rely heavily on field data as well as on mathematical and computer modeling. To the layman, whatever comes out of computer must be true if a "mathematical" model is behind the numbers. In reality it's more like garbage in, garbage out. (For the record, I am not an expert on global warming. My comments here are based on general physical and mathematical arguments that tend to be universally true.)

Mathematical models are, figuratively speaking, a dime a dozen and nearly every university professor from anthropology to zoology has a pet model for one thing or another. And in many cases the models or research using the models were funded by special interest groups. However, that in itself is not the problem, as long as the peer review process is allowed to proceed unhindered by political baggage.

Like any specialized industry, there are probably a set of global warming models that are more respected than others and have undergone a screening process to ensure some sort of reliability. But even the best models have limitations, especially those that deal with very complex systems like climate. For technical reasons I can't get into here, even the best climate models are so temperamental and unstable that only a few trained people know how to use them correctly, and even in these cases the experts can't always agree on or are often stumped by the outputs. In the class of problems that climate models belong to, small changes in assumptions can often lead to large differences in outputs.

Furthermore, even as we continue to improve these models and include more and more variables, we also continue to run into lacking fast enough computers to adequately run the simulations, which in turn force researchers to make compromises in assumptions. Think of this as similar to never having a good enough camera to take high resolution photographs. You can make out Uncle Harry, because no one has a gut like that, but who is that standing next to him? (However, it is erroneous to flippantly ask how can we calculate the climate in 25 years, when we can't even get tomorrow's weather right. As an imperfect analogy, think of the difference between estimating the increases in your general financial portfolio in 25 years given your current investment trend, your financial history, and typical market conditions versus predicting the exact amount of money you may have on any particular future date.)

When someone says their model predicts a 1.3 degree average rise in the next 50 years due entirely to bovine flatulence, I'm sorry to say that I'm not impressed because I have an idea of how those models work, including uncertain input assumptions that often drive the output. And it's important to remember that in the 1970s the alarmists were predicting a massive global cooling coupled with overpopulation and worldwide famine.

On the other hand, I'm also not in a position to dispute the "It's our fault" claim outright. But I do know this: as in other legitimate issues we have covered, environmental science has been hijacked by an anti-American and anti-industrial movement. The responsibility for "fixing" global warming now rests mostly on America, and the fix is so expensive that going it alone will definitely cripple the nation's economy. That in itself makes me question the results.

The rest of the world is essentially given a pass, even in countries that are grotesque pollution violators such as India and China. And even the European Union, one of our main accusers, has not met its own pollution reduction goals even though it continues to set more goals that member states have no intention of meeting. And that is the real rub with the whole global warming issue. So before I give up my beef I want to see a real and open scientific debate without the interference of congress or the UN. If this debate concludes that the warming is manmade, then the discussion has to also include the best reasonable worldwide solution that does not include destroying America.

That's all I'm going to say about this subject but will close with this. If any environmental nut tries to argue with you that even if they're wrong, wouldn't it be smart to be on the safe side? Remind them of the story of the young French prodigy, Blaise Pascal (June 19, 1623 to August 19, 1662).

Pascal was a brilliant mathematician and scientist that had a near death experience in 1654 when his carriage nearly fell off a bridge. After that incident Pascal devoted the rest of his life to theology. Pascal tried to convince non-believers that even if God doesn't exist, wouldn't it be wise to believe in him anyway just to play it safe? So tell your environmental friends that you will believe in global warming and mankind as its cause just in case they are right, if they become devout pro-lifers because the fetus may be human, just in case you are right.

Don't worry, they won't make the trade.

Does this class make my butt look big?

Let's tie all this looniness together with the following story as originally reported by the New York Times, and summarized in the December 18, 2006, National Review.

It turns out that just when you thought that all the victimhoods had their own college departments, our friends at the University of Wisconsin are offering a course on "The Social Construction of Obesity." As printed in the National Review:

> There is no such thing as being fat, you see; "fatness" is just figment. Nor is there any substance to claims by "scientists" that "obesity" is "linked" to diabetes, hypertension, or heart disease.

The course will be taught by "fat scholars." Do you notice the similarity between the statement above and Barrett's quote given earlier? I don't know if the University of Wisconsin has a medical school, but if it does, are the doctors upset over this? But it doesn't matter; because victimlogy trumps science.

◆   ◆   ◆

Many students who take PC classes often say they are afraid to say anything that goes against the professor's views for fear of grade retaliation, and sometimes that's a valid fear. But keep in mind how some of these courses are taught, that is, the course material could be just the rants of the professor.

Although some wacko professors are vindictive, often the only difference between agreeing with professors and giving them a hard time is the difference between an A or a B, because any other lower grade would require them to justify the grade against standards that don't exist, or even public exposure of their teaching manners or views. Peeps are afraid of public exposure because the public has higher standards than their peers or administrators.

Peep exams typically have questions formulated so you are forced to answer in the way that the professor wants you to. For example, a question might read: "According to animal psychologist and rights advocate Dr. So-and-so, what is the last thing a deer thinks before being shot?"

There is nothing preventing you from answering this question truthfully *according* to Dr. So-and-so. This verifies that you understand the course content as defined by the professor. But you can always end the answer with: "But I don't believe any of it, and here's why. According to hunting expert, Ted Nugent, they aren't capable of that kind of thinking. All they care about is: 'What am I going to eat next? Who am I going to screw next? And can I run fast enough to get away? They are very much like the French in that way'."

You just have to size up the professor and see if he or she is a wacko or just a run-of-the-mill PC Liberal. You also have to accept a lower grade if it comes to that. In the teacher-student relationship, the teacher holds the power and you need to decide if you want to risk "bringing truth to power" and the consequences of doing so.

American and Western Culture, although not perfect, are the end results of thousands of years of social thought. Yet the foundations of our liberties, including the concepts of capitalism, free will, property rights, and personal responsibility, are being trashed in our colleges for the sake of a politically correct socialist ideology.

When the second-to-last chapter is written on the history of the American nation, it will conclude that America was the greatest country in history. The last chapter will deal with trying to understand why we destroyed the greatest country in history.

The stakes are too great to let this butchering of the truth go unhindered. As a student, it is your right to question your professors (but not to disrupt the class). *If you decide to question your professors, be prepared for the worst, but keep your cool, be sincere, do your homework, know your facts and always exert professionalism even if some of your professors don't.*

The worst thing you can do to egotistical professors is to challenge them, but your goal is not to change their minds. Your goal is watch them make fools out of themselves. Years later you will look back on your actions as some of your finest moments.

◆   ◆   ◆

Most Peeps get their degrees paid for by taxpayers then realize that they are unmarketable in an insensitive business world that only hires graduates who actually know how to do something. So like dogs that bite the hands that feed them and never get hit by a newspaper, the Peeps understand that they can get paid well by the government for indoctrinating the next generation about American failures without worrying about academic or other standards. Modern artists have elevated this to an (pun intended) art form. I know this because I have no artistic qualities, leaving me to use the following very simple metric in determining whether something is or is not art: It is not art if I or an animal can recreate it. Most art today meets that criterion.

People who live and work in the real world have little appreciation for the level of arrogance that exists in the academic world toward them. But to understand where the Peeps are coming from, you have to remember they work in a world where they are typically the "smartest" one in a room filled with mostly young, as Rush Limbaugh would say, "minds full of mush." Couple this with the countless accolades that they pass onto each other and it must be difficult for Peeps to look out their office windows and not have contempt for the great unwashed. Narcissism is a burden some bear better than others.

When non-Peep professors say anything hinting of criticism about any of the protected PC topics, the Peep establishment jumps onto the highest rafters to proclaim the need to rid the university and society of the hate warlords. But when Peeps say the most incredibly stupid and hateful things about Whites, men, America, etc., the Peep establishment jumps onto the highest rafters proclaiming the need for academic freedom and diversity of thought. That is, until the public hears about it, then the administrators go and hide under their desks, issuing statements through their secretaries.

In reality, all ideas are not defended on American college campuses; only the PC ones. For proof, just count the number of Republican professors in the Wymyn's Studies departments, or ask Larry Summers, former president of Harvard, what happens when you utter a discouraging word on college campuses.

If you are a serious professor in one of these disciplines and are insulted at what I wrote in this chapter: good! Fix the problem or at least speak up about it. On the other hand, if you fit the criteria in this section then there may be a place for you in one of many American colleges and universities as a distinguished Peep in da Hood.

Weapons: The power to influence generations of "minds full of mush"
Strengths: Willing to "lie for justice"
Weaknesses: Peeps have two major weaknesses: (1) they are easy to identify outside the classroom by the lack of calluses on their hands; and (2) taking a bath after eating a hearty meal of various bean based foods, they confuse their bath water for champagne.

10

Propagandists and the Knights of Narcissia

The first casualty of war is the truth.

—A statement said in various ways by various authors

Propagandists: News as Entertainment

Bernie Goldberg wrote a whole book on the news media called, *Bias: A CBS Insider Exposes How the Media Distort the News.* In addition to that book, Goldberg's *100 People Who Are Screwing Up America*, O'Reilly's *Culture Warrior*, and a host of other books also capture much of the problems in today's media. Therefore, I'm not going to duplicate that information here. I will only present a few important points that need to be included here for continuity.

◆   ◆   ◆

Phil Graham, former publisher of the Washington Post, was reported to have said that journalism is the "first rough draft of history." However, students at journalism schools today often say they are going into journalism to correct the wrongs of the world, which you would be correct to interpret as *western culture*.

The Left has increasingly controlled American news media since the Vietnam War, and thus in effect these important institutions have turned into nothing more than Liberal Propagandists in the culture war. It wouldn't be so bad if it were restricted to differences in topics such as whether we should or should not privatize social security, or even the greater argument of the overall role of government. As we have seen on the war on terror, it's deeper than that; it includes giving aid and comfort to our enemies, while hiding behind free speech and the patriotic right to criticize the government. Speaking for myself, although I may not be enlightened enough to be able to define the difference between duplicity and legitimate criticism, like pornography, I know it when I see it.

In regards to the Education Industrial Complex, the national and local papers and broadcast media serve in the Education Industrial Complex's Communications Department. At the national level, the Propagandists keep guard against any conservative attempt to change national education legislation. If any attempt is made that might potentially set back the socialist principle of an all encompassing government school system, you can count on the Propagandists to provide the disinformation. Ronald Reagan, Newt Gingrich and others couldn't stop or even dent the Federal Department of Education. They learned quickly that the Department of Education is a cash cow you can't tip.

Local newspaper editorials always stress that taxpayers must support all educational initiatives that call for more spending, even for districts and programs that are failing if for no other reason than *for the children*. These editorials come from the same two templates and go something like this:

Small Middle/Upper Class Districts

Although there may have been some questionable spending initiatives, overall district officials have been good stewards of the taxpayer's money. The superintendent did apologize for the installation of the Italian marble tile in his office and test scores have been improving following the reduction of the student to teacher ratio down to 15 to 1, which by the way was completely in line with recommendations from leading Colleges of Education and had full support of the district's teachers union.

The annual cost per student of $15,000 is not excessive when you consider that you are getting not only an education for your child but a foot in the door of the college of his/her choice. That's quite a bang for the buck. You must support this $15 million levy in order to keep the improvements coming. Spending cuts at this time would be unwise. So join this paper, the Chamber of Commerce, and the teachers union and vote YES in November.

Poor/Urban Districts

Although there may have been some questionable spending initiatives, overall district officials have been good stewards of the taxpayer's money considering the cuts in educational funds by Republicans that unfairly tied funding to district performance. Although test scores have not significantly improved in the last 10 years, it should be stressed that the current superintendent inherited all of his problems from the previous administrations.

The annual cost per student of $20,000 is not excessive when you consider that you are investing in the future. You must support this $50 million levy in order to prevent further district slippage. So join this paper, the Chamber of Commerce, the Urban League of America, the NAACP, the ACLU, Planned Parenthood, the National Council of La Raza, PETA, the Sierra Club, the UN, the teachers union and other independent non-partisan organizations and vote YES in November.

Across the country, many newspapers and electronic news media organizations are experiencing financial problems. At the time of this writing, NBC announced massive layoffs in its news division, and the New York Times has reported large profit losses. These follow other announcements that readership is down at the LA Times and other major newspapers.

The reasons given publicly for some of these problems are the accessibility to alternate forms of news delivery systems such as the internet and cable. But I'm sure that inside the board rooms or the editors' offices another truth is known but unspoken; that with competition readily available, those idiots in the Red States are actually making consumer decisions.

The Dayton Daily News is so liberal that locally it is sometimes referred to as the Dayton People's Daily or the Dayton Workers Daily. In December 2006, the paper's editor announced his retirement. His biography listed a degree from Antioch College in Yellow Springs, Ohio. Many of you probably never heard of Yellow Springs, but if you ever drove through the town, located on State Route 68 just east of Dayton, you would swear that you just went back in time to the 1960s, except the hippies look older and thankfully tend to keep their clothes on.

If the name Antioch rings a bell, it's probably due to its sexual offense prevention policy first published in the early 1990s, which required that individuals ask permission for each phase of any possible sexual act. The policy generated a bit of a national uproar and the usual comic relief in print and on TV. But this procedure was necessary because, as Antioch puts it, they had to change their "rape culture." Fortunately, the policy also clears up some confusing situations like did you know that a person can't give consent while sleeping? A somewhat complete herstory is available as *Addendum A, Herstory 1990-1996*, on the college's website.

It's usually a good thing to give an example or two to support your arguments; so here's a subtle one. Recently a high school teacher retired at the nearby town of Huber Heights, Ohio. One of her last official duties was as the faculty advisor on the year book staff. It turns out she must have wanted to go out with a bang, so she paid for a half page ad in the year book and published a "final report card" on students, teachers, support staff and school administration.

She gave the secretarial staff an A, which was very smart of her since it's not wise to get the secretarial staff mad at you because everyone knows they run the show. She gave the teaching staff a B+, which may have been a little high, but she probably still had some friends that she wanted to keep. She gave the administration an F for failing to support the staff, being inconsistent, lacking preparation, and making the school someplace you want to escape from. Finally, she gave the student population a C. Her notes on the justification for the C were: "improvement needed, lack of effort, don't pay attention, more study time needed."

I thought this was kind of funny, but sort of agree with the official response that it was a little underhanded. However, what was interesting was the response of disappointment to her overall student body grade of C.

The Dayton Daily News acting true to their liberal roots and mission to support the Educational Industrial Complex at any cost, couldn't just report the incident. One of their many liberal columnists (sorry for being redundant) that are disbursed throughout the paper, acting on statements from the school principal that the C was unwarranted, wrote an opinion column defending the school and gave the guilty teacher an F for her assessment of the student body. She also criticized the teacher for having the nerve to even attack the system—it just isn't done, especially from someone from the inside.

I can understand the principal being mad because he has an image to uphold. But isn't C the average grade you would expect from a typical student body? Sure, there are a few schools that might score above average against some national benchmark, but on *average*, the *average* school is *average*, and C is an *average* grade. The teacher may have displayed poor judgment, but no doubt she was absolutely correct in her assessment. And what school does not have students that need improvement, show little effort, fail to pay attention, and need more study time? I get suspicious when a district claims a very high number of students with very high grade point averages. In effect, the retired teacher really said nothing.

The Education Industrial Complex wants everyone to think that the average grade should be a B or maybe even an A. That of course is meaningless, but give them enough money and they'll see to it! By the way, according to the media, a whistleblower from the Educational Industrial Complex giving away secrets is always a traitor, but a whistleblower from the Military Industrial Complex giving away secrets is always an American hero.

The Dayton Daily News recently revamped its entire format hoping to stem the tide of readers dropping out. It now looks a little like a USA Today Lite. But thinking that bigger fonts and more colorful pictures will make Conservatives understand Liberalism is a lot like thinking that talking louder will help someone understand a foreign language.

It would be nice if the news media outlets would just admit their political leanings, but they play this game that assumes we're all too stupid to read past the headlines. Here's how a typical newspaper might cover the campaign stops of Republican and Democratic presidential candidates as written through their headlines.

Republican Candidate: GOP candidate visit creates traffic jams.
Democratic Candidate: Dem candidate draws large crowds.

You shouldn't just chalk this up to biased field reporters. No article goes into a paper without several levels of editing. So whether this type of reporting happens intentionally or unconsciously, the slippage of liberal favoritism in news headlines and articles is a testament to disingenuous journalists and their senior editors.

TV coverage is just as bad. Here is how a bridge collapse would be covered in the local or national news by your typical field reporter babe (TFRB):

Dateline: sometime well into the 21st Century

TFRB: [Talking to the county bridge inspector.] Mr. Inspector, what caused the railroad bridge to collapse?

Inspector: Well, the tanker truck traveling 20 miles per hour above the speed limit hit one of the bridge's support beams and the explosion weakened the structure causing the bridge to fall as the train loaded with lead traveled over it.

TFRB: Thank you Mr. Inspector. Susan, viewers should also know that money that was to be appropriated to improve the bridge's support beams and surrounding roadways was cut by Ronald Reagan from the highway budget in 1983. Back to you Susan.

Anchor: Thanks Katie. And now in our studios we just happen to have the wife of the truck driver who died in that accident. Jill, thank you for being here at this difficult time. How do you feel about the fact that your husband may be alive today if Reagan hadn't cut money from the 1983 highway appropriation bill?

Conservatives should try to keep their sense of humor through all this and try to enjoy the show. Some of the "neutral" and "mainstream" news sources are actually entertaining to watch as they squirm to present "balance." For example, in a typical "balanced' panel discussion of 5 liberals and one conservative the questioning may go like this.

> **Liberal Host**: Ms. Conservative, why do your support privatizing social security and potentially dooming millions of elderly to go to bed hungry every night?
>
> **Liberal Host**: Mr. Progressive, if you were a tree, what tree would you be?

That last question has been attributed to Barbara Walters, current head honcho of *The View* (the V being in very large text), a fluffy day-time entertainment talk show that unfortunately millions of women use as their primary news source. However, to be fair, she may not have actually asked the question in that exact format. The story goes that in an interview with Katharine Hepburn, Hepburn compared herself to a tree. To which Walters asked, "What kind of tree?" (If men were allowed to have a show equivalent to *The View*, would it be called *The Perspective*, with a very large P?)

The rank and file in the mainstream media may be socialists, but the ones that watch the bottom line are being taught the good old capitalist principles of profit and loss. One reason why the various news media formats are becoming aggressively left leaning is because they realize they are fighting for a smaller and smaller piece of the market. They lost the Red state market because of alternative news choices and now are fighting for the remaining Blue market liberals who like what the media is spewing. One can only expect it to get nastier.

Weapons: Words and images

Strengths: Control over print and broadcast technologies, processes, and resources

Weaknesses: The increase in internet use and the rise of a plethora of alternative news sources have left many Propagandists preaching to empty pews.

◆   ◆   ◆

The Knights of Narcissia: Entertainment as News

George Voinovich makes a great Democratic senator from Ohio. The trouble is Voinovich is a Republican. Nevertheless, he did do one thing to his credit; in

June 2002, he boycotted the Senate Environment and Public Works Clean Air Subcommittee because the coal mining expert Kevin Richardson from the singing group *Backstreet Boys* was scheduled to testify on coal extraction processes and water quality.

Getting celebrities to testify before congress is not new. Earlier in the year superstar swimsuit model and nuclear physics expert Christie Brinkley was invited before the full committee to discuss nuclear energy. In 1985, a House agricultural committee asked several actresses who played farm wives in movies to testify about the suffering farm families undergo during rural recessions. The renowned agriculturists Jessica Lange, Sissy Spacek, Jane Fonda and Sally Field all made appearances. And let us not forget the great Alar apple crusade headed by the famous actress and part time toxicologist Meryl Streep in her testimony before congress in the 1980s that crippled the apple industry.

When you rely on expert testimony to support your position it is said that you are *appealing to authority*. The special interest groups and their Government Class counterparts clearly understand the emotional appeal that having a celebrity speak on an issue can mean to their cause. But technically, using movie stars to promote an issue falls under the category of appeal to an *unqualified* authority. The idea being that "I'm not a doctor, but I play one on TV," adds credence to the message. Personally, I think mostly it's just a con job.

When celebrities truly care about a cause, they must be 100 times more careful than the average person in how they conduct and present themselves in advancing the cause. But many celebrities just come across as shallow. I'm amazed at how many very talented actors are absolute numbskulls when interviewed without a script. But that's okay, I just wish they would continue making great movies, songs, and shows, but lay off discussing *Utilitarianism*, by John Stuart Mill.

Celebrities make a living reading other people's words and acting out other people's lives. In their world image is everything. To them fantasy and reality become too confusing to sort out, so why even bother, and besides beautiful people don't have to. And what scares me as much as congress asking expert nuclear advice from swimsuit models, is the real possibility that the celebrities actually believe they are experts.

So any narcissistic tendencies of previously discussed groups pale in comparison to these "Knights of Narcissia," otherwise known as the celebrities of Hollywood, where they serve in the Education Industrial Complex's Audio and Visual Department. (Narcissism is derived from the Greek myth of Narcissus, a very handsome man who rebuffed the advances of the nymph Echo. He was punished by being doomed to fall in love with his own reflection in a pool of water. Sounds like Hollywood doesn't it?)

Ironically, America fought a war to get rid of loony royalty, but there must be a natural human tendency for society to have a pampered and well paid group of people to provide us entertainment on and off the throne or stage; as the case may be. The Knights of Narcissia are America's loony royalty.

But loonies they may be, the Knights of Narcissia are formable warriors in the culture war. And what's a good culture war without a few battles over sex.

The Left likes to claim that many people on the Right are sexually repressive, while they are the enlightened ones. But when I think of the Left and sexuality, why is it that the images I get are of horny furry ferrets? Not just a few horny furry ferrets but millions and millions of horny furry ferrets led mostly by their mascots the bimbos and himbos (male bimbos) of Hollywood.

Liberals, and bimbos and himbos in particular, zug-zug everywhere and with anything. They zug-zug on TV in prime time. If your embarrassed by the zug-zugging on channel 11, don't bother changing the channel; they're zug-zugging on all the channels. When they're not zug-zugging on TV, they're talking about zug-zugging on the radio.

They sing about zug-zugging over your car radio as you drive your kids to school. But hey, it's not all bad. You actually have a choice: country zug-zug, rock-n-roll zug-zug, rap zug-zug, and even easy-listening zug-zug (although this tends to be soft zug-zug).

They zug-zug on the magazine covers at the check out line; they zug-zug on highway billboards; they zug-zug in PG movies; and they love to zug-zug in public. But when you catch them in public, and ask them to please get a room to zug-zug in private, they'll tell you to go zug-zug yourself.

Education doesn't just happen in the classroom. While all this zug-zugging is going on, our children are watching and learning. And our young girls figure if it's okay for Hollywood stars to be single moms, it must be okay for them. Unfortunately, there's usually a minor difference between the typical teenage girl and a Hollywood bimbo, and that's about 100 million dollars or more. And the himbos tell our young boys not to sweat it, because it doesn't matter who the father is; it's all good.

The problem with the Knights of Narcissia doesn't stop at zug-zugging. The entertainment industry has joined many other American institutions that have passed the point of providing constructive criticisms to downright America bashing. There are many examples of this that have been documented in a number of books and publications, including some of references cited in this book. A recent but very subtle example is the latest Superman move, *Superman Returns*, when Perry White asks his reporters, "Does he still stand for truth, justice, all that stuff?" All that stuff? What happened to the *American Way*? Well we know what happened. America is not worth fighting for; not even for Superman. In today's entertainment industry, saying something good about America would be as shocking as Rhett Butler's "Frankly, my dear, I don't give a damn," in the 1939 movie *Gone with the Wind*.

Am I being nitpicky? That depends. A Liberal reading this would think I'm nuts. A Conservative would understand what I mean. So you decide. But I have to admit I now have more personal empathy for the complaints that minority groups used to lodge about how they were portrayed in movies. Anyone remember when Marlon Brando turned down the Academy Award for Best Actor for his portrayal of Vito Corleone in the *Godfather*? His boycott was based on how American Indians were depicted in films. (Response to his boycott raised the question on why wasn't he just as upset over how Italians were portrayed in the *Godfather*.)

There is nothing wrong with any particular required theme or message when put into the proper context. But today's movies, TV shows, and songs are filled with gratuitous sex, cursing, violence, or other covert or overt messages that have no legitimate thematic function except to shock or to mock. Since my children were born, and particularly the past 5 to 10 years, there were fewer and fewer shows on TV that I felt comfortable watching with them. I became the fastest remote channel changer in the west as I switched from whatever I was watching to cooking shows whenever my kids entered the room. I often think about whether they ever wondered why their parents seemed to watch only the Food Channel.

As time marched on, the situation only got worst. Now I'm even embarrassed to watch some TV shows with my wife. Call me old fashioned if you wish.

When you go into a grocery store you have an expectation of being able to buy groceries without undue surprises. But what would you do if every time you went into a grocery store to buy food, the store manager and staff ridiculed you for wearing a cross around your neck, or an American flag pin or brooch on your lapel? What if you went up to the counter to ask the price on a can of corn, only to find a clerk and a cashier having sex, and you got this for a response: "That #$%& can of corn costs *&^% cents, you piece of patriotic Christian crap. Do you want paper or plastic sir?"

Why is it any different then when you go see a movie, listen to a song, watch a TV show, or go see a live performance, only to find yourself being lectured about how wrong your religion, your country, and your conservative political beliefs are? There is no difference.

Weapons: All forms of entertainment media
Strengths: Beauty sells
Weaknesses: According to the web version of Diagnostic and Statistical Manual of Mental Disorders (DSM), published by the American Psychiatric Association, unbridled narcissism may lead many to *Narcissistic Personality Disorder*. A disorder characterized by five or more of the following:

Grandiose sense of self-importance
Preoccupied with fantasies of success, power, brilliance, beauty, or ideal love
Belief that they are so special, only other special people can understand them
Requires excessive admiration
Strong sense of entitlement
Takes advantage of others
Lacks empathy
Often envious or believes others are envious of them
Arrogant

That pretty much sums it up; don't you think?

11

Legal Unprofessionals

Doctors and lawyers both deal in human misery. The difference is doctors typically try to end the suffering.

—Something my father-in-law once told me

The Law in Practice

The Legal Unprofession serves as the Education Industrial Complex's legal department. It is by far the most dangerous of all the other departments or members, not just in education, but across society.

The Legal Unprofession is not necessarily welcomed by all. Over the years the more powerful members of the Education Industrial Complex have agreed to include the Legal Unprofession in a trial (pun intended) mode. The inclusion is hotly debated since at the individual district or school working level, members of the Legal Unprofession have complicated the educational process through the growth of ever increasing laws and regulations.

These changes have made life miserable for teachers and front-line administrators, but on the other hand, this complication has resulted in tremendous growth in mandated support staff functions. This includes the need for the associated funding or the need for additional funding that naturally follows, and thus an ever larger Education Industrial Complex; making the higher-ups very happy (and wealthy).

Forcing federal policies on local education programs helps achieve the long sought after national socialist goal of weakening parental control over children and transferring that control to the state. Thus, one aspect of the over-legalization of education is the loss of any vestige of the legal and real authority of parents (specifically) and adults (in general) over children. An example of this is in how tort laws are slowly dissolving the privilege that adults once had over children in the administration of discipline—and I'm not even necessarily talking about corporal punishment.

Prodded on by all of the various proclamations represented by Peeps in da Hood, this trend is accompanied by the loss of any real local control over meaningful educational policies at the district level. The beatification of children results in an increasing societal emphasis on children over adults, war zone classrooms and teacher contracts that have to include "assault clauses."

The growth of litigation in America is well recognized. When I was growing up the working phase was "Don't make a federal case out of this." Today the operating policy is to make a federal case of anything. Laws that were created to fix specific problems, such as the Americans with Disabilities Act, Title IX, and others, have been butchered by activist judges under a legal culture that replaces the rule-of-law with the rule-of-whim, while corrupt and cowardly members of legislative bodies hide under their desks.

By making everything a federal civil rights issue, individual district best practices in any real sense are essentially nonexistent and a national educational legal culture is created. The teacher-pupil relationship has been stripped of its human component, and is just a legal contract. Schools and teachers are told what to teach and how to teach it. Attempts to improve education processes are challenged in courts of law in endless appeals. Every district decision is monitored for political correctness, and decisions are made from fear as opposed to logic. This includes no longer being able to play tag, dodge ball or many of the other games we had fun with during recess, because they may hurt self-esteem, are non-inclusive, or can result in a personal injury lawsuit. And one by one, the districts fall in line.

Recently there have been several stories in the national news about elementary boys kissing female classmates. The boys were charged with sexual harassment. You see, sexual harassment is not necessarily about sex or sexuality; it involves the use of gender to differentiate power. So apparently those young boys were exhibiting their full elementary school caveman-like control over the girls. Dragging them by the hair into the lunch room was surely to follow.

Even after all of the explanations, most sensible people still don't understand how this could be sexual harassment. And there's the problem: Legal Unprofessionals in conjunction with Psychosocial-babblers, Educationologists and other Peeps in da Hood are not sensible people. In fact, by the reaction that occurs within the PC community whenever a discouraging word is uttered or a questionable action displayed, you might say they suffer Idiocy Explosive Disorder.

Counseling by the district's Psychosocial-babblers was no doubt provided to both the boys and the girls who in turn probably didn't understand a thing that was told them, but the effect this overreaction will have on the children in the long term is clear. One possible outcome is that boys out of fear of further trouble will not be able to socialize with women and eventually become father rapers and mother stabbers (Arlo Gunthrie's *Alice's Restaurant*). The girls may not turn out that much better; they may end up as directors of university wymyn's centers or on the faculty of some university's Wymyn's Studies department. If you think this is all made-up; do an internet search on "elementary school sexual harassment" or anything similar.

In essence the Legal Unprofessionals, along with the other Peeps, have killed common sense. This is said eloquently in the following ditty; one of those countless e-mails from friends and coworkers that make their rounds and end up in your inbox and whose origin is unknown.

> Today we mourn the passing of a beloved old friend, Common Sense, who has been with us for many years. No one knows for sure how old he was since his birth records were long ago lost in bureaucratic red tape.
>
> He will be remembered as having cultivated such valuable lessons as knowing when to come in out of the rain, why the early bird gets the worm, life isn't always fair, and maybe it was my fault.
>
> Common Sense lived by simple, sound financial policies (don't spend more than you earn) and reliable parenting strategies (adults, not children are in charge).
>
> His health began to deteriorate rapidly when well intentioned but overbearing regulations were set in place. Reports of a six-year-old boy charged with sexual harassment for kissing a classmate; teens suspended from school for using mouthwash after lunch; and a teacher fired for reprimanding an unruly student, only worsened his condition.
>
> Common Sense lost ground when parents attacked teachers for doing the job they themselves failed to do in disciplining their unruly children. It declined even further when schools were required to get parental consent to administer Aspirin, sun lotion or a sticky plaster to a student; but could not inform the parents when a student became pregnant and wanted to have an abortion.
>
> Common Sense lost the will to live as the Ten Commandments became contraband; churches became businesses; and criminals received better treatment than their victims. Common Sense took a beating when you couldn't

defend yourself from a burglar in your own home and the burglar can sue you for assault.

Common Sense finally gave up the will to live, after a woman failed to realize that a steaming cup of coffee was hot. She spilled a little in her lap, and was promptly awarded a huge settlement. Common Sense was preceded in death by his parents, Truth and Trust; his wife, Discretion; his daughter, Responsibility; and his son, Reason.

He is survived by three stepbrothers; I Know My Rights, Someone Else is to Blame, and I'm A Victim.

Not many attended his funeral because so few realized he was gone. If you still remember him pass this on. If not join the majority and do nothing.

The Legal Unprofession has taken away the ability of teachers to control their classrooms. If teachers can't control their classrooms, teachers can't teach. And students know what buttons to push to punish the adults and continue to avoid the responsibility of learning.

Is it any wonder with the state of teaching today, and the issues that teachers have to put up with, that great teachers are being driven away in droves? When concerned parents shake their heads and wonder if we haven't lost our minds, all they have to do is ask themselves who is benefiting from this state of affairs. Can you guess who? I'll give you a clue: it's not the kids and it's not society.

◆　　　◆　　　◆

Lawyers and physicists both deal with laws. Lawyers just deal with the laws of man, but physicists deal with the laws of God.

—Me

The Law in Theory

What would you do if you woke up one morning and found out that the Supreme Court just up held a lower court ruling that reduced Newton's Laws of Motion to Nigel's Views on Things Moving About? Furthermore, the decision also decreed that the fundamental Laws of Thermodynamics are not to be so fundamental anymore. And as a free bonus, the Court decided that hereafter scientific truth is no longer the end goal of science. Rather the end goal is just to agree on an outcome that meets the expectations of one or more participating parties.

At first you might not care, because to most folks it's all gobbledygook anyway. But scientists and engineers would care, and eventually you would too when you found out that the entire technological system of the United States had just crumbled.

Yet that is exactly what has happened to our legal system. The Constitution our founders put together was not based on random thoughts. It was based on the observation, developed over thousands of years of human thought, that there existed "natural laws" and man came to understand these natural laws through the use of reason. Remember studying *the Age of Reason* in school?

These natural laws evolved to "natural rights" (human rights in modern terminology) shared by all humans. These rights were encoded in the Declaration of Independence by Jefferson through his use of *unalienable rights* that are *self evident* and endowed by a *Creator*, i.e., an authority greater than man. But man is also a social animal, thus natural law must take into consideration man's desire or need to live in an orderly social construct. However, when we enter society we surrender only those rights necessary for our security and for the common good.

The rule of natural law is one of the foundational aspects to any successful society. In American jurisprudence, there used to be a commonly held belief that, despite the gray that can exist within legal questions, there was a "right" answer, and that our judicial system was man's attempt to try to provide a framework to attain and grasp the truth. After all, if a divine Creator gave mankind certain unalienable rights, which were everlasting and unchanging, then "gray" is made only when man chips away at what is really the black and white truth.

Everything that was bad in society was the result of man being imperfect, or as James Madison said in *Federalist 51*, "If men were angels, no government would be necessary." As a result, judges and legal professionals established *rules* within the law that were not to be broken. These rules were imposed to control the chipping away at freedoms and rights.

Under this system, legal professionals would advise and guide their clients, ensure that their clients' rights were upheld against what would otherwise be unchecked governmental power, and look for the "right" answer. Under today's system, the gray within the law is celebrated, because no one in the mainstream legal community wants to talk about absolutes, or bright lines, or any determinative measure of establishing right from wrong, truth from untruths.

In today's legal system, instead of rules, judges encourage the adoption of *standards*, which are much more malleable. Rather than natural law theory, today's Legal Unprofessionals have adopted legal *realism*, a euphemism for administering *situational* justice, a legal remedy that meets arbitrary standards, usually defined by the particular judge's viewpoint given the situation at hand. The outcome of all this is the "living constitution" movement.

In today's law school, students are taught that words are a lawyer's tools to craft and mold the outcome. This is possible only if words have no meaning and seeking the objective truth is no longer a requirement. ("It depends on what the definition of 'is' is." Thank you again President Clinton). Thus, there is a good chance that an attorney operating in today's legal system, believes in objective truth as much as he or she believes in Santa Claus.

One of the first things that needed to be done in order to achieve the above was to break the connection between God and natural law. Once you got God out of the picture, there was no support for the concept of natural law, and thus no absolutes; no right and wrong.

With consideration to the discussion above, it should not be surprising to find judges that view just interpreting the law as boring. Without the shackles imposed by natural law, judges are free to create new laws from the bench, and that is power and power is sexy.

American legal philosophy is in a state of crisis, and the Legal Unprofessions have harmed America more than any other group because it has more direct access to the Government Class than any other group. It has accomplished this harm through a scorched-law policy across all aspects of American society.

Weapons: Bad laws
Strengths: A sympathetic and activist judicial system
Weaknesses: None. However, it appears that internal cannibalism is prevalent including eating their own young.

12

Opportunists

A shortage of trousers and a surplus of wine may be a great strategy for a fraternity party, but a crazy way to run an education system.

—My modification to a statement from an unknown source
regarding Europe's handling of Chinese textile imports

Every industrial complex has an Opportunist group that directly benefits when the Government Class raises taxes or expands programs. I have already discussed some examples in the chapter on the Education Industrial Complex, and will discuss others in later chapters, so I will only summarize some important points here.

Since Opportunists always approach education taxes as a way of using public money to increase their own power or net worth as the end to itself, they will always support educational initiatives regardless of need or value. There are some low-level small "o" opportunists, such as employees, who are just doing their jobs and support the next levy because of the promised 3.2% pay raise; just as a soldier may realize that a new weapons system is nothing more than pork, but continues on doing the best he can knowing that this pig may also get him a promotion.

In some respects the difference between a small "o" opportunist and a big "O" Opportunist is their position in the pecking order. In this section I'm referring to big "O" Opportunists with the power to influence the carnage as opposed to individual small fry who usually are just caught up in the feeding frenzy, and usually end up only getting scraps.

Teachers unions provide an excellent example of Opportunists. But so much has been written about teachers unions that there is little original I can add, and encourage you to read up on the subject. Keep in mind the potentially vast differences between national and local bodies as well as possible differences between locals.

Teachers unions are some of the strongest unions in the country. Their influence is felt directly in developing curriculum content and educational operating directives or indirectly through political influence via campaign contributions. Even the most sincere school board members soon realize who really pulls the strings in their district.

What makes teachers unions even more formidable is the fact that they lobby for many non-education initiatives. These initiatives almost always fall under the umbrella of political correctness. Many of these initiatives are forcing fundamental changes in our society, and with help from the Legal Unprofessionals and the Peeps in da Hood, some initiatives come back and actually hurt rank and file teachers as they try to carry out their teaching duties.

Having said all that, the single most important reason why unions exist is because of bad management. Good management does not breed union shops.

Other big "O" opportunists include powerful high level administrators at federal or state levels. At the local district level, examples are Real Estate agencies that worry about property values if local levies are defeated, and thus fight vigorously to support levies regardless of need or justification.

Weapons: Money
Strengths: Political influence
Weaknesses: They have no image in a mirror.

◆   ◆   ◆

Whether you are talking about the Government Class, Psychosocial-babblers, Educationologists, Peeps in Da Hood, Propagandists, Knights of Narcissia, or the Legal Unprofessionals, they all have one thing in common: they all belong to the *Intelligentsia*. The word intelligentsia comes from the Russian *intelligentsiya,* which in-turn comes from the Latin *intelligentia*. It is used to depict the "intellectuals" who form an artistic, social, or political "elite."

If you didn't know already, you do know by now that members of the Intelligentsia are so Liberal in their outlook that they make Karl Marx look like Adam Smith (for those of you educated in government schools, Adam Smith is credited with being the father of Capitalism). In fact, how ironic is it that this group, that is often associated with espousing noble socialist egalitarian goals, is also officially associated with the word "elite."

Members of the Intelligentsia do not officially acknowledge that Opportunists exist; because that would imply that some people are into their cause celeb for monetary reasons versus their noble motives. However, members of the Intelligentsia do accept salaries and grant money from Opportunists following the tradition of the world's oldest profession.

13

Guerrilla Warriors

Guerrilla warfare: a method of unconventional combat by which small groups of combatants attempt to use mobile and surprise tactics (ambushes, raids, etc) to defeat a foe, often a larger, less mobile, army.

—From Wikipedia.com

Up to now we have looked at Education Industrial Complex members that operate mostly at higher formal levels. Let us now look at some local informal and disparate but allied groups.

Like probably most states, Ohio has an outdated education funding process that has both state level components from sales, income and sin taxes, and at the local district level is also heavily dependent on property taxes. Also as in most states, the formula used to distribute state-wide revenues is so convoluted that the details are not worth discussing here. However, what is worth noting is that the Ohio Supreme Court has ruled four times since the late 1990's that the system needs overhauling, yet the state legislature has done nothing to change the fundamental funding process.

In the mean time, school districts fight tooth and nail for every property tax penny, and understandably property owners fight back. "Rich" districts get reduced state funds, thus not only do the rich district property owners end up paying excessive property taxes for their local government, but the other taxes they pay ends up in somebody else's districts. The whole process becomes nasty at every levy request, which seems to occur continuously. In some cases the fights really become nasty with the end result that communities are torn apart; taking months or years to settle back to normalcy. School supporters accuse the holdouts of being anti-children; and property owners accuse the district of waste and arrogance.

Anyone who has observed how local school levy dynamics work should be able to recognize the groups below because the dynamics are universal. So when you read the following descriptions, picture the letters in newspapers or statements made during your district's levy campaigns especially at community meetings held to discuss these issues and see if you can associate certain statements with the groups below. Think about some of the extreme antics displayed by your district's supporters during these campaigns; the name calling, the emotional but empty meaning "We are for kids" signs and slogans; and the various methods the district and its supporters may use to exploit kids to promote the levies. Then finally think about where the thousands you pay in taxes are actually going.

Jocks

The name gives this one away. Fanatical soccer moms, basketball dads, and so on, are examples of people that view sports as the most important reason for government schools and thus have centered their children's lives around sports. Before you jump out of your seat, keep in mind that I'm referring to fanatics. From people who subscribe to multiple cable or satellite services just for the 250 sport channels, to parents who run onto playing fields and attack coaches or players. This includes people who actually watch TV pre game shows for tactical insight from players and coaches like, "We plan to run and pass the ball today."

Jocks get along with Opportunists, but have difficultly understanding the Intelligentsia. They do a lot of heavy lifting during levy campaigns. In fact, the Jock lobby is so powerful that it ensures that extracurricular money is diverted from useless activities like the math club to character building efforts like team horseshoes. This transfer of money is supported by the district, but is often a public embarrassment. You can tell it's an embarrassment by asking your district for a cost breakdown on extracurricular spending (including salaries).

Here's how it works. Your sweet little Sabrina joined the Math Club and you learn that the club has barely enough money to buy chalk, but you read in the paper that the district's horseshoe team just hired three more coaches and got the okay to travel to Capital City for the state tournament. At the same time the district is using the need for new text books (on face value a legitimate request) as one justification for its new levy. So you ask the superintendent for the district's extracurricular cost breakdown.

In most cases, the superintendent will ignore you or refuse to give you the information. You rewrite the superintendent again and get a response about how important academics and athletics are to the total education picture and rest assured that your district professionals work hard to strike this balance.

You then write your board of education and they ignore you or refuse to give you the information. You rewrite the board again and get a response about how important academics and athletics are to the total education picture and rest assured that your district professionals work hard to strike this balance; then they recommend you write to the superintendent.

At this point most people would drop the issue; as is hoped by the district chiefs. However, being the determined person you are, you file a freedom of information request. The district sends back a statement that they are not required to provide you this information for a number of bogus but legal sounding reasons. Sometimes this letter is from the district's lawyer, which should automatically make everyone suspicious of the response.

But remember you are determined. So you research your state's website and find out that your state has sunshine laws and all state and local government bodies must provide approved public information when asked. So you quote the law back to them and tell them that unless you get the information you requested you will yell and scream, tell the governor, call the papers, write the story on your blog, bring formal charges and so on. They cave in and tell you that they will provide you the information but the law allows charging you for the duplicating costs. You agree. You show up at the district office and the secretary gives you a stack of 300 pages filled with information that may or may not contain the data you requested or in any understandable format; but that's your problem. You also get a bill for $30.

By now it's clear that you feel passionate about the amount of school funding that is going into nice to have extra-curricular jock activities while the district is struggling to replace history books that contain statements like, "Someday man may indeed land on the moon," or science books that say, "Scientists have currently discovered 77 elements." You find from the information you collected that that extra-curricular funding is larger than what the district publishes because of word games played by what "extra-curricular" really means. So you set out to tell the community because you feel that sensible people will realize that math is more important than horseshoes. You publish your experiences and findings in a letter to the editor of the local paper, and even circulate a flyer that calls for not supporting an increased levy request until the district comes clean on where its priorities are.

Oh you poor naïve wretched soul.

You soon realize from the repercussion that you don't pull on Superman's cape, you don't spit into the wind, and you don't question the Jock lobby. The repercussions can come from your neighbors, from your children's classmates, or from the district itself.

In the most extreme cases the retaliation can turn ugly. Maybe you would be shouted down at a community meeting, called vicious names, and in an in-your-face confrontation with a district teacher or supporter told if you don't like it here why don't you just leave. Maybe that car you've parked for years in the driveway now has been vandalized—not bad, just a few scratches here and there just to make a point. But in most cases the retaliation might be more subtle; a gym teacher recognizes that there can only be one family with the last name Zywxrek-stanski and decides not to pick your son for starting line ups during phys ed classes; or that neighbor you've known for years with the young volleyball daughter all of a sudden pretends not to see you at the grocery store.

Fear of retaliation or the stigma of being anti-child is a major contributor to many parents or taxpayers not being more critical of their local school system. Remember you are not fighting just a government program; you are attacking a belief system.

It is also at this point that you realize that boards of education, or at least some members, do not represent you, but rather are just cogs in the Education Industrial Complex.

Weapons: Helmets, knee pads, athletic bras and supporters and other body armor

Strengths: High testosterone levels, even in the females, making them formidable warriors

Weaknesses: If you find yourself being chased by soccer moms driving minivans loaded with kids sporting shin pads, you can use the minivan's lack of maneuverability to escape (unless you drive a minivan too, in which case you're screwed).

Schmoozers

People in this group are basically brown noses that have made their lives revolve around schools. The Schmoozers can't stop saying good things about their school district or education in general no matter the state of affairs. Some of them attend practically every school board meeting (trust me when I tell you that if you've never been to one, that this is a Herculean effort). Their primary goal is to continue to rack up brownie points by demonstrating their undying admiration for the Education Industrial Complex. Some of the Schmoozer extremists have school support signs on their front lawns 24/7.

The relationship between Schmoozers and the local school officials reminds me of the Warner Brothers cartoon characters Chester the Terrier and Spike the Bulldog. Chester is a small lively dog with floppy ears that idolizes Spike, a brawny grimacing bulldog sporting a sweater and a derby hat. Chester bounces around Spike saying things like: "What do you want to do today Spike, do you want to chase some cats? I know where we can find some cats. I'll do anything you want Spike cause you're my hero, Spike."

Schmoozers differ from the Intelligentsia in that Intelligentsia members argue from complex sounding academic viewpoints whereas Schmoozers say things like: "We have to pass the levy because the school board and superintendent say the district needs the money." Another favorite is, "Sure there are problems in this country's education system, *but not in our district.*"

Schmoozers get along well with Opportunists, are in awe of the Intelligentsia, but as in high school are still uneasy in the company of Jocks because of the wedgie memories. They are easy to spot by the position of their heads relative to the colons of educational bureaucrats. While driving, Schmoozers can be identified by those cute vanity plates with captions that read something like, "Put Kids First," with a box of crayons on one side and a little kid's hand on the other.

Weapons: Single issue concentration
Strengths: People in power enjoy suck-ups
Weaknesses: The inside of the colons of educational bureaucrats provide a severely limited view of the world

Moochers

Next to the Legal Unprofessionals, it is safe to say that Moochers comprise the second greatest threat of all the other groups because of how prevalent mooching has become in all sectors of society. If your school district were passing out free government cheese, the Moochers would be first in line. If government services were illegal drugs, Moochers would be the addicts.

In education, Moochers are parents that basically do not want to pay their fair share of the educational burden, and thus will always vote and support reaching into other people's pockets to fund their children's education, beyond any reasonable amount that can be justified for the public good. Thus, all Jocks and most Schmoozers are Moochers, but not all Moochers are Jocks or Schmoozers.

Here's one example, out of many, on how tax mooching works at the local level. Parents A have 4 children and their income allows them to live in a modest home. Parents B have 2 children and the lower number of children and/or a higher income allows them to live in an upscale home. Since a large part of the local education bill is based on assessed property and/or income taxes and not on use of services as measured by the number of children in the school system, Parents A are potential Moochers.

Parents A are only potential Moochers because Moochers must at least meet the following three criteria:

1. They do not want to pay their fair share of their children's basic education bill because they feel strongly that it's the public's duty to pay for every program whim that they feel necessary.

2. They insist that it is your constitutional duty to help pay for their children's education because you won life's lottery and they didn't.

3. They vote yes on all tax increases until their kids are out of school, after which they reserve the option to vote no.

Moochers will eventually force government school systems to provide comprehensive taxpayer supported food, clothes, school materials, and pre-school and other day care services. It is inevitable because the need for these services come from a pull and a push action. The pull is provided by the Do-gooders and Socialists that make up many school administrations and boards of education. The push is provided by Moochers who would love to pass off even more of their child rearing responsibilities to the general public.

Of course it really makes no sense to base educational funding on property taxes instead of a "user pays" system or even a more general tax base? Exceptions can be made for true poverty status. Paying for education based on the size of the lawn you mow or the number of bedrooms you have, instead of the number of children you've spawned, makes as much sense as charging you for groceries by the size of your car. (The historic connection to land ownership as a basis for collecting taxes is recognized, but that connection has been lost for a variety of complex reasons as government has taken on more social responsibilities, providing more services, and alternative tax processes have been established. Besides, it used to be the norm that only property owners could vote, limiting mooching as a source of political power.)

As mentioned above, we see tax moochers throughout American society, and with the support of politicians, tax mooching in itself has become a cottage industry in property, income and other taxes. Thus as our nation continues to shift tax burdens to less than 50% of the population, the majority will always vote for the status quo, ensuring no checks and balances to an ever growing and wasteful government.

Weapons: The constitution's "general welfare" cause and several subsequent laws and amendments
Strengths: Easily ally with pandering politicians; acquired eternal life through the New Deal and Great Society programs
Weaknesses: Strong tendency to lose bladder and/or bowel control when told to accept personal responsibility

The Jean-Baptiste De La Salle Club

Jean-Baptiste De La Salle is considered by Catholics as the patron saint of teaching. He developed the idea of teaching children in groups rather than individually, and introduced many other modern practices.

In this book you will find both praise and criticism of the teaching profession. At the individual level there are many teachers who are worth every penny they make (or are even under paid) and are truly dedicated individuals. On the other hand, there are many teachers that aren't worth their weight in chalk dust. In other words teachers are like anybody else.

But during levy time, many teachers and their supporters will remind us of the tremendous saintly sacrifices that teachers make *for the children*. Any vote against a levy is a vote against teachers and against children.

I think this is a good time to try to understand why the *suffering teacher* emotional appeal works so well on the general population. For what it's worth, here is my theory.

Originally, parents were responsible for raising their children including training them in any needed subject or life skill. When public education became the norm, parents relinquished that aspect of their parent-child relationship. Parents began to see teachers as virtual extensions of themselves, and children saw teachers as virtual extensions of their parents; and under those limited conditions, all three parties agreed to operate as a virtual family under the same shared set of societal and cultural expectations (this was the "privilege" I referred to in the Legal Unprofessionals chapter). The rich had this relationship with their nannies, but this was new to the middle and lower classes. The public school teacher became, in effect, the common man's semi-private non-resident nanny. The natural outcome of all this, after all we are human, was the creation of emotional attachments within each group pair: parent-child, parent-teacher, and teacher-child.

These types of relationships fall under the idea of *in loco parentis*, or "in place of the parent," which refers to a transfer of parental responsibility to some other adult or organization. However, *in loco parentis* can only work if the parents and teachers (or adults in general), operate under the same cultural norms and expectations.

The problem we now face is that all three relationships have greatly unraveled from their previous conditions. There is no longer a common set of societal or cultural norms. Although some emotional attachments still exist, they have weakened to become, in various degrees, just legal relationships; as cold as Antioch College's permission-based intimacy. The legalization of an ever increasing set of human interactions has destabilized the family, the entire educational process, and society as a whole. The Legal Unprofessionals are spear heading this effort with the support of the other Intelligentsia.

According to the U.S. Department of Labor, in 2004 more than half of all elementary, middle, and secondary school teachers belonged to unions—mainly the American Federation of Teachers and the National Education Association. I don't know about you but it bothers me when professionals join unions. I know there are many professional unions or quasi-unions, and the problem is not that they exist, because as I said before, unions exist because of bad management. It has to do with more with attitude.

When I board an airplane I want to see a pilot that is (excuse the sexism) a middle aged man with a chiseled jaw, graying hair, about 6', 2" tall weighing at around 200 pounds. If there was a sign on the cockpit door describing the pilot's abilities, it would read like this:

> The captain behind the stick has 12,000 hours of flying time including 6,000 hours over the European Theater, the Pacific Theater, North Korea, North Vietnam, Granada, Kosovo, Afghanistan, and Iraq I & 2. He once guided his aircraft for 30 miles without fuel and with only one wing and safely landed without landing gear on a moving carrier deck. During this flight he was able to give mouth to mouth to his severely wounded copilot and was able to save his copilot's blood gushing leg by applying a tourniquet which he made from cockpit electrical wire and the rear throttle.

It takes away my respect when I see that same pilot in a picket line blowing an air horn at passing cars while holding a sign that reads: *Airline Execs are Fascists.*

When I go into a classroom I want to see a teacher that is (excuse the sexism) a middle aged woman with a soft but stern face, graying hair held in a bun, about

5', 4" tall weighting around 130 pounds. If there was a sign on the classroom door describing the teacher's abilities, it would read like this:

> The teacher behind the desk has 30 years of teaching experience including time in East St. Louis, Detroit, and Los Angeles. She is qualified in and has taught math, science, music, art, reading, writing, and history. During a field trip to an aquarium, she once rescued, one by one, her entire 7th grade class pinned in an upside down school bus at the bottom of a 20 foot river flowing with Class IV rapids.

It takes away my respect when I see that same teacher in a picket line blowing an air horn at passing cars holding a sign that reads: *School Board Members are Fascists.*

Now that we got the fairy tales out of the way, can we talk? The truth is that Mother Teresa is a saint and as a group, teachers are fairly well paid (exceptions noted). According to the U.S. Department of labor, in 2004 median annual earnings of kindergarten, elementary, middle, and secondary school teachers range from $41,400 to $45,920; the lowest 10 percent earned $26,730 to $31,180; the top 10 percent earned $66,240 to $71,370. These numbers are in line with union figures. You should also note the many federal and various state tax credits/deductions and low cost loan programs for teachers. You can find out about some of these by doing an internet search on "teacher tax and loan credits" or something similar.

Keep in mind that teachers work 180 or so days a year and many have tremendous pension and health plans. (Yes, yes, yes, some teachers work more than 180 days, but how many come close to 240 or so days of a typical American worker? Just as important, how does the system reward those that do work more than 180 days?)

The teaching profession is desperately trying to hold on to its "Mary Poppins softness" while becoming a cog in the Education Industrial Complex. So are teachers more dedicated than soldiers, police or firemen? Are they more dedicated than the cleaning men and women who work with no benefits to support their families? Or for that matter, are they any more dedicated than the countless people who perform the endless list of society's dirty jobs? Are they more dedicated than you at your job? Does your profession have vocal supporters backing you when you decide to go on strike, or is your function in life *unimportant?*

I'm not saying that teachers may or may not warrant these salaries or benefits; if allowed to, the free market takes care of determining that. I'm only saying let's look at the entire pay and benefits packages as well as performance before we jump to conclusions. During the late 70s and early 80s there were countless reports of military families living on welfare because the military pay was below the poverty line for some of the junior troops. After some attention in this area, I think it would be hard for someone to argue that today's military personnel aren't paid well given the entire military pay and benefits package, including retirement. And it's important to note that there is no military union; at least not yet.

But troops and teachers have one thing in common; since they are both government paid employees there is horrible compensation for those that truly outperform their peers and those that are poor performers generally get paid the same as others of the same rank or tenure. And people that have critical skills are often paid the same or nearly the same as those with more common skill sets.

Ironically those teachers who deserve more should take note that what is preventing them from making a market based salary is not anti-children taxpayers, but the very system that they work in and often support. In a more market oriented system where districts that had to *compete for results-based-funds against charter schools or other competitors*, great teachers could, like many other professions, negotiate their own salaries as districts would scramble for their services.

Weapons: The ability to assign time-outs and weekend and holiday homework assignments
Strengths: Mary Poppins imagery
Weaknesses: Apples

PART III
It Takes a Village: The Schoolhouse

The enlightened reader is now introduced to the world of local education politics, where neighbor is pitted against neighbor.

14

Teach Us, Oh Children, the Wisdom of thy Years

Despite the resurgence of anti-government extremism, it is becoming clear that most Americans do not favor a radical dismantling of government. Instead of rollback, they want real reform. And when a strong case can be made, they still favor government action, as they have demonstrated recently in their support for measures like the Family and Medical Leave Act, the Brady Bill, and the new Direct Student Loan program.

—Hillary Clinton

Hillary makes a great observation in the quote above. Her pro-government argument is appealing, and she is absolutely right in her observation. But why is she right? Part of the reason is that so many people are getting a piece of the government pie, it's almost impossible to roll back government.

Let's take the Family and Medical Leave Act (FMLA), which essentially allows for 12 weeks of unpaid leave for every 12 months of employment. A Conservative purest would argue that the free market should take care of that issue. The Do-gooder or Socialist would argue that the free market doesn't cover the exploited "working poor" or other disfranchised workers. When you peal back the onion on this, you would find that the FMLA is strongly tied to women's issues and had strong backings from the usual feminist groups. Some opponents of the FMLA cited that since women would tend to exercise their rights more than men (for a host of reasons; some even sensible), that the FMLA would hurt women because companies would avoid hiring them.

Okay, who cares? Sure, Pink Republicans made the Libs compromise on a number of fine points, but it's the law of the land now. So let's assume that the FMLA as enacted was a good idea and the Conservatives who opposed the law were just a bunch of windbags. Let's also ignore any hidden negatives opponents

131

claimed the act would have on women, businesses, or on the economy, if any. Finally, for the sake of argument, let's invoke the modified Brezhnev Doctrine, introduced when we first discussed the Government Class, and decree that since the FMLA is in place, it will always remain in place.

Or will it? Oh, it won't be eliminated, but it will be modified, because the law was just the first iteration of the thesis, antithesis, and compromise process. What will follow is a greatly extended FMLA that includes *paid* leave. In effect, the modified Brezhnev Doctrine is only partly correct and requires the addition of the Corvo Corollary (with apologies to Newton's First Law of Motion): *All liberal laws once in place will remain in place, until acted on by a Liberal force, in which case the resultant motion is always leftward.*

How do I know this? The benefits provided by the FMLA are not as comprehensive as those in some other countries, such as Sweden. According to Widipedia.com, Swedish law provides 480 days (16 months) of paid leave (80% or more of wages). The Swedish law also includes the goal of stimulating national gender equality (whatever that means). So you can bet that the American Government Class is busy working on a law similar to Sweden's policy. The timing just has to be right. But don't worry, the Pink Republicans will hold firm and demand the law only specifies 450 days.

◆   ◆   ◆

The full title of Hillary's famous book is, *It Takes a Village: And Other Lessons Children Teach Us.* Essentially, it is an argument for society—read government—to meet all a child's needs. Hillary always starts out saying the right stuff about parents being the primary care givers, that people know what's best for themselves, and so on. She keeps saying this until her audience falls into a mindless stupor. Once she notices their eyes glazed over, she begins dropping the bombshells. By the end of her speech, article, or book, there are government programs, agencies, and laws for buying socks. So no one should be fooled by any of this; Hillary's real belief is that child rearing is too important to be left to parents.

I think it takes a village also. My village is a community where parents are responsible for those darling little by-products of their unbridled and lascivious sexual desires—and also much of their other personal life choices—not me or other taxpayers. Considering that we are often told we can learn so much from our children, they aren't teaching us very well, since it seems a lot of parents, and citizens in general, don't seem to understand this.

15

Vote Early and Vote Often

Look that up in your Funk and Wagnall's.

—A recurring gag from *Rowen and Martin's Laugh-in;* a 1960s TV
show

Communities are seeing more and more uniformity in their classrooms across our nation's government school systems, leaving little choice or competition at the local level. However, whenever someone even attempts to question the government school system, the educational elite have only one answer: the finger (not a finger, but *the* finger).

Considering the dynamics discussed in the previous chapters, do taxpayers have any chance of bringing sanity to the educational system? Maybe not, but for right now, let us acknowledge that occasionally the good guys win a battle or two.

In Ohio, 47% of school levies passed in March 2004—a record low. For the greater Dayton area, the rate was a somewhat higher 58%. However, noteworthy is that some of the levies barely passed including those seeking simple renewals. In August 2004 the failure rate was nearly 75% (out of nearly 100 levies)!

So why did these schools have such a hard time passing levies in 2004? Since Eisenhower's councils of government have failed us, for a brief moment in time maybe the taxpayers decided to take care of it themselves. And let's not forget that disgruntled taxpayers have middle fingers too!

Do the failed Ohio levies show a growing public distrust that the educational system has become bloated, promising services it cannot afford or should not even be providing at public expense? Maybe people believed that politicians, school administrators at all levels, and local school boards abandoned their roles as councils of government responsible to the entire community, and have just become advocates for the Education Industrial Complex.

Maybe citizens that bear the burden of funding government schools through property and other taxes recognize that they are receiving less and less direct or indirect benefits from many of the educational programs they pay for, even when the lofty "for the public good" argument is used.

Thus, as taxpayers struggle to pay their taxes and are aggressively compelled to support a school levy, many are beginning to ask: "What are we paying for?" The answer they are given is "It's for the children," but then are surprised when they peel the onion and find questionable programs backed by a host of special interests—all looking to be subsidized by the taxpayer.

Remember special interests are not just organizations, but also individuals. In a recent Beavercreek levy campaign, the parents (Jocks/Moochers) of a student argued the levy must pass because their child's horseshoe scholarship would be in jeopardy. (Of course it wasn't a horseshoe scholarship they referred to, but I'll use horseshoes as a placeholder to protect their identity. But to be fair, I also need to mention it wasn't exactly a sport you would normally think of.) Does a publicly-funded school have a mission to provide opportunities for horseshoe scholarships or education?

So every once in a while a few brave souls have the courage to ask the fundamental question: "What is the role or purpose of a publicly funded education system?" Is it more than just *reading, riting, and rithmetic*? If it is, then how much more? Of course, when any hint of this question arises, the Education Industrial Complex goes on the offensive.

People who question their local Education Industrial Complex affiliate i.e., their school district, especially during a levy campaign, experience a full backlash. Hell hath no fury like a soccer mom scorned. As mentioned earlier, this backlash could be anything from public condemnation about you, your family, or your ancestry, to verbal abuse at public forums, to even damage to your personal property.

Maybe school levies are failing because school systems, prodded on by many eager for a piece of the public pie, have lost sight of their core mission. Taxpayers are beginning to see that the only control they have over bloated, unresponsive, and often arrogant school systems is at the ballot box.

If public officials (the councils of government) fail to understand these issues, assuming they care, there will be further levy failures, poorly served children, and badly damaged communities.

Change will not come about from within because industrial complexes reproduce asexually, with genetically identical offspring in leadership positions. Sanity and accountability will only come when taxpayers demand a system truly for the children, not for an Education Industrial Complex. Our children will inherit a workable system or a bankrupt one. The choice is ours to make. But to make a difference, you must get involved.

16

Gentlemen, Start Your Buses

Public money is like holy water, every one helps himself to it.

—Italian Proverb

When I got out of bed on February 7, 2003, I wasn't planning on becoming a radical activist, hated by every soccer mom in town. Like millions of other Americans that day, my first wakeful thoughts centered on finding the bathroom.

A few minutes later, as I was reading the morning Dayton Daily News, I came across an article with the headline: "Beavercreek school board to pick levy proposal." I was a bit confused.

"Didn't we just vote on a levy increase?" I asked my wife.

"I think so." She responded.

A second cup of coffee refreshed our memories. Yes indeed Beavercreek voters did approve an annual $11 million levy just two years earlier in February 2001. A third cup of coffee brought back the additional memories when voters approved a very expensive construction bond issue just a few years before that.

The $11 million February 2001 levy was the second attempt by the school district that school year. A few months earlier, in November 2000, the district lost a $7.7 million levy by 88 out of nearly 23,000 votes. (Why did the levy request go from $7.7 million to $11 million in just 3 months? Stay tuned.)

The school board started the first November 2000 levy campaign on a bad note and things went down hill from there. The Three Stooges, the Keystone Cops, and the Marx Brothers combined couldn't have choreographed a more comedic entertainment spectacular that year.

Although the school board claimed a levy would have been put on the ballot that November anyway, a $4.5 million accounting mistake forced the issue with gusto. Now not only were the taxpayers asked to dig into their wallets to fund educational programs they were not allowed to question, but also to bail out a

$4.5 million dollar accounting error. After learning of the error in March 2000, Beavercreek taxpayers were also told:

- The individual who made the error was released from her contract without penalty and with a severance pay consisting of a sizable portion of her remaining annual salary.

- The early construction of the new administration building could not be stopped due to the cost of terminating the contract. (The building was located on a street called Kemp Road and the relative opulence of the building led citizens to dub it "The Castle on the Kemp." Taj Mahal was another popular name. It currently stands as a monument to egotistical wasteful spending, and causes the grinding of teeth to those that pass it on regular basis.)

What made things worse was that the superintendent and the school board refused to take responsibility for the error, refused to apologize to the community, and displayed an unbelievable level of arrogance that could only be surpassed by the French.

The following quotes are two out of dozens of quotable quotes that help capture the District's approach during this financial crisis:

We're running a heck of a program with minimum number of people, we're not overspending; we are underfunded.

The Superintendent

We're in this situation because of the way the state funds schools.

The School Community Liaison

Knowing something had to be done, the school board decided to hold a series of public forums leading up to the November ballot. The meetings didn't go over very well. In one meeting, as reported by local papers, written questions by taxpayers demanded apologies from the school board. Yet the school board continued their arrogance. One board member even said, "I have my "I'm sorry page" right here. I'm sorry for increasing teacher salaries, I'm sorry for...." As she continued reading her list, the audience became agitated and began to stand up and shout in the direction of the podium. It was not a pretty sight.

Although the applicable board members later wrote public apologies, things were getting ugly and taxpayer anger was literally oozing, like Steve McQueen's *The Blob*, into every city building and home. Yet, the district and its supporters were arguing to ignore the misdeeds of a few and vote yes to the levy, if for no other reason than to do it *for the children*.

This is not to imply that ardent district supporters were not angry at the district for the $4.5 million spending mistake. But reading or listening to their statements, one can't help but conclude that they weren't really mad at the mistake. No, they were mad because now they had work harder to get the next levy passed. Sort of like President Clinton's supporters who didn't really care about what Clinton did, but were angry at him because his actions made it harder to get their agenda passed.

In any case, the District held their forums and the superintendent made his speeches. The district used its tax supported literature, employees, facilities and other resources to promote the levy, including using children as propaganda routes to parents: a common procedure used by most districts.

But the Education Industrial Complex could not exist if it had to operate within the confines of laws, regulations or official protocols, so it turns to its army regulars and guerillas for support. Thus, the local papers and various business and civic groups all endorsed the levy (as they always do) reminding taxpayers to put their selfish motives aside and do it *for the children*. To everyone's surprise (ahem) even the local teachers union endorsed the levy, but of course only to ensure the continuation of a quality education *for the children*.

Finally, a political action committee (PAC) of private district supporters raised a war chest of slightly more than $21,000, a fair amount for a town the size of Beavercreek. The district enjoys the support of a PAC during every levy campaign. The PACs may have different names for each campaign but they're usually manned by the same people and supported by the same organizations.

A private PAC supporting the district is a useful tool. First, the PAC budget makes a nice supplement to the districts use of tax dollars for levy promotion. Second, the PAC can make statements and organize activities that the district would be unwise to promote or is not legally allowed to do.

Normally this formidable force would have been enough to ensure victory against the largely unorganized great unwashed resistance. A resistance described by many school supporters as mean-spirited, anti-child, anti-school, greedy property owners. But the levy was defeated by 88 votes. Now 88 votes is hardy a landslide, but this is an indication of how hard it can be to defeat school levies in some towns when you consider the very deep animosity toward the district in

2000 because of all the mismanagement and poor community relations. Without the tremendous work from the district's army, the failure would have been very much greater.

So what do school districts do when faced with a levy defeat? All the important district leaders get together and announce both a short term and long term plan. The long term plan is to place the levy again on the next ballot. The short term plan is to stop busing and threaten to drop advanced math and science programs. Stopping busing reminds everyone who's really in charge, and threatening to drop math and science programs scares parents and preserves the really important programs like bowling and horseshoes and other extracurricular athletics making the Jocks happy. There are no math-warrior parents on the same level as Jocks.

With the defeat of the levy it was time to carry out the threats made during the campaign, so busing to the high school was cut (Ohio state laws prohibit or restricts cutting busing to the younger grades). With this elimination came the warning of pre and post school-day traffic jams; a primary concern of working parents who have to get to work on time, especially the Moochers who often see the school district as a baby sitting service.

Beavercreek High School is located on a busy two lane street called Dayton-Xenia Road where traffic often backs up even on normal school days *with* bus service. Dayton-Xenia is one of those roads that should have been widened years ago, but as discussed in a later chapter, the city had to first fund an emergency golf course.

A local paper described the traffic congestion as being not as bad as expected. However, that afternoon at the height of traffic to pick students up, a fire alarm went off at 3:15 p.m. causing—yes—a traffic jam. Officials weren't sure why the alarm sounded but the point to stressed-out parents waiting 45 minutes to pick up their kids was made nevertheless. It could have been a prank, but if you are into conspiracies, and I'm not saying it was intentional, then the person who pulled the alarm knew exactly what he was doing. Again the most aggravated were the Moochers, who now had to actually take care of their own children.

The defeat of the levy was making all district supporters nervous. Understanding the gravity of the situation, pressure was placed on the school board and superintendent to give the community the pound of flesh it wanted. So in addition to three board members agreeing not to seek reelection, on January 25, 2001, the superintendent "offered" to retire at the end of his contract.

Some taxpayers wanted an immediate resignation of the responsible school board members and the superintendent, but the amount of organized energy needed for that to happen just wasn't there. So with the promised eventual departure of the three board members and the superintendent, many taxpayers finally got their pound of flesh and in February 2001 approved by a 60 to 40 margin the $11 million levy.

So why did the levy amount go from $7.7 million to $11 million in just 3 months? Well you see, the original $7.7 million levy, if approved in November, would have coincided with an existing levy set to expire in a year. Thus for one year taxpayers had the privilege to be double taxed. But since the November levy failed, the money in the tax overlap was lost and the February levy had to be increased to compensate for that loss.

As time passed, the Beavercreek community began to settle back down to normalcy and tried to heal the bitter wounds. Except there were two more itty-bitty problems just festering in the background just dying to rear their ugly heads.

The first itty-bitty problem had to do with the teachers and other district employees. Remember how I said how concerned they were for the welfare *of the children*? How concerned were they?

After all the talk about working together; all the talk about property owners making sacrifices; all the talk about everyone pitching in; all the talk about putting *children first;* and all the talk about forgetting the past; after all that talk what did the teachers and district employees do after the levy passed? On August 14, 2001, they voted to go on strike.

◆   ◆   ◆

The second itty-bitty problem was that there were pretty good indications that the district knew in 2001 that they were going to be short again in a matter of a few years. Since the District knew that they were not out of the woods yet and going to soon need more money, there were some attempts at nibbling at minor peripheral funding. But it's worthwhile to list the top three big ticket actions the District took between 2001 and 2003 to reduce the cost of operations so that the 2003 levy could be eliminated or at least greatly reduced from the original 2001 estimate:

- Nothing

- Nothing

- Nothing

The district did enact some procedural measures to ensure that mistakes like the 2000 accounting error would not occur again. Two major steps were the hiring of a professional treasurer, and the establishment of a citizen's financial oversight committee manned by individuals knowledgeable in accounting principles and laws. The oversight committee's mission was to ensure all accounting actions were legal and proper and aligned with the budgetary forecast. A third step was hiring a new superintendent with a personality.

Before going on with my story, I need to say something more about the new superintendent. The new superintendent is a nice guy. He practices management by walking around. He can be seen in the morning at different schools waving to parents dropping off their kids. He visits the lunch rooms during lunch to talk to students and often helps clean up the tables, and can often be seen at major school events. He is well liked by his staff, students, and the community. The man must put in 80 hours a week into his job. When soccer moms see him I'm sure they can only wish their loser husbands were more like him. As superintendents go, when measured against the constraints and culture posed by the Education Industrial Complex, Beavercreek's current superintendent is one of the better ones, but that doesn't make him immune to policy criticisms.

Now back to my story. The real problem was that though the district now knew where the money was going (a good thing), there was no apparent substantial attempt to assess, or even begin to assess, if the money was being well spent at the programmatic level, including what programs should be funded, how they should be funded, or how efficient they were being run. In short, many in the community felt that the District continued to operate with little regard to a critical A-Z programmatic analysis, or with any regard to exactly what type of educational program *the community* was willing to support.

Furthermore, many in the community felt that the board of education, even with some new members, still operated with a "We know what's best attitude." There seemed to be no fundamental change in the District's operational philosophy. In fact, the Board's only documented metric in their 2003 Strategic Plan to measure success was passing levies. Thus, we may have gotten a new board that was forced to initiate formal financial control processes, but the thought that entered my mind was the message in the song *Won't Get Fooled Again* by the Who, "Meet the new boss, same as the old boss."

In mid February 2003, just two years after voters passed an $11 million annual levy, the district announced five possible levy options they were considering for the May ballot as mentioned at the beginning of this chapter. These ranged from $15 million down to $10 million. Justification for the request was based on the fact that without the additional revenue the district would be in debt again, this time to the tune of $8.9 million!

A few days later the district announced it had decided on the $10 million levy. The chosen levy was continuous, meaning that once enacted it would always be running like a perpetual motion machine taking money from taxpayers and giving it to government bureaucrats, who, since the tax was continuous, had little incentive to operate in a fiscally responsible manner. This is just human nature. *To sum it up: all districts operate and suffer under the same Education Industrial Complex cultural umbrella, and although many inner city districts are bankrupt because of mismanagement, many suburban districts find themselves broke because they are spoiled.*

I was furious. So I wrote a Letter to Editor to the Dayton Daily News that was published on February 24. The letter called for cutting fat and used the high school's Ultimate Frisbee physical education course as an example. It ended with: "In the past, the Beavercreek School Board has successfully used the marketing jingle, 'Keep the Creek Flowing,' (read: 'Keep the money flowing') when requesting budget increases. However, I would like for every Beavercreek voter to think that maybe it's time to 'Dam the Creek'."

At a later school broad meeting, a board member would publicly denounce my letter. If they had the power of the Inquisition, I would have been charged and burned at the stake for heretical actions and words against children (remember they are the new gods). As several board members held me and tied me to the stake, another board member would be charged with setting the wood on fire. As the fire danced around me and I was seeing my last few moments on earth, another board member would be holding a 20 foot pole supporting a Frisbee at the end, pressing it to my burning lips, allowing me a last chance to kiss the Frisbee and recant and maybe save my immortal soul.

I recognize that what should be taught at public expense is a complicated issue, but questioning any aspects of the Education Industrial Complex isn't even allowed. But when a school budget gets out of hand, defined as consistently rising much faster than inflation, the district leadership needs to apply program prioritization, but prioritization implies possible program cuts, and that is verboten. Program cuts also forces districts to address the following very difficult question: *What is the fundamental goal of a publicly funded primary and secondary education given the realities of a limited budget, the desires of those actually footing the bill, the responsibilities of the parents, and the new demands of an ever increasing technical world?*

So why are we surprised when we see local school levies fail due to a taxpayer backlash? Government School supporters would argue that seeking revenge on school systems for lousy tax legislation is not fair. To a point they are correct. However, it's more than just the unfairness in the property tax process. Although some people will always vote against a school levy, or for that matter any tax, fundamentally Americans are the most charitable people in the world.

Let's look at just how ridiculous the school funding process is through the "Am I a Moocher" index (or AIM). The physicist Stephen Hawking once said that for every equation in a book, you lose half of the potential sales—or something like that—so at great risk here's how it works (for you mathophobics out there just skip this part and begin where indicated about 8 or so paragraphs down).

1. Assume your kids will be in the system for 13 years

2. Define N as the number of kids you have in the government school system.

3. Find the cost per student in your district. Call this C. (See discussion below.)

4. Determine your annual school taxes. Call this T. (See discussion below.)

5. Estimate the number of years you would be paying school related taxes. Call this Y.

The AIM equation is: $AIM = (13 \times N \times C)/(T \times Y)$

If AIM is about 1 then you more or less have broken even, that is, you paid for the "services" rendered for your children. If AIM is less than 1, you are paying for somebody else's DNA progeny. If your AIM ratio is above 1, you're a potential Moocher. Now before some anal retentive person who specializes in educational costs objects to my model, let me say that the formula is meant to provide only a relative estimate, and obviously better models would provide better estimates.

One of the hardest numbers to get from a school district might be the average annual cost per student. You would think that the number is just the total budget divided by the number of students, but nothing is that easy with the government. If you did use the total budget divided by the number of students you more than likely would not get the same number that your school district uses, at least not in Ohio. That is because you first have to define what you mean by the number of students. Is it the average number? Is it the peak number? Or is it the number that shows up on some chosen day of the year that for official purposes determines state funding levels?

More to the point, the State of Ohio when comparing districts uses a formula that excludes certain budgetary items. This process is used to establish a consistency in comparing diverse districts across the state and has some validity if used properly. However, this also has the affect of confusing what the real cost of education is in a particular district. Therefore, in Ohio, a district's published annual cost per student figure can be thousands of dollars less than the effective amount. If the amounts used in this book for the annual cost per student seem to be inconsistent, it is because they are, but not by mistake.

So given that, using rough numbers and considering only property taxes at first, let's look at the parents I mentioned earlier who complained about their child's "horseshoe" scholarship being at risk if the levy failed. I happen to know the number of children they had and the typical 2003 annual school related property taxes for homes in their neighborhood. Given the district's figure of the cost per student of C = $7,500, and assuming they would pay property taxes for about Y = 50 years gives their AIM result of about 5! In other words, you can think of this as a 500% return on their investment!

What a deal! This couple will never pay for the education their kids have received, yet they complained that people who voiced concern about higher property taxes were mean spirited and their child had a right to a horseshoe scholarship. I spent the next 2 weeks rereading the constitution but I didn't find the clause that says taxpayers have to pay for horseshoe scholarships, but I might have missed it. Here's how the argument would go:

> **Moocher**: My child has a right to a taxpayer supported horseshoe scholarship.
> **Founding Father**: Why?
> **Moocher:** If someone likes math, the system offers avenues for that person to pursue his or her dream. The 14th Amendment gives my child equal protection under the law. So taxpayers have to pay for his or her interests, no matter what they are.
> **Founding Father**: Just shoot me.

Just for the record, my property tax AIM ratio is just below 1. That means in terms of property taxes alone, my wife and I are more or less breaking even.

Now you must be asking yourself, what the hell am I mad about? Well, two reasons. First, the calculations above only included property taxes. As you include education bound state and federal income and other taxes, these AIM ratios would drop, that is, the chances of you getting screwed increases, and the screwing gets even uglier if you live in a rich district or, God forbid, make a good salary. But the important number is the ratio of one AIM to another, in the example above, the horseshoe parent's ratio to mine based only on property taxes was about 5 to 1; what a great deal—for them!

Let's now add income and other taxes and assume that both of our households paid a total education tax burden twice the value of our respective property tax burdens. Both our AIM values would be cut in half but our ratios would remain the same, i.e., the ratio would still be 5 to 1, but their AIM would still be high at about 2.5 and mine would be about 0.5. The bottom line: even with including nominal income and other taxes they would still be big time Moochers, and I would be even more of a big time sucker. I guess the good news is that I'm not alone.

(Mathophobics start here)

You can play with tax numbers if you wish, but the bottom line is that there will always be people willing to ask for government provided perks without realizing that they are effectively reaching into other people's pocket. If you asked most of these people if they would put a gun to someone's head to steal their money, you hope they would say, "I would never dream of doing something like that." However, they have no qualms about having the government, through its police powers, put a gun to someone's head and take their money. And they can find many members of the Government Class who would volunteer to hold the gun. This is the difference in taking care of others according to Jesus, and taking care of others according to the Government Class.

The second reason why I'm mad is the shear waste of hundreds of billions of dollars annually that the Education Industrial Complex uses to either fatten itself or execute poorly conceived educational policies at the expense of where the money should be going. I don't want that message to be lost as I talk about whether an affluent school district like Beavercreek should offer Frisbee lessons. Our taxes are being wasted at a rate that should be criminal. Our national education system is broken, and more money won't help it. Our affluent suburban schools are bloated and our inner city schools are in chaos because of actions by the Education Industrial Complex and the Government Class. We are using 19th century teaching models in a 21st century world. Our vast wealth allows us to sit around with our heads in the sand and discuss ways to increase cultural sensitivities, address made up disorders, and play Frisbee. But our vast wealth is rapidly vanishing.

◆   ◆   ◆

Although there are legitimate reasons to help the truly needy, as in many other aspects of our society, people who are sociably responsible and work hard to enjoy upscale living standards are penalized, and Moochers are rewarded (or bought off) by the Government Class. So I find myself in March 2003 wondering if I was the only one angry about all this. It turns out that I had company.

17

PAC Mentality

Political Action Committees (PACs): groups of typically politically aligned members that raise funds and use those funds to influence candidates and/or the legislative process.

—Me

Little did I know that another group of folks were just as upset as I was and were about to publish their own letter-to-the-editor when I wrote my Frisbee letter. The unofficial ringmaster of this group was a retired Navy captain, who I will refer to as the Skipper. In early March 2003 the Skipper sent a letter, with multiple signatures, to the local papers titled, *It's full speed ahead with levy.* In that letter the Skipper called on the district to knock off the spin and hype.

I didn't know any of the letter's signatories, and I also didn't know that Skipper was fanatically trying to hunt me down after reading my February 24 letter. My phone number was unpublished, so he couldn't find it in the phone book, but he was finally able to find me, and mailed a letter to me. In that letter he outlined a meeting he was planning on holding at his house and wanted to know if I was interested in attending. I called him at the phone number he provided, and I said I would be there.

When I arrived at the Skipper's house several people were already there. The purpose of the meeting was to try to organize some unified opposition to the May 6 levy. Whatever we decided upon, we had to act fast. It was already late March, and we only had about 5-6 weeks before the vote.

At the risk of sounding melodramatic, it was a classic David and Goliath scenario, with Goliath having a well oiled and extensive support infrastructure. In fact, execution of the district's standard battle plan had already been started. The employee union infantry were cleaning their weapons; the soccer mom cavalry was ready to ride; air support, provided by the local Propagandists, was ready to drop supporting editorials; special ops, manned by the local business and civic groups, were camouflaging their faces; and as reserve forces, ready to be called up if necessary, they had the children in the classrooms making street signs to wave at motorists and practicing their pleading and whining to save their future.

Several immediate problems had to be addressed at the first meeting. The most important was how do we get our message out? Besides the Propagandists, the district had a paid staff whose full time job, once the offensive campaign started, was to officially or unofficially promote the levy. The Propagandists gave direct access to their newspaper pages or TV time whenever the superintendent or school board wanted to pronounce this or that. The District ran a website and a local cable access channel all paid for by tax dollars.

Meanwhile back in the Skipper's basement, except for a few retirees, many of us had a day job. We didn't run websites or cable access channels. We didn't have access to 15 second TV news spots. And if we were lucky to have our letters printed in a paper, they were often edited in content and word count.

So I offered the idea of using e-mail based on the theory of six degrees of separation, or that anyone on earth is connected to any other person through a chain of 4 other connections. We may have only been 10 people in that room, but each of us knew at least a few other Beavercreek voters, who in turn knew a few others, and so on. By using e-mail we could theoretically reach thousands of voters literally overnight (and cheaply).

It worked! Within a week we had a well established and extensive e-mail roster. (God bless the internet. Information technology has always been the great liberator, which is one reason why governments everywhere are trying to control the internet.)

In that first meeting and in the next few meetings we also agreed to chip in money to prime the pump. However, the question was what pump were we priming? Clearly, the money would pay for signs, pamphlets, or other related costs if we decided to go that route. But obviously if we were going to be organized and maybe even receive donations we needed an organization, leadership, and a name.

Within that first week or two, Skipper and I along with Skipper's backyard neighbor, who I'll call Wilson, agreed to organize and lead the group. The Skipper, as a 30 year retired naval captain, had the right people and leadership skills to chair the group (besides it was his house). Wilson had extensive business experience and agreed to be treasurer and co-chair. I had no specific skills to offer but agreed to do whatever I could.

So the Skipper and Wilson became co-chairs and I became the Director of Communications; a rather pretentious title that I always hated. But it did give the organization a bit of formal legitimacy. We also agreed at that time that no decision affecting the group would be made unless all three of us had concurred. Later that was relaxed to a simple majority rule, so it was fortunate that we had an odd number.

Now that we had a leadership team, we needed a name. We kicked around several names and I don't remember who came up with the final name of *Keep Beavercreek Affordable* Political Action Committee, but it stuck. To tell the truth, I didn't like the name at first because to me it opened the possibility of the opposition to pick up on the "Affordable" and turn that into "Selfishness." I was opting for "Accountable," putting the emphasis on how the dollars are being spent, rather than the amount. Later I came to realize that no matter what we would have called ourselves, we still would have been lowered on the evolutionary scale to somewhere around the Proterozoic era, more than 550 million years ago, right around the time blood sucking cesspool scum appeared. (Later on, one letter writer stated that KBA stood for "Keep Being Asinine.")

Nevertheless, the Keep Beavercreek Affordable Political Action Committee, or more simply the "KBA PAC" was born. Wilson registered the KBA PAC with the county on April 1, and we were off.

One of the smartest things Skipper, Wilson and I agreed to was that the KBA PAC was not to have paying members. This was a rather unusual move, but proved beneficial in the long run. Paying members meant organized periodic meetings with members voting on important issues. The biggest problem with formal membership was the required commitment in time and resources that we just didn't have. Limiting the KBA PAC leadership and membership to us three resulted in a streamlined organization that could decide and act quickly. If people liked what they heard and saw, they contributed, if they didn't, well that's life. However, without our supporters and volunteers, Skipper, Wilson and I would have been as successful as political activists as Larry, Curly, and Moe were as plumbers. (For you Three Stooges fans, that's *A Plumbing We Will Go,* Columbia Pictures, 1940.)

Limiting the PAC leadership to just three people also had a secondary but very important benefit. As we began to write our opinion pieces, the local editors became aware that only the Skipper, Wilson and I officially spoke for the KBA PAC.

We also agreed to the following three general operating principles:

• The PAC's focus will be for the long term.

- PAC activities must remain professional and positive.

- As a matter of policy, the PAC would not meet with government/school officials proposing levies except in extenuating circumstances.

The feeling behind the third bullet is that it is the responsibility of the officials proposing the levies to adequately justify the need for the added property tax burden. Additionally, it would be detrimental to the intended purpose of the KBA PAC to put itself in a position where it could be compromised, or where it might be might lose control over its agenda.

Our plan was simple: write more letters, get other people to write letters, get our name and our mission statement out, and try to collect some money with the hope of buying signs or paying for a mass mailing. We looked into placing ads in the local papers and concluded that was cost prohibitive. In short: our goal was to provide some organized opposition to the locally organized Education Industrial Complex.

Now we had to decide on a message. "Vote No to School Levy" is okay for an attention getter, but somewhere we had to explain why. After a few nights of work, we came to a longer list of talking points. It wasn't all inclusive but it was a start. Detail was to follow.

Having established an e-mail roster we began in earnest in April to distribute our information via e-mail. We began nearly all our e-mails with an introductory sentence explaining what followed, then a request or the recipients to pass on the e-mail to their family and friends living in Beavercreek. Something like this: *The following article was originally published in the (date and paper). It discusses the (issue). Please forward this e-mail to your Beavercreek family and friends.* At the bottom of the e-mail we would add a sentence providing information on how to contact or contribute to the KBA PAC.

Although we established an extensive first level e-mail roster, without a sophisticated tracking system, we had no way to know how far our e-mails were getting. But the Six Degrees of Freedom theory must have held. Indications seemed to support that our e-mails were reaching the superintendent and the school board. And if the theory was indeed correct, someone in Mongolia was reading an e-mail concerning a tax levy in some never-heard-of town somewhere in the United States, whose name when translated into Mongolian probably meant *the bucktooth rodent that lives in shallow running water.*

The district clearly had no idea how earnest the KBA PAC was. The superintendent wrote us a letter in April stressing how he understood our concerns and that he too had accountability high on his list of responsibilities. He offered to meet with us privately to discuss our concerns in more detail. As letters go it was a nice letter, but it was one of those letters that superintendents learn to write in Superintendent Charm School where they take such classes as:

Mastering Levies 101

The student is introduced to concepts needed to pass levies. Smooth Talking and Side Tracking are discussed. Students will learn never to address concerns publicly and to channel all questions to private one-on-one conversations. Successful completion of the course requires mastery in making statements such as: "The levy increase will only cost the taxpayer an extra cup of coffee a day"; "There are no sacred cows"; "No stone will be left unturned"; "We are being good stewards of taxpayers' money"; "We're putting the children first."

Early in April, I was contacted by an editor at the Dayton Daily News. She wanted to know if we were willing to be interviewed along with the superintendent at the newspaper's offices. I checked with the Skipper and Wilson, and we decided to decline the invitation. When I told her assistant we decided not to attend, she seemed rather incredulous, and I bet it threw the superintendent for a loop too, since it wasn't expected to go that way. I suppose normally a group like ours would have jumped at the chance for their 15 minutes of fame. But we had our reasons, not the least of which was that we had just barely organized as a group and still were struggling to get our sea legs.

Organizations experience problems when they lose their core mission focus. It is important to remember the KBA PAC's third operating principle was that we would not meet with government/school officials because that only produces compromising situations. And we wouldn't act in any way that would put the PAC in a position where it could be compromised or where it might lose control over its agenda (remember the definition of Pink Republicans). This last standard was lost on many people who criticized us for not officially meeting with district officials. Another reason we declined the offer to meet with the superintendent at the newspaper's office is that as part of the Education Industrial Complex the media is not impartial, and we looked at this as a set up.

Remember, this is the paper that is locally referred to as the Dayton People's Daily. As in most papers across the country, occasionally some hard hitting news story about education is reported on. But in most cases the articles typically cover important news such as how some third grade class learned about diversity through the use of paper-mache (or papier-mâché if you're a purest).

We had things to say, but this wasn't the right time or place. Later the Skipper and I did do an interview on a local 30 minute early Sunday morning radio show that the government forces radio stations to broadcast as community services but no one listens to.

Around this time the district began touting a study the district paid for by a professional accounting group. The 100 page performance report was a mixed bag for the district since it contained both good and bad conclusions. Understandably, the district pulled out the good stuff to support their point of view. Understandably, the KBA PAC pulled out the bad stuff to support our point of view.

So was it just a "he said/she said" problem? No, it was more than that. The report gave the district some kudos but also contained numerous improvement recommendations for the district to consider. These recommendations would have made substantial improvements to some of the district's processes and provided a corresponding cost reduction. Yet the district knew the report would not come out in time before the May levy to allow them enough time to consider the recommendations, make appropriate changes, and then, based on any cost savings, go to the voters with a comprehensive financial plan supported by an independent assessment. So, as arrogant government organizations typically do, they just went ahead and put the levy on the ballot anyway.

Later the PAC would challenge the district of having no intentions of using any of the report's recommendations. They just wanted to use it as a leverage to support the levy by arguing that their sincerity in running a tight ship was proven by their funding of this study, and hoping no one would lead such miserable pathetic lives, so devoid of interests, that they would actually read the report. The problem was that Skipper, Wilson and I read it.

So as the KBA PAC started to gel, we were getting criticized by many in the community for not being more specific in detailing our issues. So on April 21, 2003; just barely three weeks after forming, the PAC produced 3-4 pages of detailed talking points.

Between the talking points and the actual vote, the PAC published several more articles concentrating on the lack of justification for the levy. The fun was just beginning!

18

Victory

"Well, in our country," said Alice, still panting a little, "you'd generally get to somewhere else—if you ran very fast for a long time, as we've been doing." "A slow sort of country!" said the Queen. "Now, here, you see, it takes all the running you can do, to keep in the same place. If you want to get somewhere else, you must run at least twice as fast as that!"

—Lewis Carroll, *Alice's Adventures in Wonderland*

A few weeks before the May 2003 voting day, the superintendent and school board decided to hold a community forum at the high school. I like to think it was because the district sensed an organized resistance due to KBA PAC activities above and beyond the typical ranting of the usual anti-levy nuts. The official purpose was to explain the reasons for the proposed levy. I attended that forum with my wife and we sat in the front row.

One thing I will always remember from that forum was the discussion between one of the board of education members and the superintendent. This discussion occurred before the start of the forum, and was only between the two, but since I was sitting in the front I was able to overhear some of it.

Just prior to the forum the KBA PAC e-mailed a letter listing our talking points referred to in the last chapter to our e-mail recipients, and that e-mail must have ended up in the inboxes of the district leaders. The board member, standing next to the superintendent, snickered, "Did you see that letter that was sent out?" That snicker followed by a chuckle, more than anything else, solidified my desire to defeat this levy.

Prior to this event, I never met the superintendent or any of the school board members, so they didn't know me from a hole in the wall. Therefore, I was surprised when the superintendent later came over to talk to me as if we had been buds for years. I found out later how he ID'ed me. (Actually, it turned out that he was also raised in Cleveland, so that meant we had a hometown thing going.)

The forum presentation had the typical number of pie charts and tables and the treasurer attempted to explain school district levy laws, which of course make no sense to lawyers let alone real humans. After the presentation, as my wife and I were leaving, we were approached by a young lady who had gone to school with my oldest daughter. I didn't know who she was at first, but apparently she remembered me from an appearance I made at the behest of my daughter to speak on jobs and professions.

The young lady wanted to know if the presentation changed my mind. "Of course not!" I told her.

Within a few minutes we were joined by her mother who turned out to be a teacher in the Beavercreek School System. I figured that this girl outed me to her mother who in turn outed me to the superintendent, and that's how he identified me.

We spoke for nearly an hour, with neither party convincing the other of anything of significance. Her mother did become speechless once I reminded her how the teachers thanked the community after taxpayers bailed out the district a few years back by voting to strike.

As I was leaving the school that evening, a tear fell down my cheek as I realized that this young lady never met a government program that she didn't like (except possibly the military, but that didn't come up). Here was a person of legal voting age, who owned no property, who paid little if any taxes, yet had the same voting power as me. She had the power to tax me without any responsibility for her actions! Exactly as the Government Class wants it to be.

Although I can't prove it, soon after this meeting, a letter to the editor appeared in the Beavercreek News Current that I think may have been written by the girl and/or her mother. However, whoever the authors were, they accused me of wanting to cut programs *after* my older daughter had graduated with honors and won a full scholarship at a local private college.

The letter claimed I wanted to cut everything: gee, I would have been happy with just Ultimate Frisbee. The reference to my daughter was one of several that were published along those lines of argument over the coming months. The explicit message in the statements was that I was out to destroy the same system that helped my daughter get a college scholarship. The old "You got yours now you want to stop me from getting mine" argument.

The only problem with that is what is missing from the paragraph. First, there is the arrogant message that all the success my daughter was due to the Beavercreek School system. Again, the Beavercreek School system is not a bad system as school systems go, but I like to think that the 1-2 hour daily dinner and post dinner discussions that her mother and I had with her and her sister over the past 14-18 years on history, art, literature, philosophy, religion, all other topics helped just a little. I like to think that the time her mother and I helped her on her homework and other school activities, including non-school related science fairs helped just a little. I like to think about how getting my kids to all 50 states and discussing the historical and political perspectives of the sites we visited helped just a little. Finally, I like to think that my daughter going out on her own and winning several non-school related state and federal competitions helped just a little. (She would later go on to be selected as a White House Intern in the summer of 2005.)

The second problem with the letter is it doesn't address the fact that with the total taxes my wife and I paid, we supported our children's education as well as the education of two to four other children. Yet we were the evil ones. Considering that we are still paying education taxes even though our children are out of the system, you would think that at least we would get photos and monthly progress reports on the other children we're supporting.

Another published letter whined about how the public doesn't see the employees using scrap paper for messages, not taking lunch and breaks because they're too busy, and listed several other hardships. The letter is one of those pity-the-teacher letters whose authors think they're making a point in support of a cause, and actually anyone with at least one neuron firing can see beyond the words.

First, let's be clear here: Beavercreek is a relatively upper middle class town, the district in 2003 was spending around $7,500 to $9,000 per student, and if the levy passed well over $10,000 per student (depending on what numbers you want to believe). It enjoyed and continues to enjoy a tremendous amount of community support through PTO, booster clubs and other volunteers, all of which possibly provide hundreds of thousands of dollars in free labor, add to this fund drives and other community fund raising activities ... AND TEACHERS CAN'T GET STICKY PADS!!! And let's not forget that starting in 2002 (and I assume is still on), qualified educators were given a $250 federal tax deduction for qualified school supplies. Hmmm, I guess there is a problem here, but I don't think it's a lack of money? Could it be priorities?

Since letters-to the-editor had to pass the paper's editorial boards, they paled in comparison to what we were getting in e-mail. As the PAC's Director of Communication, or in more layman terms, the stuckee that had to manage our e-mail account, I had the pleasure of being the first to read our fan mail.

There's no need to cite detailed articles from the superintendent and members of the board of education since they all come from the same Education Industrial Complex cookie cutter. "We are good stewards of your money"; "Quality Education costs"; "This is absolutely the minimum we need to sustain quality in our schools"; "If this levy does not pass, our children will suffer": are examples of the more important talking points.

What was missing were statements that defined what they meant by quality and what was done to lower costs. The reason why these statements were not made is because they couldn't define what they meant by quality; in fact, as mentioned earlier the district's quality performance document in 2003 only mentioned passing levies as the major metric. Personally, having "passing levies" as a quality statement to me is like saying "raising taxes" is their quality goal. As to explaining what was done to lower costs: saying we've done nothing of substance because Plan A always calls for raising taxes first, was obviously too embarrassing.

Over the coming years, I noticed several recurring themes or myths that the district and its supporters kept repeating hoping that if said enough times, they would become fact. Some of these may apply only to Ohio but it is worth going over these myths.

> **Myth 1**: Businesses should pay more taxes; impact fees should be levied on new construction; or we need a greater ratio of business to personal property.
> **Myth 2**: What we need is a school income tax.
> **Myth 3**: It's the state's fault. The state needs to revamp its school taxes to be more "equitable."

These myths all have a common theme: playing a shell game with how education is paid for.

First of all, businesses do not pay taxes. Taxes and impact fees on businesses are just operating costs passed to consumers. Many people don't understand this, and it doesn't help when this concept is often sold from "get the rich" angle. Some people do understand that even though businesses can only act as tax collectors, they still like to use businesses to distribute the burden to a greater tax base because it gives the false impression of easing the load on property owners. Of course, effective out-of-pocket educational expenses are still the same, but more importantly, the taxpayer's perspective of costs will suffer since education revenues are mixed between direct property taxes and hidden increases in business consumer prices. Is it ever wise to buy a service or a product before knowing how much you are paying for it? Will there be a one for one reduction in personal property taxes for each business tax dollar raised? I doubt it.

This criticism has nothing necessarily to do with the integrity of any specific district leadership. It's just that governments are inherently inefficient and government officials often find themselves acting under conflicting interests with the interests of the taxpayer often last. In other words: even good people have bad ideas. And everyone reading this knows it. There are just some who refuse to acknowledge it. Part of those who refuse to acknowledge this fact are parents shirking their responsibilities to provide for their own children, opting instead to reach into other people's pockets. Public officials who support the "business tax argument" are just pandering to a number of constituency groups.

The second myth of an educational income tax is often sold under the guise of spreading the burden of educating *our* children. Personally, when I use the expression "our children" it is usually in reference to the two wonderful cherubs that my wife downloaded. When members of the Education Industrial Complex uses "our children" it is in reference to Hillary Clinton's *It Takes a Village* nonsense.

Rising educational and health care costs have many similarities. As we have discussed, revenue for education comes from a variety of taxes, and are not tied to a household's number of school age children, thus costs are spread to third parties. People using the service (first party) do not bare the true costs of the service and thus there is no incentive by the service providers (second party) to lower costs.

In another example of double talk, parents who avoid their responsibility to educate their children by forcing the community to bear the costs are praised for the Education Industrial Complex community spirit and compassion for children. Taxpayers who argue that parents should bear more of the routine costs are vilified as being non-caring.

Who is doing the praising and vilifying? The first and second parties will always vote to support the tax shell game, especially parents with multiple children who are getting quite a break. Service providers support this process since a user-fee based system would induce parents to demand lower costs and higher quality.

Occasionally grandparents proudly proclaim happiness with paying taxes to support their grandchildren's education. Ironically, under a user pay system the money would be better spent if the grandparents would provide a stipend directly to their grandchildren, and probably save money in the process.

The final myth continues with the shell game, shifting the discussion from parental responsibilities and skyrocketing operating costs to how can we continue the revenue flow and hide the costs to the taxpayers. It assumes of course that the state and federal governments get their money from some sources other than your taxes. It assumes that somehow it is more efficient if someone collects taxes from Cincinnati and gives some to Cleveland then takes some from Cleveland and gives it to Beavercreek. Where do the taxes collected from Beavercreek go? Duluth?

◆   ◆   ◆

During the lead up to voting, the KBA PAC purchased several hundred campaign signs. These were the typical signs you see lining the road way during any election period. The signs basically said to vote no to the upcoming school levy in white letters against a green background. We didn't have the political machine the district had so the purchase of these signs represented a major investment to the PAC, representing a big chunk of our contributions.

Unfortunately, from putting up the first sign to the actual election day, we lost about 50% of them. We tried to replace some of the lost signs but couldn't keep up with the loss. There could have been only three reasons for this loss: (1) pesky rabbits pulled them underground like you see in cartoons, (2) people saw them as collector items that would be worth millions in twenty years, or (3) the district's rabid supporters stole them.

I'm inclined to lean toward the last reason.

I'm not saying that this was the first time that political signs were stolen, but the high number is quite unusual, at least around this neck of the woods, since in some respects, Beavercreek is a rather Norman Rockwell sort of town. And I'm not saying district leaders sent out marching orders to steal our signs. They didn't have to do that. The Moochers, Jocks et. al. were scared. All that is needed to initiate these types of actions is the cult-like support of the members of the Education Industrial Complex.

After all that was said and done, the voters decided on May 6, 2003, by 63% to 27% to turn the levy down. I can't say how much influence the PAC had in defeating this levy. I'd like to think we had some affect. I will say, however, that I would soon realize how naïve I was about how the whole process worked. Like Alice in Wonderland running as fast as she could and getting nowhere, the KBA PAC was about do the same.

19

Armageddon

Dr. Peter Venkman: *This city is headed for a disaster of biblical proportions.*
Mayor: *What do you mean, "biblical?"*
Dr. Raymond Stantz: *What he means is Old Testament, Mr. Mayor, real wrath-of-God type stuff. Fire and brimstone coming down from the sky. Rivers and seas boiling!*
Dr. Egon Spengler: *Forty years of darkness. Earthquakes, volcanoes ...*
Winston Zeddemore: *The dead rising from the grave!*
Dr. Peter Venkman: *Human sacrifice, dogs and cats living together—mass hysteria!*

—From the movie, *Ghostbusters*

The wrath of God has nothing on the wrath of the Education Industrial Complex when it is confronted with the possibility that some part of its gravy train may be taken away. With the levy defeat on May 6, things were about to get interesting.

The first responses to come out of the levy defeat were statements published in the morning papers made by the superintendent, members of the school board and various Grim Weepers. None of these were unique; you probably have seen similar statements from your local Education Industrial Complex representatives: "this will only hurt the children;" "this is an insult to teachers;" and "quality will suffer" pretty much capture everything. The Grim Weepers get their name from their tendency to look like there are about to break out in tears as they go on how crucial the levy was, and its failure now means they are going to have to try to explain to the children why God made such mean people that they would even hurt children. (Don't worry, in this context "God" is mentioned outside the classroom.)

However, of particular interest is the following statement from the superintendent: "What we've said to the community this time around is that this is what we absolutely, positively have to have. So I can't go back and say that we only needed X amount of dollars. The bottom line is this is what we believe we have to have to run an efficient and an effective and an excellent school district."

Basically the superintendent was saying how can the district leaders ask for a lower levy if they just spent several months trying to convince people that the prior request was the absolute lowest necessary to maintain quality. Good question. The answer of course is what all good politicians learn early in their career: just ignore what was previously said.

Since the district's leadership was always expounding how they were interested in hearing from the community on education issues, the KBA PAC promised the school board and the community that we would publish a comprehensive paper dealing with district funding issues. We fulfilled that promise in June 2003 by sending the district a 33 page point paper and placed that paper on our website. We also offered to meet with the board to explain our positions (not to compromise). We never got a direct response from the Board. But that was understandable, because when school boards say they are interested in hearing from the community, they really mean only from their sycophants.

The closest response we got from the board was a newspaper article they published ridiculing some of our suggestions. We didn't get a direct response from the school district until the superintendent sent us a 7 page response in September, but by that time, everything was already said and done through a myriad of articles and forums.

Soon after the levy defeat the publishing company that ran the local Beavercreek News Current paper decided to offer a weekly special edition named the Beavercreek News Current Extra. The Extra was delivered free on Wednesdays to all city residents. The reason why I bring this up is that the Extra played an important early role in the KBA PAC's ability to get its message out to the taxpayers.

The Extra's editor allowed the KBA PAC to publish extended guest articles sometimes reaching 1500 to 2000 words. That summer we published numerous articles on a number of issues school district topics as well as a host of other local government matters. The public response, both negative and positive, was tremendous. The Extra soon was inundated with more letters-to-the editor than it probably could handle. Many of these letters were heated and ill-mannered diatribes from both sides, but most of the rants were coming from the district's supporters, including teachers, mostly aimed at the KBA PAC and other persons daring to criticize the district.

This was an exciting time for Beavercreek. Muhammad Ali may have had the *Rumble in the Jungle* and the *Thrilla in Manila*, but we had the *Reek in the Creek*.

The heated debate spilled over into a July 2003 community meeting held at the high school. This meeting was well attended by the community and was also understandably well represented by teachers and other district employees. The meeting didn't go very well as tempers got the better of many. I remember one incident in particular because the shouter, who I believe was a retired district teacher and administrator, basically said you either support the district or get out of town.

Besides community letters-to-the-editor, the KBA PAC received many "interesting" e-mails. Both published letters and e-mails fell into the following major categories.

Oliver Twist Letters

Oliver Twist letters are letters supposedly written by students pleading for every portion of academic gruel they can get, much like Charles Dickens wretched character, Oliver, who asks the workhouse master, "Please sir, may I have some more?" Oliver Twist letters tend to depict a future of poverty and despair if a levy isn't passed.

I only have two problems with these letters: (1) they are emotional but probably do have some impact on voters, and (2) adults exploiting children is rather disgusting but unfortunately rather normal in the Education Industrial Complex.

In some cases you can tell that a letter may not have been written by a student by its grammar and sentence structure especially those that claim to be from younger kids. You know you got a fake when it starts out:

> Greetings, I am a 8th grader in a Beavercreek middle school and I'm rather concerned about another possible levy failure and its impact vis-à-vis Ohio Revised Code and the most recent Ohio Supreme Court decision concerning property tax as used to fund public education. Wishing to avoid a life of drug addiction and prostitution, I beseech the voters of Beavercreek to consider voting YES in November's ballot. As most of you know in John Doe vs Ohio....

I don't expect kids to understand all the issues that were being discussed, and although I understood why they were saying what they were saying, being free from Liberal Psychosocial-babbler guilt, I really didn't care. We used to have a saying in the military aimed at young recruits who thought they knew everything: "I have more time in the chow line than you have in the service."

Students say a lot of stupid things; yes even in college where they seem to know the solutions to all the problems in the world. How many college kids in such hard hitting classes like *Social Services in a Democratic Society 101*, say things like: "I think its okay for rich people to pay 75% of their income to pay for education." Then years later when they finally get a job and pay taxes they seem to change their minds.

When students start paying taxes and have more time on the planet than I have in the chow line, then I'll start listening to them.

Mother Teresa Letters

Schmoozers and teachers wrote most of these. They put every teacher on saintly par with Mother Teresa. The only problem was the *average* teacher was making $45,000 for 9 months of work and Mother Teresa ate worms to survive.

I addressed this whole teachers-are-suffering routine in the Jean-Baptiste De La Salle Club section. I'm sure there are many districts such as in Appalachia and inner city schools where it is difficult (mostly due to the policies of the Government Class and the Education Industrial Complex). But in most cases the worse suburban and equivalent teachers have to put up with are spoiled American teenage knuckleheads and their idiotic parents.

Rodney King Letters

These letters pleaded for everyone to just get along. Most asked for compromises, but remember what I said about compromises and Pink Conservatives. Many others asked that we approve this levy then we can talk about the future later (yeah right).

American Flag Letters

These letters talked about how important education is to a free society. They called on your patriotism to ensure the future of our community and country by voting YES to the levy. The only problem was many of us thought that we were ensuring the future of our community and country by voting NO to the levy since the issue is not education but accountability in education.

Opportunist Letters

These letters came from individuals or businesses that were going to make a buck from a levy passage. Real estate agents were prominent writers. Real estate agents understand that the three most important things about selling a home is location-location-location. The 4th, 5th, and 6th most important are bloated-school-systems.

The biggest Opportunists of course are the teachers union. Strictly speaking, union representatives seldom actually write letters. They let their teacher soldiers do that because unions want to present themselves as above the fray. They do however exhibit support through paid advertisements and these can get quite interesting. For example, one ad could show a line of adults with several grayed out. The caption reads: If this levy fails, 3 out of 10 teachers will lose their jobs. The sub caption reads: Your child's math or science education is at risk. The hope of course is that no one asks: "Why isn't volley ball at risk first?" (You know the answer to that now; there is an organized Jock lobby, but there isn't an organized geek lobby.)

When the levy passes, and the district is flush with money, the union wants its payback. It will threaten to strike or actually go on strike. But whatever it does; rest assured it's doing it *for the children*. In 2006, teachers in the city of Huber Heights mentioned earlier, went on strike one week after school started. After about a week of the typical ugly name calling and fighting between parents, board members, administrators, and teachers, the strike was settled. The newspaper quote that stuck in my mind was by a teacher who said, "We did it for the children."

District Letters

These letters came mostly from the superintendent and board of education. The superintendent just kept stating they were good stewards of taxpayer money (except for one particular article discussed below). The board letters were more interesting. Sometimes the letters were signed by all five members. Sometimes individual members wrote their own.

Although you hate to generalize, it seems that many school board members across the country seem to agree with *it takes a village* philosophy. The board members who support this trend are typically Do-gooders and Socialists. But wouldn't it be great if boards of education acted like real councils of government and leave parenting and grand parenting where it belongs? And you wonder why we have problems in our education system or government leadership in general?

During the second Clinton-Bush-Perot Presidential Debate on October 15th, 1992, in Richmond, VA, a long-hair-hippie-1960ish looking guy in the audience asked the following question [emphasis mine]:

> The focus of my work as a domestic mediator is meeting the needs of the children that I work with, by way of their parents and *not the wants of their parents*. And I ask the three of you, how can we, as *symbolically the children* of the future president, expect the two of you, the three of you to meet our needs, the needs in housing and in crime and you name it, as opposed to the wants of your political spin doctors and your political parties?

There was no doubt that millions of Moochers, Peeps in da Hood, and other Intelligentsia were marveling at such an insightful question, especially the part about ignoring the wants of the parents. But for me, my stomach began to churn as soon as I saw who was asking the question, followed by severe projectile vomiting after he finished.

Feminists usually don't like to talk about the traditional feminine side of women unless it's to their advantage. For example, Feminists like to claim that women are natural nurturers and thus are better suited for government office instead of warmongering males. You see ladies and gentlemen, this is why we desperately need a female president. Only a female president can supply the nurturing leadership so government can provide the suckling to the awaiting American public. You can hear the piglets snorting now from all across the fruited plains.

Deep Throat Letters

Occasionally the KBA PAC would get letters giving us some seemingly insider information on the goings-on in the city or school governments. Sometimes the writers just wanted us to know about the shenanigans, other times the writers wanted us to do something about the issue.

We had no investigative capabilities to chase down every lead and of course we had no clue if any specific lead was valid or not. Furthermore, many of the leads involved questionable but otherwise probably legal processes whose details would have been lost on the general public with the background of screaming that was going on.

Deep Throat writers typically wanted someone else to do the dirty work, so the quickest way to shut them off was to recommend that they pursue the issue. Some did, if only in a letter to the editor, but most just dropped the issue.

Burn in Hell Letters

These letters were directed against the KBA PAC, its supporters, or people just voicing their concerns about particular school issues. *The Burn in Hell* letters all had the same message, they differed only from where the writers started from: "My son's horseshoe scholarship is in jeopardy, so burn in hell." "It's your duty to pay for my daughter's education, so burn in hell." Or finally, "Without a good education kids won't be able to make enough to pay for my social security, so burn in hell." The e-mail versions were quite nasty, sometimes telling us to perform certain acts upon ourselves. Many of the e-mails were unsigned.

◆   ◆   ◆

The title of this chapter is Armageddon and this was the prevailing battle cry from the local Education Industrial Complex. Nothing captures this better than a letter from the superintendent published on October 22, 2003 entitled *Levy Failure Would be Disaster.*

In that letter he mentioned the usual reductions in "enrichment" activities, increased class sizes and so on. But he also mentioned the potential increase in crime because students would have more time on their hands. He bemoaned the possibility that we might lose the opportunity to proclaim in the future that one of our students discovered a cure for cancer, became President, or saved our environment. But the real kicker was the following statement: "Vote yes for the students, vote yes for the community, but most of all, vote yes for yourself—*your life may depend on it.*"

Needless to say, this article generated a bit of an uproar. I think later the superintendent backed away from the article and I think I heard that he claimed it was not his article and his picture and name were erroneously printed with it. I don't know what really happened. Maybe it was written for him and he didn't take the time to really read it. Nevertheless, I'm sure that it won over all the Beavercreek cancer patients, environmental Chicken Littles, and most of all, senior citizens afraid of roving gangs of Beavercreek teenagers parking their Mercedes and BMWs on the wrong side of the street, blocking their way to their shuffle board match.

Actually, cultivating fear is a typical tactic of not only school districts but federal, state, and local governments across the country? In response to these fear tactics, many people buy signs supporting school levies and prominently place them on their front yards hoping that their houses get passed over from roving gangs of teenage angels-of-death that have too much time on their hands. These signs take the place of lamb's blood and are much more hygienic.

By August the school district had come up with their offer of a new levy for November. This levy was about a 25% reduction and was temporary rather than continuous, which meant that they would have to go back to voters again in the future in order to renew the levy. They claimed they were able to bring the amount down because they found $2M to cut. They couldn't find this $2M before the failed May levy. I guess the money was playing hide-and-seek and didn't hear the superintendent and board say "ollie, ollie oxen free."

Prior to the district coming out with its plan, the KBA PAC asked the district to consider a temporary annual $2.5 million levy representing enough money to pay off the debt caused by previous administration. Our argument was that this would give the district enough time to come back to the community with proper justification for whatever subsequent amount it can really justify as opposed to the amount it wanted. We did not specify any program cuts, we did not dictate to the district how to run the schools, and we weren't telling teachers how to teach: our positions were clear and well documented.

In the history of our KBA PAC, the most we ever had in our budget was about $2,000, but typically our operating budgets were much less. The pro-district PAC raised many many times more than we ever did to support their campaign.

When all was said and done, the district won the reduced levy approval by 8,258 to 8,208 votes. The day after the vote, the superintendent wasn't claiming victory yet since there were a number of absentee and provisional ballots that had to be counted. It's hard to say whether he was sincere or being coy since a rumor was circulated in town that the district, or the pro-district PAC, mailed out hundreds of absentee ballots to former graduates attending out of town colleges. Since these kids had heart, but their brains were still in development, their YES votes were guaranteed and thus also demonstrating how people who do not pay taxes have the power to tax others.

Over the coming year Wilson left the KBA PAC and the Skipper and I found a guy I'll call Thomas Paine to take up the open slot. Paine was a retired Air Force civilian Intel Analyst. Paine did a great job at maintaining our version of "common sense" on our website.

We had other run-ins with the district over the years. Two are of particular interest and summarized briefly here.

The first was a rather embarrassing act on the part of the district, but demonstrates the arrogance and power of government especially the forces that drive industrial complexes.

Acting on a tip from a well known district Schmoozer, in the spring of 2005 the Beavercreek School District, through its hired legal counsel, attempted to squeeze a few extra bucks from 13 specific properties. The plausible deniability reason given was to ensure that "everyone is paying their fair share." Thus, the district leadership decided that besides education they wanted to do the county tax collector's job too. The Greene County auditor was not amused.

Apparently the Schmoozer went about looking up property tax assessments in an attempt to report discrepancies and hopefully raise more money for the district. Since this was in the spring, I assume he was hoping for a teacher to place a rainbow sticker on his report. If it had been autumn, it may have been a pumpkin or a scarecrow, but it can't it be a witch anymore, since that would be offensive to some people.

The district's core supporters often claim how Beavercreek is lucky to have such caring individuals in charge of our education system. Yet these individuals didn't hesitate to use the full weight of the government to intimidate taxpayers. As one letter writer wrote: "You can almost see them now—the lawyer holding the taxpayer upside down by the legs as the district leadership scramble to pick up the fallen lose coins."

When all was said and done, it turned out that the targeted property owners were in compliance with the law. The icing on the cake was that one of the targeted property owners was a strong school advocate who contributed thousands of dollars to the district. As the same writer put it (paraphrasing): *It looked like the district was starting to eat their own. It would have been funny if it weren't so disgusting.* Yet isn't this typical of the Government Class?

The second major run-in with the district was when the KBA PAC decided to support candidates for the school board in 2005. Three slots were coming open and all three current board members decided to throw their hats back into the ring. Their campaign slogan was "We A.R.E. for Kids"; where A.R.E. were the initials of the three candidates. Pretty clever.

The KBA PAC was supporting three other candidates. One candidate was active in educational affairs for some time, and another ran for a board position in 2003 but lost. The third candidate was a newbie.

The incumbents had been very nice to the local Education Industrial Complex and thus had full backing of the district, its supporters, and the teachers union. It was comical to watch the district officially try to maintain neutrality during the election. It was twice as funny to watch the union try to maintain an air of impartially (they later of course endorsed the incumbents). After all, these three incumbents, along with the other two board members, vote 5-0 on nearly all, if not all, administrative initiatives.

The high point of the campaign occurred at that year's Beavercreek Popcorn Festival. The Popcorn Festival is an annual town event held in September on the weekend following Labor Day, where the city closes off the major Dayton-Xenia road to inconvenience local residents for two days, so vendors can sell tacky wood carvings of wildlife, your kids can pester you for 15 tons of cotton candy, and you get to buy some sort of sausage sandwich that might be a grade above carnie food. Oh, and some booths sell popcorn. (There are of course some charity, church, and other booths of local interests.) Several other local communities have similar events but with different themes: strawberry festival, sauerkraut festival, and so on. Interestingly, I found on one website that the Popcorn Festival was rated one of the top 100 events in North America by the American Bus Association. No, I'm not kidding!

Now before you say I sound like a grumpy old man: hear me out. There are several large local parks that this event could be held at without disrupting citizens not interested in attending or the local merchants not interested in having their parking lots turned into dumpsters. But it is what it is.

During election years, candidates rent booths at the festival to grip and grin with the voters and pass out brochures. In August 2005 I called the city and asked if any booths were left for rent for our school board candidates. The city person said no, all the booths were taken.

So on the weekend of the festival, the A.R.E. folks had a booth and one of our candidates, I'll call her Bonnie Parker, was walking around passing out campaign literature. As soon as Bonnie was spotted and reported on by A, R, or E the festival marshals (identified by green shirts) descended on Bonnie and told her she couldn't pass out campaign literature unless she rented a booth. On the face of it, that sounds reasonable. After all, some folks played by the rules and rented booths, so shouldn't all participants obey the same rules? Just hold that thought for the moment.

The Green Shirts surrounded Bonnie and tried to intimidate her into leaving, and even the police were called in. The problem was that Bonnie was stubborn as a mule. In the end, the Green Shirts and the police couldn't find any law that prohibited her from passing out campaign literature on public property.

That was Saturday. The next day, Bonnie Parker was inciting anarchy once more. The Green Shirts showed up again along with the police. This time the police were able to point to a piece of paper torn out of the internationally recognized Beavercreek Popcorn Festival Book of Rules and Guidelines. Chapter 3,

Section 4, Subsection 2, Paragraph 5, line 16 indicated that solicitation, political or otherwise, outside of booths was prohibited.

The Skipper and I were at the event on Sunday and we agreed to rent a booth space that opened up when the original renter canceled. For those of you familiar with Arlo Guthrie *Alice's Restaurant* cited earlier, this whole affair was even bigger than Arlo's arrest for littering (and creating a nuisance). The PAC and the candidates got a lot of bad PR on this, but besides the fact that for Beavercreek this was the crime of the century, what's wrong with this story?

If Bonnie was selling turkey sandwiches out of her backpack, then I would agree she should have gotten a license like all the other food vendors. But let's remember what she was doing; she was passing political literature in America on public property. Apparently the authorities never heard of the Constitution that allowed such hideous acts, or maybe they really believed that the Beavercreek Popcorn Festival Book of Rules and Guidelines voted on by a no doubt distinguished group of community elders trumped the Constitution.

The A.R.E folks had lots of money, put out some pretty impressive literature, and paid for notable print and TV ads. Our candidates went on and lost in November by a margin of about 2 to 1.

♦   ♦   ♦

It's hard to put into words the work that the Skipper, Wilson, Thomas Paine and I put into fighting the school district and other local government initiatives. During the summer of 2003, the Skipper and I spoke on the phone more often than my two teenage daughters. Along with other volunteers we hand delivered (because we couldn't afford the postage), tens of thousands of brochures on several different election cycles covering local issues. The Skipper, Wilson, Thomas Paine and I put our reputations on the line, because many in the town weren't happy that we were trying to soil our collective nest.

The Skipper and I alone must have put in thousands of hours into KBA PAC activities. So did we accomplish anything? I think we did. But it's the kind of victory that will never be recognized and won't last.

The district administration and school board in 2000 were a collective train wreck running on the fuel of arrogance. The new board that was elected and the newly hired superintendent were relative major improvements, but the Education Industrial Complex is not just made up of individuals; it is a culture and cultures don't change easily.

Although I have beaten up Beavercreek's Board of Education in this book, I believe being a member of a modern school board is a difficult job, but it is difficult because the Education Industrial Complex has made it so. However, as I mentioned earlier, I also believe that for the most part many members of boards of education tend to operate on the principle of expanding education programs at whatever cost as opposed to an overriding philosophy of what should or should not be included in a government school system. For many board members, the only obstacle is finding the money and justification to expand the programs.

So being on a school board may be a difficult job, but it is an impossible job if you try to break ranks and stand on principles. The few board members that do show some philosophical restraint are typically hounded by the Educational Industrial Complex, which in some cases may include lawsuits or threats of lawsuits for something as *silly* as trying to enforce dress, academic, or behavioral standards.

When the new Beavercreek district leaders decided on the continuous levy for May 2003 they were operating just like their predecessors, because they were using the same play book. I believe the levy defeat and the constant pressure put on by many in the community shocked them. Since that levy, they have not asked for a tax increase and have consistently sought cost cutting measures to hold costs down. By the time this book is released, they may have even paid off the debt they inherited. I think within the limitations given them, the superintendent and board have done a respectable job in certain critical areas, but are dealing with problems far bigger than they may or may not realize, and in my opinion, are contributing to the problems through implementation of seemingly well intended but misguided programs and policies.

Today they take credit for being good stewards of taxpayers' money. At the same time, observant people have noted new programs being added along with new employees being hired.

In education, programs are created but never destroyed. Eventually, I believe another financial crisis will occur. At that time, the then superintendent, board, teachers union, Moochers, Jocks and all of the other players will ask the Beavercreek taxpayers to dig deep into their hearts and wallets *for the children*.

In reality what is needed is a complete overhaul of America's education system even in successful communities such as Beavercreek. I will leave this chapter with the following ditty I wrote that captures the frustration of working against the Education Industrial Complex. This poem was later published with some additional text by a KBA PAC supporter in a longer letter-to-the-editor.

As background for the poem, the superintendent was doing a visit to one of the city's elementary school dressed as the Cat in the Hat. After reading about the Cat in the Hat event, and remembering the old adage that everything one needs to know in life is learned in kindergarten, it dawned on me that maybe what we have here is a failure to communicate. In the hopes of breaking through the communication barrier, I offered the following, hoping that it will be understood by the board of education and the school administration.

How much does it cost to run a School?
Would you tell us if we were in a pool?
One mil, two mil, new mil, old mil.
To pay a bill or to pay a frill?

Would you tell us all before the Fall?
Or only if to you we each make a call?
Would you, could you, before November?
Would you, could you, try to remember?

How is all that money to be spent?
To pay for jocks or for the rent?
Please tell us, cause we like to know.
Taxes, taxes, they continue to grow!

High in the castle the school board sits
While down in the city the people throw fits
You don't understand, they often say.
For mandates, mandates, you must pay.

Mandates! People ask for cost reports.
Don't ask that question, the board retorts!
Questions, questions, stop the fuss
You will be happy if you'd trust us.

Together the people begin to band,
It is the District that fails to understand.
It is in God we trust, we wish to clarify,
But in the District we need to verify.

20

Declaration of Educational Independence

Democracy and socialism have nothing in common but one word, equality. But notice the difference: while democracy seeks equality in liberty, socialism seeks equality in restraint and servitude.

—Alexis de Tocqueville

The Beavercreek superintendent wrote an editorial column in 2006 expounding on the fact that education is the foundation of a free society and America is great because of our public education system. His statement is correct.

However, I say that our government school system is destroying America and I would argue that I am also right. So how can we both be right?

The Superintendent, of course, was talking about America's public education system prior to the birth of the Department of Education on May 4, 1980. I'm talking about America's government education system since May 4, 1980.

The Department of Education didn't just pop out of nowhere. However, we don't have to go through all the historical links that led to that momentous event in 1980 that has led to where we are today, all we have to do is look at three major events of the 20th century: Franklin Roosevelt's New Deal, Lyndon Johnson's Great Society, and the Vietnam War.

Roosevelt took advantage of the Great Depression to introduce a quantum jump in governmental activism. Many historians still argue over whether most of the measures taken by Roosevelt's New Deal programs actually helped cure the depression including the massive unemployment. In 1933 unemployment was about 25%, but by 1938 unemployment was still at about 19% even after the tremendous amount of federal expenditures.

Although some of the New Deal programs were later ruled unconstitutional, what the New Deal did do was introduce, once and for all, an all powerful federal government sold on the concept that the welfare state can bring about social harmony and can replace individual responsibility: Social Security comes to mind. State and local governments followed suit.

Lyndon Johnson continued with Roosevelt's quest and introduced the Great Society concept and associated welfare programs in the 1964 to 1965 time period. Specifically in 1965 he introduced several federal education initiatives that helped lead to the creation of the Department of Education in 1980. (In what has to be one of the greatest displays of political pluck and doubletalk, I read in a July 20, 1966 Cleveland Plain Dealer article, entitled, *LBJ Urges Crackdown on Spending*, that Johnson asked Congress to hold down non-military spending! The way these people think is absolutely amazing!)

But Lyndon Johnson's legacy to the welfare state was not just the Great Society. In many respects that was a continuation of the New Deal. Johnson's legacy to the Government Class was the Vietnam War.

There is much debate on whether it was necessary for the United States to enter Vietnam to prevent the feared communist domino effect of country after country falling into the Soviet sphere of influence. But hindsight is always 20/20. However, given the realities of the time, John Kennedy decided to go beyond Eisenhower's "military advisory" involvement and eventually Johnson decided to really step up the tempo. It's just too bad Johnson and the military leadership didn't decide to conduct the war as it should have been conducted: you know something silly like actually trying to defeat the enemy. (There are many schools of thought on these issues, but fortunately there are enough papers, books and speeches that address these different views, freeing us from the burden of discussing them here.)

By the time the Vietnam War was well underway, the last remnants of what might be called classical Liberalism existed mostly in Martin Luther King's civil rights movement. Modern Liberalism, as defined by a desire for a large socialist state *coupled* with modern cultural (politically correct) beliefs, was still mostly being expressed through the rants of various non-cohesive single issue groups. What the socialists, communists and other modern liberals in the 1960s lacked was a unifying rallying cry. The Vietnam War provided that opportunity; or more to the point, how we conducted the war provided that opportunity. (For a great discussion on some of the points covered here see Robert Bork's book, *Slouching Towards Gomorrah: Modern Liberalism and American Decline.*)

By 1968 it was clear that America had squandered its treasure and blood on a badly managed war; so much so that even the middle class was wobbling. The many diverse and disparate left-leaning groups that were operating as separate entities were given the opportunity to unite under the anti-war/peace movement that was nothing more than a front for an anti-America mob. The Modern Liberal coup that finally tipped the scales happened in August of that year in the streets of Chicago during the Democratic National Convention. Although the rioters got the snot beat out of them by the Chicago Police, and some ring leaders (the Chicago Seven) were prosecuted, they were later all acquitted and the Left would eventually go on to win the culture war.

In many respects these domestic events mirrored what happened earlier that year in Vietnam during North Vietnam's January 1968 Tet Offensive. The Tet Offensive was a crushing military blow to the communists, but we all know who won the war.

(Here I differ with Bill O'Reilly. I believe he would argue that the secular progressives, as he calls them, are losing the culture war, but I don't agree. The few examples he cites as proof are to me nothing more than temporary glitches in the secular progressive movement. I would also argue that the way the Bush administration has conducted the Iraq war mirrors the Vietnam fiasco, and the Democratic win in 2006 was just the beginning of another major opportunity to shift public policy to the left.)

In the next few years, the Democratic Party would convert completely to Modern Liberalism that started under the pretenses of a peace movement. The Classical Liberals that were left or are still around are like the little toe: kinda cute and occasionally useful, but mostly ignored. They're like the little pig in the *This Little Piggy Went to Market* nursery rhyme that gets to whine: "Wee, wee, wee! I can't find my way home."

Following the victory in Chicago, Modern Liberals began to really nip at the foundations of American culture. Big government in itself was only half of their goal. Because having a large socialist government wasn't good enough if the government didn't share their cultural view of the world, and government is a great enforcement mechanism.

Members of the Intelligentsia were sent into high gear. Institutions such as the family and religion had to be destroyed and recreated in a new mold and life and death were both redefined. Where once existed only male and female sexes became a collage of genders. All love between a man and a woman became rape. Women were told they no longer needed a man for fulfillment, leaving many women and specifically single mothers to find out the hard way that it also meant men no longer needed women for fulfillment. This created a new class of poor women and a subsequent lost generation of children. Fatherhood and husbandhood were replaced by governmenthood. Success was the result of life's lottery and not tied to hard work; if you didn't win life's lottery, then someone else was living high on your portion; paying taxes was a duty only for the rich and the more excessive the better; receiving welfare was a constitutional right; and only big government can bring about solutions to social harmony and personal fulfillment.

In order to achieve power you must tear down the old guard, and thus all concepts of established right and wrong were labeled as just culturally relative. Western culture in this scheme was denigrated to the lowest levels of contempt. One of the favorite cultural areas Liberals love to muck in is sex in school, where sex is not just for adults anymore.

The Vagina Monologues has appeared as a high school play in Amherst, Massachusetts, with support from the superintendent and other school officials. (This play is extremely graphic and even depicts the sexual seduction of a teenage girl by an adult woman where afterwards the teenage girl states, "If it was rape, it was a good rape.") The superintendent was reported to have said, "We hope that there are ways for our students to find their voice in their years with us." This was the same district where school officials decided to display a photo-text exhibit in the *elementary* schools titled "Love Makes A Family: Living in Lesbian and Gay Families," but banned West Side Story because it was racist. It looks like in Amherst, some voices are more easily found than others.

How about that girl in Winona Senior High School in Minnesota in 2005 that thought it would be a great idea if she wore a button that said, "I (heart) my vagina"? This is a good story because it shows how the Intelligentsia doesn't pussy foot around to screw America. (Wow, was that last sentence a quadruple entendre?)

The principal in this case told the student that she couldn't wear the button. (This is a good thing, but unfortunately the reasoning behind the ban was rather convoluted.) Remember what I said about the tension between lower level administrators and Legal Unprofessionals. Guess who came to the girl's rescue? That's right, the ACLU. Not only that, but the director of Winona State University's women studies, helped design and sell the vagina buttons at a local production of the Vagina Monologues. The director claimed that because of the context of the button, she believes it is different than if it contained a male sexual organ. Go figure that one out.

Is it all about sex? No, across the country we find teachers burning American flags in classrooms, leading students to recite the Mexican National Anthem, or asking students to write essays on how we should prosecute George W. Bush for war crimes (defense essays are not allowed). And it's not all political. An Associated Press article in the fall of 2006 reported on a school in Columbus, Ohio, that gave points to students to improve their test scores based on how many points their parents earn for volunteering at the school.

These are just a few of countless examples of insanity occurring in our government schools. Sure, there are schools that are doing very well, but these schools are fighting an uphill battle against a deeply broken system. And let's not forget that for the most part, to conform to legislation by large states such as California, most text book publishers kowtow to rigid PC rules. So we have a national system of PC books used by teachers across the country all trained by PC Educationologists.

Even the better schools graduating students that may do well in science and math, are short changing them on the advantages of free enterprise, or any historical perspective of America and its proper place in the history of human social evolution. Instead, our students are taught that the U.N. is mankind's salvation, the world would be a better place if America didn't exist, or America would be a better place if we were more like ... France!

Don't try to figure any of these out ladies and gentlemen, there is a point in PC stories where the discussion becomes too absurd for normal people to discuss; it just causes too many short circuits in the brain, or paraphrasing radio commentator Glenn Beck: "It's like blood shooting out of your eyes." On the other hand, I feel sorry for many administrators and teachers because I think a lot of the zaniness we hear about, even the Columbus example above, *are from good people trying to make a lousy system work.*

Moderates would argue that these are isolated incidences. Okay, maybe on a PC scale of 1 to 10, these examples may be rare 10s, but there are a lot of sevens, eights, and nines out there.

I mentioned earlier that many elementary schools are eliminating certain playground games due to worries of law suits from Legal Unprofessionals resulting from playground injuries, and the fact that these games promote violence, discrimination, insensitivity and a host of other social harms. They know this because the Peeps in da Hood have so decreed it. Did you know that dodge ball was evil?

These are all skirmishes in the culture war, but the culture war is pretty much over, although some mopping up still needs to be done. The new education system is now run by the Government Class and its armies and no longer represents the education system that the Beavercreek superintendent alluded to.

What about Beavercreek? Is Beavercreek PC? Earlier in discussing the levy defeat in May 2003 I mentioned that I had no idea how much the KBA PAC contributed to that defeat, but one thing that didn't help the district was the little military recruiting incident that happened a few weeks before the ballot. It turned out that a bunch of teenage leftists who objected to the Iraq conflict were protesting the presence of military recruiters on campus. These are the type of students we see at high schools and college campuses everywhere that know all the answers to the world problems. The fact that most of them can't find Iraq on the map shouldn't deter us from seeking their sage advice on this heavy issue.

The Beavercreek Superintendent's solution was to restrict and isolate the military recruiters from the main student commons area. Now remember this is an Air Force garrison town. Many taxpayers were angry. Ironically, many members of the school board had strong ties to the local Wright-Patterson Air Force Base. So how did the military recruiters get the short end of the stick?

That decision was more than just the solution to quiet a few loud leftists, because the same types of incidents, mostly notably in San Francisco, have occurred in districts throughout the country. These represent skirmishes between cultures as embodied by their respective industrial complexes, and the Education Industrial Complex has been winning most of the battles.

All districts suffer under the weight of political correctness. The time that students can use to further study the real issues in their respective classrooms is wasted on making sure we deal with our sensitivities. Conservative taxpayers are paying for their own destruction. This is equivalent to paying the Mafia to put a hit on yourself. That is why the Education Industrial Complex fights tooth and nail against any voucher or alternative education system. They need your money. They could not survive under an open competitive system.

Nationally, we spend over 2-3 times the amount on education as we do on the military. If this were poker, the Education Industrial Complex would see the military's 400+ billion and raise it another 600+ billion. Yet there are those that sport bumper stickers stating cleverly (remember Liberals have great bumper stickers): *Wouldn't it be wonderful if the Air Force had to hold a bake sale to buy another B-2?*

If the Military Industrial Complex's entire budget went over to the Education Industrial Complex, our kids would still perform as poorly as they do now, because it ain't the money folks, it's the culture that the Government Class has created with the help of the Education Industrial Complex armies.

If you think that the solution is to accept the status quo and work together with your district for the sake of the children; go ahead. If you want to write letters to your state or federal congress members; go ahead. If you think the answer will come from voting for the right Republican or right Democrat; go ahead. If you want to believe in Santa Claus; go ahead.

So what would it take to truly achieve academic success in America? America's education "business model" or "operational model," whichever you prefer, is broken. All solutions offered are merely variations of a theme working within the confines of the same broken system. Special interest groups offer plans that just benefit themselves, and politicians are too gutless to recommend any real changes so they just offer useless solutions that tinker with the problems. It comes a time when consumers have to realize that sometimes a product is not meeting the performance specifications printed on the box and its time to return it to the store. To flip President Clinton's line when he was referring to welfare: *It's time to end it, not mend it.*

In an earlier chapter I mentioned that I didn't have the answers to our education problems but I knew where to look for the answers. The place to look is in competition.

Yeah, I know. I heard and read much of the objections to that argument. But those objections are almost always emotional and usually come from folks that might have something to lose in that transition, are afraid of change, or don't understand or want to understand what is really meant by that recommendation.

It doesn't necessarily mean that all government schools are shut down. It means that schools must be given quasi autonomous status. Of course, this scares the PC crowd because they will lose control of their agenda.

As both a real and symbolic first step, I would start with eliminating the Federal Department of Education. This would not be a cure-all, but it is the thread you need to pull to begin unraveling the Education Industrial Complex. By eliminating the Department of Education, you would begin to reestablish the condition that the federal government has no constitutional authority in education

This would start the process allowing states to run their own programs and let the best states win. One state might decide to keep centralized control. Another state might introduce open competition starting with offering vouchers between districts and between government and private schools, including home schools. The argument that public schools would be at a disadvantage because by law they would be forced to accept students the private schools can reject, could be addressed through a myriad of options. The end result will be the states that adopted successful plans would float to the top of the list.

In some states, administrators might be given wide discretion in setting school policies and establishing curriculums and standards, even in areas such as enforcing strict dress codes. In these states, administrators would be amply rewarded for

success and fired for failure. There would be no need to come up with complicated or archaic methods to decide what is success or failure. No need to hire
Peeps in da Hood to come up with new pin-head theories of cognitive this or that
to be forced on all districts as a national PC standard. Parents would know where
the good schools are and vote by their selection. School districts will either compete or hire professionals who can make them compete.

Of course, how we pay for education would have to change also. Following
the passage of a November 2006 levy, one Beavercreek school had their outside
marquee sign read "Thank you voters," followed by, "Word of the week,
DEMOCRACY." Here's a word of the week I bet you won't see on that sign:
VOUCHERS.

There would still be plenty of work to do, especially in the legal arena, where
decades of bad law has to be undone. Without a federal role in education, we
might be able to re-establish parent's and teacher's moral authority over children,
but it will require overturning decades of court decisions. Districts could make
decisions based on logic and not fear because children would not have the same
perceived constitutional rights as adults in areas such as freedom of speech and
search and seizure. Parents could once again ease drop on their children's phone
conversations or e-mails without fearing a lawsuit from the ACLU because their
precocious little Archibald had his privacy rights violated.

But where would all the answers come from to solve all of the near endless
details that have to be addressed and make this transition successful? From people
much smarter than me. *From the countless teachers, administrators, and other staff
members who are currently suffocating under the Education Industrial Complex, in
unison with their customers: parents and taxpayers.* That's where the answers lie.
Not with the Government Class or the Intelligentsia.

Hillary Clinton once claimed that she sensed Eleanor Roosevelt's ghost in the
White House and had "imaginary" conversations with the spirit. She got a lot of
flak for that, but I can understand where she was coming from. I often speak with
Thomas Jefferson's ghost, who for some unknown reason decided to haunt my
house.

Tom (after a few conversations, we were on a first name basis) was acutely
aware of the education problems in America, so I asked him if he wouldn't mind
writing a declaration of independence for people who wanted to opt out of the
current mess. He said he would be happy to. The following is what Tom wrote,
which I offered to rewrite it in more modern terms, but he got angry so I left it as
he wrote it.

The Declaration of Educational
Independence of these fifty States

In Congress, Date To Be Determined

The unanimous declaration of parents in the fifty United States of America

When in the course of student events, it becomes necessary for parents to dissolve the educational bands which have connected them with the government school system, and to assume among the powers of the earth, the separate and equal station to which the Laws of Nature and of Nature's God entitle them, a decent respect to the education of their children and the future of this great land requires that they should declare the causes which impel them to the separation.

We hold these truths to be self-evident, that all parents are created equal, that they are endowed by their Creator with certain unalienable rights, that among these are life, liberty and the pursuit of educational free choice for their children.

That to secure these rights, governments are instituted among men, deriving their just powers from the consent of the governed.

But whenever any form of government schools become destructive of these ends, it is the right of the parents to alter or to abolish it, and to institute new educational processes, laying their foundation on such principles and organizing their powers in such form, as to them shall seem most likely to effect their children's education and this country's future.

Prudence, indeed, will dictate that school systems long established should not be changed for light and transient causes; and accordingly all experience hath shewn, that parents are more disposed to suffer, while evils are sufferable, than to right themselves by abolishing the forms to which they are accustomed. But when a long train of abuses and usurpations, pursuing invariably the same object evinces a design to reduce them under absolute despotism, it is their right, it is their duty, to throw off such government schools, and to provide new educational processes for their children's education.

Such has been the patient sufferance of these parents and taxpayers; and such is now the necessity which constrains them to alter their former systems of government education. The recent history of education in America is a history of repeated injuries and usurpations by the Government Class, all having in direct object the establishment of a culture not inline with what made this nation great.

To prove this, let facts be submitted to a candid world.

- They vilify America, teaching only the bad and out of context with other history.

- They have forced upon students readings and other literature of secondary status, and have eliminated those readings paramount to an orderly and free society.

- They have eliminated the citing of those pledges that bound us to fundamental truths.

- They teach moral relativism as defined by the new cultural elite.

- They have changed the meaning of our Constitution so as to weaken those common notions important to keep order and tranquility.

- They have watered down all academic standards, resulting in lower skills and abilities of graduates.

- They have refused assent to student disciplinary laws, the most wholesome and necessary for the public good.

- They have wasted through broken philosophies and ideologies the futures, lives and treasures of urban communities.

- They have called together legislative bodies at places unusual and distant from the depository of their public records, for the sole purpose of lobbying them into compliance with their measures and for looting of the public treasury.

- They have ignored pleas from representative groups repeatedly, for opposing with manly firmness their invasions on the rights of parents and taxpayers.

- They have endeavored to prevent the population of these states and communities to establish their own standards and norms.

- They have obstructed the administration of justice by refusing their assent to laws for establishing meaningful results-oriented academic accountability.

- They have made teachers dependent on their will alone for the tenure of their offices, and the amount and payment of their salaries.

- They have erected a multitude of new offices, and sent hither swarms of administrative officers to harass our people and eat out their substance.

- They have affected to render military recruiters into less than honorable positions on campuses.

- They have combined with others to subject us to a jurisdiction foreign to our constitution, and unacknowledged by our laws; giving their assent to their acts of pretended legislation and unfunded mandates.

- For quartering large bodies of unnecessary teachers, staff and administrators among us whose functions are of questionable necessity.

- For protecting them, by a mock trial from punishment for any injuries which they should commit on the students and taxpayers of these States.

- For cutting off meaningful educational competition with other parts of the industry.

- For imposing taxes on us without proper consent.

- For depriving us in many cases, to petition out of the system.

- For transporting students beyond their districts to be educated under pretended circumstances.

- For rendering our own local school legislatures impotent, and declaring themselves invested with power to legislate for us in all cases whatsoever.

- They have abdicated government here, by declaring us not capable of educational self rule and waging war against us.

- They have plundered our purses, ravaged our schools, incited our towns, and destroyed the lives of our children and our nation.

- They are at this time transporting large armies of lobbyists and other mercenaries to complete the works of student indoctrination and parental isolation, already begun with circumstances of cruelty & perfidy scarcely paralleled in the most barbarous ages, and totally unworthy of a free and civilized nation.

- They have created tax levies that constrain our fellow citizens to bear malice against their fellow citizens, to become the enemies of their friends and brethren, or to fall themselves by their hands.

- They have excited domestic insurrections amongst us, and have endeavored to bring on the inhabitants of our districts new rules of social interactions that result in undistinguished hostilities between all ages, races, sexes and other conditions.

In every stage of these oppressions many people have petitioned for redress in the most humble terms: but those repeated petitions have been answered only by repeated injury. A bureaucracy, whose character is thus marked by every act which may define a tyrant, is unfit to educate a free people.

Nor have we been wanting in attentions to the Government Class brethren. We have warned them from time to time of attempts by their fiats to extend an unwarrantable jurisdiction over us. We have reminded them of the circumstances of our emigration and settlement here.

We have appealed to their native justice and magnanimity, and we have conjured them by the ties of our common kindred to disavow these usurpations, which would inevitably interrupt our connections and correspondence. They too have been deaf to the voice of justice and of consanguinity. We must, therefore, acquiesce in the necessity, which denounces our separation, and hold them, as we hold the rest of mankind, Enemies in War, in Peace Friends.

We, therefore, the people of the United States of America, as parents or taxpayers, assembled, appealing to the Supreme Judge of the world for the rectitude of our intentions, do, in the name, and by authority of the good people of all communities, solemnly publish and declare, that all students are, and of right ought to be free and independent, that they are absolved from all allegiance to the current educational establishment, and that all political connection between them and the Government Class, is and ought to be totally dissolved; and that as free and independent people, their parents have full power to choose schools, conclude contractual educational alliances, establish standards, and to do all other acts and things which independent people and communities may of right do—and for the support of this Declaration, with a firm reliance on the protection of Divine Providence, we mutually pledge to each other our lives, our fortunes and our sacred honor.

◆   ◆   ◆

If you are a member of the Government Class or of the Education Industrial Complex, you can quit laughing. You and I know that none of this will ever come about.

For everyone else, you can start crying. The persons who will make you cry is none other than Jesse Jackson and his bouncing baby boy Jesse Junior (D-Ill). For whatever you think of him, Jackson is a smart man: when Jesse Jackson Sr. speaks about education, the Government Class and Education Industrial Complex are also thinking it.

Jackson Sr. and Jackson Jr. would like to see a constitutional amendment forcing everyone to send their children to government schools. Here is what Junior had to say as reported by the Harvard Gazette on February, 27, 2003:

> The word "education" does not exist in the Constitution, and therefore, the right to an education in America is a state right. It is time we move this democracy forward for every American. Every American deserves the constitutional right to a public education of equal high quality—a 28th amendment. These rights are inalienable and I'm arguing that we should be fighting for inalienable rights.

Let's make sure we understand what is between the lines here. The only way to ensure that all students have access to "equal" education is for the federal government to take over all educational processes and instill the same high quality (ahem) education we have today in government schools. (Notice the use of the word "inalienable" as opposed to "unalienable" as in the original Declaration of Independence. I'm not sure if Jackson actually used "inalienable" or whether it was transcribed in error. In any case, both words are acceptable. In this book I have used "unalienable" only to keep in line with Jefferson's original usage.)

How can the government do that? You have to think like the Government Class to understand this. First, everyone knows that government schools are failing either their students directly or America in general; even "successful" suburban ones. If some parents can choose a private school for their magnificent petite seraphs, some kids will have a better education than parents who cannot afford the better schools and have to send their kids to failed government schools. This is in clear violation of the 14th Amendment's Equal Protection Clause. Nuff' said.

Even if Jesse Senior and Junior don't get their way, remember the thesis, antithesis, compromise process. Ask for an amendment, settle for a law.

For those of you that are even thinking the government can't do this because, after all, they are your kids; aren't they? Oh you miserable misguided fools. One by one we have lost our parental rights. What makes you think Uncle Sam is going to stop now?

PART IV
It Takes a Village: The Town Hall

Where now the educated reader, having graduated from the affairs of the schoolhouse, enters the affairs of the city.

21

Zzzzzz

What gives you the right to question the hard work of our elected officials?
What makes you an expert on all of these subjects?

—Common e-mail questions to the KBA PAC to which I always
replied: "I'm a taxpayer."

I want to apologize up front for Part 4 of this book, because this section of the book covers issues that only a mother could love. In fact, I bounced back and forth between including it and deleting it, but the final decision is staring at you.

My agony was based on the fact that the material isn't too exciting when compared to education, the Iraq War, or what the newest hot Hollywood bimbo is wearing under her skirt—if anything. We too often look at social or political problems cruising at 35,000 feet; but sometimes you have to land and get your feet dirty. That's why I wrote Part 3 on local education politics.

Is the material important? Well that depends. Government no longer just installs traffic lights, fixes roads, prints and mints currency, and protects our borders (ahem). We covered why this is so in previous chapters. In any case, I did try to jazz it up a bit here and there. I hope it isn't too painful.

22

Photons, Protons, Neutrons and ... Govitons?

Sandy: Carl I want you to kill all the gophers on the golf course
Carl Spackler: Correct me if I'm wrong Sandy, but if I kill all the golfers they'll lock me up and throw away the key.
Sandy: Not golfers, you great git! Gophers, the little brown, furry rodents!
Carl: We can do that. We don't even need a reason.

—From the movie, *Caddyshack*

The field of Physics that deals with studying how the forces of nature interact is called High Energy Physics but is also often referred to as Particle Physics. It's called Particle Physics because nature's forces interact through hundreds of atomic or other more elementary particles.

Physicists speak of gravitational, electromagnetic and nuclear forces: each force exhibits itself in a distinct way. For example, you can blame gravity for skinned knees; electricity and magnetism for internet porn; and nuclear forces for the cold war. But Physicists have overlooked the Golf Force.

So what does the Golf Force do? The golf force acts through the Government Class and causes them to build a number of 4 ¼ inch holes in the ground to throw taxpayer money into. Golf is just another excuse for the Government Class to violate the taxpayer's wallet.

The original discovery of golf is open to debate, but golf is usually recognized to have been started in Scotland in the 14th to 15th centuries and building a community golf course has been a goal of nearly every city council ever since. But, a golf course is not just another city park with a few baseball diamonds and some basketball courts. A municipal golf course is a big business that carries a big risk.

When one looks at the substance (or lack thereof) behind the decision to build a municipal golf course, the only logical conclusion is that operating golf courses in the majority of cases should not be a legitimate city function. Yet many communities have built golf courses and many of these operate in the red forcing many city managers to transfer money from the general fund to balance the golf course budget: which of course means that other necessary city functions like police or street services get the shaft.

How do cities fall into this predicament? Without argument, a municipal golf course has a certain aesthetic community appeal, so much so, that Busy-bodies and Do-gooders can't help working themselves into a golf course building frenzy. Up till now we discussed some antics of the Government Class, but let's have some fun with this and look a little deeper; at the Government Class atomic level.

Nature's forces act through a host of elementary particles like the ones listed in the chapter title. For example, an atom can interact with another atom by emitting a photon of light, which is absorbed by the receiving atom. I'm going to call the class of elementary particles that are emitted by members of the Government Class *govitons*. Govitons are particles emitted by members of the Government Class to influence other members of the Government Class.

In some ways you can think of a goviton as the basic unit of Liberal thought. Govitons are often generated in a moment of emotional outburst. For example, if you hear a school board member say something like, "Now that we have established a pre-school program, I think the district needs to hire wet nurses for mothers that can't breast feed their babies," then you have just experienced the process called *goviton emission*. When another school board member lights up and shows agreement, then you have just witnessed the process called *goviton absorption*.

For our purposes here, we can safely say that in nature every particle has an antiparticle such that when they collide, they mutually annihilate each other; such as protons and anti-protons. This is the matter-antimatter stuff science friction writers always fall back on when they need something to blow up. But the goviton is different.

Although Conservatives in government generate antigovitons that can annihilate Liberal govitons, on average there are more government Liberal govitons than Conservative antigovitons. The remaining antigovitons generated by Pink Republicans are too feeble to annihilate the rest of the govitions; they can only weaken them. Thus, when the remaining Liberal govitons not annihilated by Conservative antigovitons collide with Pink Republican antigovitons, you have witnessed the process called goviton-antigoviton *compromise*. Some ill informed people call this bipartisanship.

Goviton-antigoviton compromises are not victories for Conservatives. They are always victories for Liberals because; remember from an earlier chapter, Liberals get their schooling from Hegel, Marx, Engels and Lenin operating under the *thesis, antithesis and synthesis* triad. In the terms used here, these would be the goviton, the antigoviton, and the compromise. The compromise becomes the basis for the next goviton emission, i.e., the next proposition or thesis, sometime in the near future. (I apologize to any reader who found the above discussion stupid. But that's how physicists think.)

Here is how a city with a five member council gets a golf course most people don't want. Can you spot the thesis, antithesis and synthesis?

Phase 1

> **Do-gooder**: Let's fund a golf course. A golf course would help make our city a wonderful place to live.
> **Conservative**: Operating a golf course is not a legitimate city function.
> **Socialist**: Oh, I suppose now you're anti-golf. You're always so negative. A golf course would generate more taxes for the city. Let's just fund a study, surely that wouldn't hurt. *Thinking to herself.* We can charge people by their income and let the poor play for free and the homeless live in the clubhouse.
> **Pink Conservative**: I don't like the idea of the city operating a golf course but I guess a study wouldn't hurt.
> **Scoundrel**: *Thinking to himself.* To hell with the taxpayer, I like playing golf.
>
> **Final vote**: Four votes for a study; one vote against.

Phase 2

> **Do-gooder**: The golf course study concluded that a golf course might prove profitable. I say let's go for it. The city could use the club house for many other social events.
> **Conservative**: There are major risks here. But risk isn't the issue. Even if the course eventually operates in the black, operating a golf course is not a legitimate city function.
> **Socialist**: I don't get you, why are you against generating more taxes. You're always so pessimistic. Golfers are typically rich white guys. We can use the profits to fund other city projects like a recreation center, women's center, senior citizens center, and feed the hungry center; just to name a few. Are

you against feeding the hungry? Okay, let's just contract an architect to lay out some designs, surely that wouldn't hurt.

Pink Conservative: I still don't like the idea of the city operating a golf course but we've gone this far so I guess looking at a few designs wouldn't hurt.

Scoundrel: *Thinking to himself.* Boy this is going to cost the taxpayers a lot of money, but having a golf course in town would save me from driving 25 miles to play in that crappy county course.

Final Vote: Four votes for an architect design; one vote against.

Phase 3

Do we need to go on any further? I think you get the point. In each phase there was no need for the members of the Government Class to press for the whole enchilada, because each phase was one step toward victory. The Government Class is good at keeping their eyes on the prize.

◆   ◆   ◆

When a city's leadership considers the development of a golf course, they need to carefully analyze the purported justifications. Golf courses are big business. When private enterprises build golf courses, you can bet it's to make a profit. When cities build golf courses it is more often based on emotion rather than a market need, leading to terrible mistakes because emotions are not foundations for making good business decisions for private or public purposes.

Most people don't know their local golf courses operate in the red because most people don't get to that depth of analysis when their city leadership claims their city is broke and taxes need to be raised to ensure the police cars have fuel. Some towns may hide their golf course financial data inside separate accounts, making it even harder to discern how much of the golf course is being subsidized.

City officials are smart enough to know that if they ask for new taxes to bail out the local municipal golf course, that most people wouldn't give them a mulligan (that's a little golf talk meaning they wouldn't get another chance to swing at the ball). Thus, demonstrating that city governments, like boards of education, can also play the old switcheroo by paying for nice-to-have programs by holding need-to-have programs as hostages.

Most town folks just want their elected officials to operate in good faith and assume they do. Once again making the mistake of assuming they have councils of government watching out for them, instead of realizing that the Government Class foxes are in the hen house.

Depending on whom you ask, Beavercreek's golf course is operating either in the red or black. At the time of this writing, it appears that the course is barely covering it operating costs, but the annual debt payment is still over $600,000. This amount of money may pay for one hour of New York City's operations, but for Beavercreek it represents a huge chunk of change. I think most officials believe that the chances of the golf course ever being able to pay off the debt under the current property based tax system is about the same as finding a Liberal rooting for a Bush victory in Iraq.

A cursory review of the golf courses in the local area (which includes Beavercreek Golf Course) revealed that all have had financial woes to one degree or another. Two reasons offered for these financial difficulties are that there are too many courses in the local area and that there are even more upscale courses available a short drive away.

The KBA PAC's position on the golf course was for the city to divest itself of the enterprise and follow the leads or Los Angeles, Detroit, New York City, Chicago, and San Francisco who have all moved toward some form of privatization of government-operated golf courses during the 1990s.

However, the loss of millions of property tax dollars for these cities in operating golf courses would have never occurred if the then responsible city councils would have understood a city government's core mission. Unfortunately, for the Government Class, the core mission is the whole apple pie, or for those cities in the southwest that have schools that recite the Mexican National Anthem, the whole enchilada.

In the mean time, in 2005 and 2006, the city put on the ballot a number of police and street levies. The PAC took these issues on and in most cases recommended a NO vote due to the lack of justification for the increased levy amounts (just for the record, we didn't always recommend NO, we did recommend YES on a number of levies). We knew that the golf course was siphoning away from these legitimate city services to pay for Government Class vanity, so we called for a divestiture before asking for more tax dollars for other services.

These levies either failed or were forced to be reduced (then passed) because taxpayers knew they were getting screwed. Screwed because money that should have been going to pay for legitimate police and street services were siphoned off to pay for the few, the proud, the golfers.

23

You Say To-ma-to,
I Say To-mot-to

March Hare: *Then you should say what you mean.*
Alice: *I do, at least—at least I mean what I say—that's the same thing, you know.*
Mad Hatter: *Not the same thing a bit! You might just as well say that "I see what I eat" is the same thing as "I eat what I see!"*

—Lewis Carroll, *Alice's Adventures in Wonderland*

Someone once said that you don't buy beer, you just rent it. One common trait that all members of the Government Class share is their uncontrolled tax thirst: but as in drinking beer, the Government Class eventually mostly just ends up flushing the taxes away. Sometimes the Government Class has to play games at quenching their thirst. One of the biggest tax games is the income tax scam.

Taxing income is a peculiar means of collecting government revenue. What makes it peculiar, as it was briefly mentioned in an earlier chapter, is that it is not the best way to collect needed operating revenue *if the main purpose is to collect operating revenue*. However, if controlling the economy, modifying people's behavior, spending money like drunken sailors, or getting kick backs, even if they're all legal, from special interest groups are your goals, then an income tax is the way to go. A few regulations here and there, coupled with a few targeted deductions, backed up by an office or agency that instills fear and leaves taxpayers with little recourse (pssst, that would be the IRS and its state and local equivalents) and you're on your way toward making people dance to your sheet of music. The Government Class has learned the lesson well.

It wouldn't be so bad if income taxes were not set up to be political footballs. But a benign income tax would inhibit the ability of the Government Class to not only raise the money they would like to raise, but also prevent them from controlling behavior through 50,000 pages of federal tax laws, and thousands more at the state and local levels. The key to getting public support for income taxes is to play a shell game with who is going to pay the taxes through class warfare, or pitting one group against another. In almost all cases, the Government Class uses income taxes to reward moochers and punish achievers.

As I mentioned in the background chapter on Beavercreek, the city charter requires a ballot in order to introduce an income tax. Since 1984, we have had four unsuccessful attempts at passing some type of income tax: two by direct voter rejection and the last two fizzled before making it to the ballot box. In fact, I had to make last minute changes to this chapter because in January 2007 city council voted 4 to 3 to not push the proposal along for voter consideration.

The council had no choice. According to news accounts, three of the council members, including the mayor and vice mayor, played footloose with the city charter regarding the ballot process. There were also some rumors that the city attorney may have provided legal advice at taxpayer expense to the private group pushing the tax proposal. Well at least four of the council members knew something was rotten in Beavercreek and did the right thing. But the tax proponents have vowed to fight on. If anything, the Government Class and its supporters are persistent little devils.

Income tax proponents have argued that Beavercreek is one of the largest cities in Ohio without an income tax, which directly limits the city's potential growth as well as its ability to manage basic operations. This is code for *Beavercreek is one of the largest cities in Ohio without an income tax, which directly limits the city's Government Class to spend more taxpayer money on questionable programs.*

I know to many all this whining makes me seem like a nutcase, but there is just too much historical data that shows that even good people in government have bad ideas, and bad law is awfully hard to retract. That is why it is important for taxpayers to insist on strict guidelines to accompany any tax legislation right up front. This is hard to do at the federal level, but it shouldn't be that much to ask at the local level.

Technically, the third and fourth attempts were for an earnings tax, not an income tax. An earnings tax essentially excludes retirement and investment related income (which remember is also money you earned but the government labels it as if you didn't). Guess what group of voters would be one of the biggest winners from an earnings tax? If you said senior citizens, you would be right. Guess what block of voters most often votes? If you said senior citizens, you would be right again.

What's unfortunate about all this is that the proposed tax, if properly executed, generally might be good for the city and its citizens, for a host of reasons too boring to include here, including specifics in State of Ohio laws regarding city income taxes. The city would get a windfall of new revenue, and in return, the proposal calls for some reduction in property taxes. But the proposal has no binding clauses on the promised property tax reductions or safeguards on how the money will be spent, except for some general non-binding spending statements. Just as important, there aren't any safeguards against abuse by city officials who may use the new tax department to harass taxpayers. All it would take is a letter to the editor that some city official doesn't like followed by an audit by the city. Or even worse, somebody who decides to write a book critical of his local government.

Members of the private committee that pushed the new proposal had publicly stated that where the money comes from is more central than how the money is spent. WOW! But the money always comes from a taxpayer somewhere, and how it is spent is important. So, earnings tax, income tax, to-ma-to, to-mat-to; if the money ain't spent right, its all for naught

For example, there are many in Beavercreek who would love to have a community recreation center. But would a recreation center become another load stone around the necks of taxpayers? I know I sound like a scrooge, but Beavercreek residents have access to many private and public recreational facilities in the city and in nearby communities.

In 2003 a person called the Dayton Daily News Speak Up section to complain about a failed Washington Township recreation center levy (the township is located a few miles south of Beavercreek). The caller asked if the owner of a string of fitness centers, who was very vocal in his opposition to the levy, would build a basketball court for his or her child since the levy failed.

The owner's response to the caller was published in a letter to the editor and goes to the heart America's moocher mentality. The owner in his response said: "Give me the millions of tax dollars the levy would have confiscated from us, and I will build a basketball court with solid gold backboards." He went on to say that we deserve good basic services from the government but: "Building and managing elegant health clubs is a perversion of the government that is done for the gratification of bureaucrats. So, the situation boils down to this, there are producers who supply goods and services to people, and there are government addicted moochers who want to steal from us to build things such as government health clubs. The moochers want to enrich themselves at taxpayers' expense."

The beauty of the full response is its sensuality. You can *feel* the author's frustration in trying to run a private business but having to compete not only against his normal business competitors, but also against taxpayer subsidized recreation centers. You can *hear* the anger in his voice as he expresses the fact that not only does he have to compete against the government, but he is taxed to support the competition. You can *see* the author's view on how community after community is going bankrupt due to violating their core missions. You can *taste* the bitterness in his disgust over the general moocher mentality. Finally, you can *smell* the putrid stench of the moocher who without remorse expects taxpayers to buy basketball courts for his/her budding NBA player.

An April 5, 2004, syndicated Associated Press article on the subject had this to say: "Municipal recreation centers can be favorites with hometown residents, but also can be taxing when the bill comes in. In northeast Ohio, there are more than 20 municipal recreation centers and almost none completely support themselves financially."

I believe taxpayers would express more of a conservative attitude to their government if every community had an active group capable of successfully taking on important issues and putting their governments to task. Unfortunately, this doesn't occur that often for a variety of reasons. One reason is many people make mistakes in organizing these groups. Another is fear of retribution from government officials as well as from moochers and other such neighbors. And another reason is that most people are too sane to spend their free time as the Skipper, Wilson and I, and later Thomas Paine, have been doing since the KBA PAC's inception. Because you can't rely on the local media propagandists, the end result is that communities only get to hear the Government Class's side of the issues.

There is also an aspect to radically changing a community's tax collection structure, such as passing a city earnings tax, far more subtle than whether or not a community ends up with a community center. Passage of new taxes without holding the city accountable would be a pivotal point in any city's history, because at stake is more than just a numbers game. Just as getting married or having children represents more than just a few more people under the same roof; poorly thought out taxes result in a life-style transformation of your city or state; just as the federal income tax drastically changed the national landscape.

With all due respect to Charles Dickens, whose *A Tale of Two Cities* involved the geographically separated cities of London and Paris, I would like to present *A(nother) Tale of Two Cities*, in this case the two cites are two views of any town USA separated in time by the passage or failure of a windfall tax. So let's hop in our Look-Ahead-Machine and see two views of what your city might look like years after passing some type of an unconstrained tax. First, we look at the city after a badly formulated earning tax passes.

Bombarded with threats that basic city services will suffer and being promised that retired pay and wages for those under 18 will be exempt and a moratorium will be placed on city-related property tax increases, city voters barely pass the earnings tax in 2008. Key to the passage was the promise that the new tax would take pressure off of property owners and thus also indirectly help the school district.

City Council immediately approves the hiring of dozens of city engineers who come up with a few initial essential projects but then realize that they would have to be more creative if they are to keep their jobs. After a few streets are fixed, some exit ramps built, and a bridge study or two completed, they go to task to build a city community center and a new city hall; both completed in 2011. These buildings make the school district's often criticized administration building look as modest as the little house on the prairie.

The traffic along the roads servicing the new community center and town hall required the roads to be widened in 2012 to accommodate the traffic. In 2013 several large retail giants inform the City that they would love to build more stores in the southern part of the city that could bring millions of dollars into the city coffers, but some zoning "issues" need to be taken care of, and by the way, the streets are rather "underdeveloped." The city engineers get to work making sure that they make the developers happy at taxpayer expense.

After years of effort, North Fairfax is now 5 lanes from the city's north to south boundaries; ditto for Big Valley Road north to south, and Temp Drive east to west. If it weren't for some obstructionist property owners trying to protect their property, Farmers Hall Road would have been completely widened by now, but all in due time and as soon as these property owners come to realize that they don't really own their properties but merely rent them at the pleasure of the government.

With the tax shot in the arm, the City aggressively courts industry to move to the city, offering them tax abatements and other taxpayer subsidized incentives. More condos and single family units are built where once there was green space. Where there were once pastures there are now huge parking lots servicing the city's multitude of Super-Duper Marts and accompanying strip malls. Some of the older strip malls are barely populated and are rapidly becoming run down. The city population has exploded.

In the battle between pasture and plaster, the plaster wins. Truthfully, did the pasture ever really have a chance? To politicians the green in the color of money always is more appealing than the green in the color of pastures.

With the influx of tax money and with no accountability strings attached, there was no need to smartly spend the funds. The separation of school and city planning continued and there was no attempt to integrate city planning with the school system. The influx of families has already made the extra middle and two elementary schools, built in 2012, too small to handle the load. The plans for the new High School were obsolete even before the blue prints dried. Property taxes needed to pay for the school system have skyrocketed.

Not wanting to be out done and to show it can be as uptown as other local communities, the city council creates a "City Historical Preservation Office" in 2015. With an initial staff of 10, this office has the responsibility to make sure any exterior modification to a home, including something as simply as the color of paint, is "officially" approved to ensure that the aesthetics of the community are not compromised. The cost to get the city to approve your paint color is $50 and takes 3 months. The office also ensures that any flags flown outside a home or building is in exact proportion in size to the home or building. This office is also responsible for investigating neighborhoods that might be "blighted" and need to be razed to make room for new buildings that will serve the public good: like for example more shopping centres.

Interior home modification approvals are left to the Department of Interior Construction and Improvements which provides the important service of watching out that any interior self-improvement project does not impact your safety and especially the safety of your children. The cost to get the city to approve any interior modification to your home is $75 and takes 6 months (city workers may have to enter your home in order to do their job).

The golf course is still being subsidized, but the good news for golfers is that now 36 holes are being subsidized by taxpayers. Overpriced modern (read "ugly") art lines the main streets. The new traffic load and the increase in traffic lights prevent you from making it from one side of the city to the other in less than an hour.

After the initial 10 year moratorium on property levies promised by politicians in order to get the income tax passed, the city begins pushing them again in 2018 to "save" essential police and street services for the "safety of our children and the elderly." By 2020 the income tax has doubled and wherever possible, exemptions have been eliminated. People who oppose these tax measures are labeled "selfish."

But it's not all that bad, city residents now have their garbage taken to the curb for them.

Now let's look at the city in 2020 after voters defeated three more attempts at unaccountable income taxes:

City residents still have to take their own garbage to the curb.

Oakwood, a nearby city, has some of the laws described above, as do many cities across the country. But the people in these towns tend to pick their noses with their ring fingers to make sure everyone sees the size of their diamonds. Another nearby community, Centerville, is at the time of this writing, considering government interior inspections of individual apartments, apparently not trusting landlords to manage their own properties. Of course today it's apartments, tomorrow it's your homes, and everyone reading this knows it. Examples such as these are numerous.

What allows governments to violate people's rights is access to revenue generated by excess taxes. Cut the taxes, limit governments to provide only legitimate services and you cut the abuse. But members of the Government Class go to great lengths to quench their tax thirst. When no income tax is available, then the only other option is full steam ahead on construction that will generate more revenue through increased property taxes.

In summer of 2006 phase I of the Greene opened in Beavercreek. The Greene is the up scale shopping centre I mentioned in the My Town chapter that resembles a small town shopping district. When the developer petitioned the city and county for approval, he asked for a long term 15% tax abatement. The county and city agreed. The board of education voted his request down for a lot of complicated reasons.

The potential city property taxes that would have been lost if the developer decided to go elsewhere was considerable. The City Council went ahead and sped the initiative through denying citizens the right to voice their concerns. They had to get their fix and couldn't wait around for democratic processes to work. When a group of citizens collected signatures to petition the city to put the abatement up for a public vote, the City invalidated the petitions based on technicalities such as font size and color!

Supporters of the Greene, including those on the city council, argued that the size and the upscale nature of the Greene justified their action. My position on all this was that as a land owner the developer had every right to build whatever he wanted to within the law, but it was not appropriate for the city or county to provide tax abatements, even if other communities did so. After all, if a private citizen was planning to build a $5,000,000 home and another citizen a $250,000 home, would the city agree to a similar deal regarding property taxes with the richer home owner? Why not just create a city ordinance to keep the low rent $250,000 home riffraff out of the city? Will the city now do this type of dealing with all future private retail or other developers? Will it be forced to because of this precedent? If not, why not? What criteria will it use to decide who gets the tax break?

The citizens group tried another petition, this time a recall petition for two of the council members that were not up for re-election that year. By this time the city populace was sick of the whole affair, and there wasn't enough interest to do a recall, so they fell short of the needed number.

The Greene developer didn't expect this kind of backlash. To patch things up with the community, when the Greene opened, the developer promised to contribute a portion of the collected revenues from the curb parking meters to local charities. The only problem was that although the buildings and possibly the sidewalks belonged to the developer, the streets in the Greene belonged to the city.

This would be equivalent to me putting up a parking meter at my curb to charge people who park in front of my house, then keeping some of the money for myself and giving some to charity. This is why rich people become rich. They're smart.

Personally, I think the developer was just trying to be a nice guy and a good businessman, but the forced taxpayer subsidized charity wasn't going to last. A guy who happened to get a Greene "parking ticket" took on the city council over the legality of the process. At the time of this writing, it appears that the council will reluctantly inform the Greene management that their charity parking tickets are a no-go.

Look, I know mistakes happen, but public money is public money. Our councils of government must always restrict entanglements that show favoritism, real or not. When councils of government try to play cutesy with public money, even legally, it almost always backfires.

◆   ◆   ◆

In 2006 I had the opportunity to meet with the city council. Actually, I was being interviewed for a council seat that opened up when a council member retired about 18 months before his term expired. (He had the opportunity to take an around-the-world sailing trip with three friends. After weighing the choice between 18 more months of hearing mind numbing zoning arguments at 9 PM on Monday nights, versus taking this once-in-a-lifetime trip, he chose the Ferdinand Magellan option. Many of us, I'm sure, would agree that he chose wisely.)

There was no love lost between the council and the KBA PAC, so I didn't expect to be selected, but I applied anyway. I figured the reason why I was called in to the interview was to allow council a chance to talk to a KBA PAC member, since our operating policy was not to normally talk to government officials.

When the topic of an income/earning tax came up, I told them that I would never support a tax if it was to be modeled after the previous versions. I offered my specific suggestions, which supported a tightly controlled earnings tax, various restrictions on spending, and dollar for dollar reductions in property taxes. There were other issues we discussed, but a week later I found out that I was not selected for the vacant seat.

The bottom line is that most people who enter government have no concept of its proper role. Most just see the public purse as a sandbox.

24

And all that Jazz

How can you be expected to govern a country that has 246 kinds of cheese?

—Charles de Gaulle

When the Skipper, Wilson, Thomas Paine and I agreed to form and operate the PAC, I don't think we had any idea about the breath of subject areas that we were signing up to tackle. If the PAC had focused its efforts on education, police, or some other single issue our work load would have been much lighter. Over the nearly four years of PAC operations, we had to become familiar with all of the local levy issues. Our workload was our own fault, since we made it part of our charter to look and comment on all local levy and other tax issues.

Besides Beavercreek City schools, police, streets, and parks, we soon found ourselves also taking on the Beavercreek Township's fire department levies and parks levies. And then there was the county.

Greene County, as I'm sure many other counties, seemed to have an endless menu of levy requests for taxpayers to consider. Levies for children services, the county hospital, parks and recreation, the library system, and so forth, in one form or another kept popping up. Some of these were a mixture of legitimate "for the common good" services and others were just well disguised welfare programs. A case in point is the county hospital which advertises itself a community hospital, but many of its services are clearly designed and restricted to welfare cases. Again, we can argue about the legitimacy of liberal welfare policies but at least be up front to taxpayers about paying for a service that they may not be eligible to receive.

From a practical point of view we had to pick and choose what issues to really tackle; remaining neutral on the others. Sometimes the issues were chosen for us by either the size of the levy request or the way the requesting agency went about asking for the money.

There were two things that distinguished the many other city and county organizations from the school district: (1) their relative budget sizes were small, and (2) they were not members of an industrial complex. Thus there wasn't the same general level of intensity during levy campaigns, or the same cultural infrastructure to call on for support when some organized group such as the KBA PAC decided to call them out on their tax levy. This was very evident in the governing bodies themselves. Whereas the board of education members seemed to work lockstep, the various other regional governing bodies tended to be more diverse in their political leanings, although there were still more members of the Government Class than not.

The one thing some of the other organizations did share with the Education Industrial Complex was relying on emotional arguments to justify their requests and to scare people, especially old folks, into voting yes on their levies. Put yourself in the position of an 80 year widower who is being told that unless the fire levy is passed, no one will be there to save you if your house caught on fire.

But isn't that statement true? That is, if the fire department doesn't get funding, there won't be anyone to save you if your house is on fire. Yes that statement is true, but it's also not the issue.

In earlier chapters I beat on the Government Class for expanding government but have never really discussed any criteria to help define *a legitimate government service*. Knowing whether or not a service is a legitimate government function makes deciding whether or not to fund it via a levy request a no-brainer. The only problem with that premise is that many people don't think in those terms, or are often parochial when it comes to certain issues, and thus the question becomes a relative one. After all, can the elderly be blamed for supporting those services that cater to their special needs regardless of any esoteric argument about whether a particular function falls under proper governmental roles and responsibilities?

In practice one can't capture the role of government, at this or that level, in a nifty simple definition or sound bite; although many have tried. One of my favorites is by William Pitt, 1708-1778, 1st Earl of Chatham. As part of a speech on the Excise Bill, the honorable Mr. Pitt said the following:

> The poorest man may in his cottage bid defiance to all the forces of the Crown. It may be frail—its roof may shake—the wind may blow through it—the storm may enter—the rain may enter—but the King of England cannot enter—all his force dares not cross the threshold of the ruined tenement!

What a great statement about property rights, and if you apply a broader definition to "property," it's a great statement about most, if not all, individual rights. I think one can make a very strong argument that all liberties and thus individual and social prosperity can only come after securing property rights. Only when a person is secure in his freedom to enjoy what he or she has worked for, can any society be successful. Yet, as we have discussed on a number of occasions, our suicidal drive to destroy "property" rights is no doubt causing Mr. Pitt to spin in his grave.

This also should be making every concerned American tremble in their homes, because going one step further, great and free societies can last only as long as there is respect for property rights; a lesson that would be taught in our government school history classes if it weren't for the fact that they are too busy bad-mouthing America. By the way, did you notice the time period the very British Mr. Pitt lived in?

However, I believe the founding fathers did a pretty good job at defining the federal role, even though subsequent generations have destroyed their vision. At the local level the philosophical approach has to be a little different because the duties of local governments are obviously different from their state or federal counterparts, and may even vary greatly between localities. In order to define those services we would almost need to write a generic local government constitution and equivalent *Localist Papers* corresponding to the *Federalist Papers*. All I can do here is relate the thought processes I used when evaluating local levies, leaving you to agree or disagree with them.

1. Clearly, a major requirement is that the function must truly (in a direct way) serve the common good. This seems like a very broad criterion but it must be stressed that a very strict interpretation of "common good" is being applied here. Funding golf courses and many art works does not meet this criterion, but funding parks, Police and Fire Departments does. Funding libraries and government schools may or may not meet this requirement, depending on a number of factors that have been discussed or will be discussed below.

2. A second major requirement is that the function cannot be adequately or practically addressed by the private sector. Examples are once again Police and Fire services. Again schools and libraries may or may not meet this requirement. In general, community recreational centers do not meet this criterion for most cities. Ditto for publicly funded hospitals. In fact, many publicly funded hospitals are often justified as a means to patch holes in our health care system; holes that were put there by government in the first place.

3. A third criterion is that the function must be put into historical perspective on its necessity and success as a governmental function as well as to its extent as a government function; in other words, a lessons learned approach is used before establishing a new governmental function and if created, strict guidelines are established and codified to limit its scope. This criterion lends support to some limited public funding of libraries and schools but in conjunction with criteria 1 and 2, the funding must be severely limited to meet those two criteria.

4. The last criterion is that the service is funded by the most general tax base possible, and where applicable, users must pay the bulk of the costs through user fees (again true poverty cases can be dealt with separately). That is, taxpayers are not forced to fund questionable services they do not benefit from, are prevented from using through some sort of arbitrary financial, racial, sexual, age, or any other discriminating factors, or finally a subset of taxpayers (like property owners) are not singularly burdened to fund the service.

I can hear the snickers from the Government Class. They know the reality is that governments do not adhere to the criteria above and taxpayers will always be forced to pay for illegitimate or questionable government services and no measly little political action committee will ever change that.

The KBA PAC knew that too. So instead of trying to change the foundations of our society from the get-go, we opted for a phase 1 approach with the limited goal of getting local agencies to run tight ships. To this end we came up with the following Voter Reference Guide (I modified it slightly to put it into proper context here).

KBA PAC Voter Reference Guide

The purpose of this Voter Reference Guide is to assist you, the voter, in determining whether approval of a proposed levy is warranted. The Guide asks questions that the KBA PAC feels a voter should consider when deciding to vote YES or NO on a levy. The KBA PAC is not implying that a government agency has to meet all criteria outlined below to receive a YES vote, only that the electorate should consider the criteria when deciding how to vote.

Question 1: Is the tax request limited to programs that are well defined, that clearly benefit the general public's welfare, and that are within the scope of the requesting government agency's core mission?

Often, levies are not justified but merely promoted without clearly defining how they directly benefit the community. Frequently this is the result of a government agency losing sight of its core mission. A tax request should be measured against an agency's core mission. The agency should provide a complete and understandable delineation between desirables and necessities.

Question 2: Does the tax requesting government agency have a readily available strategic plan outlining its core mission and goals, and does this agency work with elected officials in integrating its strategic plan with other local government agencies?

Government agencies often operate independently of each other, requesting tax increases with no clear concept of overall "community" impact. Government agencies working together helps eliminate duplication and waste.

Question 3: Has the tax requesting government agency published clear and definable goals and measurable criteria to allow taxpayers to evaluate its performance?

A government agency's performance needs to be quantifiable and readily available to the community. Generic claims made by any agency without data to support these claims should be rejected.

Question 4: Does the tax requesting government agency have a record of good financial stewardship and customer service?

Institutional "cultures" often transcend individuals currently holding key management positions within the government agency. Thus, past performance is often a good indication of future performance. Consider how you were treated as a customer when you have contacted the applicable agency for normal business purposes or assistance.

Question 5: Has the tax requesting government agency documented that all possible cost savings have been exhausted, including cutting unneeded or wasteful programs?

No agency should be given new or additional taxes unless they have completely reviewed all programs and make the necessary management decisions to cut unneeded or wasteful programs.

Question 6: Has the tax requesting government agency documented and made available to the community proof that it has sought and implemented efficient methods in carrying out its core mission?

No agency should be given new or additional taxes unless they have completely reviewed their processes and adopted improvements, including outsourcing where applicable and "best practice" benchmarking against like organizations.

Question 7: Has the tax requesting government agency clearly explained to the community the impact of its levy request in terms of any real increases to property taxes?

A levy may be marketed as a "renewal" even though you may be paying more because of property reappraisals that may have occurred since the original levy request was approved by the voters. Introduction of new taxes to spread the tax burden should be accompanied by a corresponding decrease in those taxes it supposedly replaces, or the additional taxes explained and fully justified by the tax requesting authority.

Question 8: Has the tax requesting government agency responsibly provided the community all the information it needs to determine its support for a levy proposal?

Government offices should treat taxpayers with respect, including satisfactorily answering all tax-related requests for clarification. All government agencies should also operate under full public disclosure within the limits of the law. Taxpayers should not have to hunt for tax justification. How a government office treats you when requesting expenditure clarification is a good indication of its respect for you as a taxpayer as well as its effective stewardship of your money.

Question 9: Has the tax requesting government agency provided a complete and understandable justification to the community without using scare tactics and emotional rhetoric.

Scare tactics and doomsday scenarios are an insult to the taxpayers. When specific program cuts are threatened, full justification for the choices, including a budgetary breakout and priorities, need to be provided.

How effective was this guide and other actions of the KBA PAC? I have no direct quantitative way of measuring that. In the spring of 2005 the Beavercreek Township Fire Department requested a levy that would have substantially increased their tax revenue. As typical of government agencies, there was no real justification for the request, except the typical arrogant approach that they deserve the money so shut up or when you find your house burning down you won't have anyone to call. What makes levies like this difficult is that Fire Departments are legitimate government agencies, but that doesn't mean all of their services are legit, or that they are running efficient operations.

On April 11, I e-mailed the fire chief and asked him about 7 specific questions regarding the levy request. The fire chief never responded to me or more importantly never bothered to provide the community a justification for the levy request. The KBA PAC addressed the Fire levy via e-mail and published letters and recommended a NO vote. Other citizens not necessarily KBA PAC supporters also criticized the request. The levy was defeated nearly 2 to 1.

Soon after the defeat, the fire chief wrote a short article in the local paper giving thanks to citizens for supporting their fire department and that although the levy was defeated, the community can expect to continue to receive the highest level of support from their fire department that can be provided. And, oh by the way, they will be coming back and asking for the money again.

In the mean time the fire chief carried through with his promise to cut personnel to save costs and laid off a couple of dozen fire fighters and emergency personnel. During this time, several fire fighters contacted the KBA PAC and for a time we were collaborating on a plan to force the chief to fully justify the levy request. We learned during this time that the rank and file was asking the chief to talk to us and answer our questions; his response was something to the effect that we were just a bunch of rectal openings, but those were not exactly the words he used.

In the follow-on November election, the Township reduced the fire levy request down about 25%. The PAC recommended a YES vote for the reduced levy and backed a newcomer running for Township Trustee with the justification that the real problems were with the incumbent Trustees that oversaw the fire chief and fire department operations, and new blood was needed to fix the serious management problems at the fire department. The levy passed, but our candidate lost.

◆   ◆   ◆

During the same time period as the fire levy, the county library system was seeking a small levy to restore services that had to be cut due to recent reductions in state income tax revenues. In one newspaper article a high school student, who I'll call Perky Susie, complained about her frustration over the reduced library hours. Because of the reduced hours Perky Susie had to sometimes skip after school activities and rush over to the library in order to finish her studies or research. Perky Susie said: "I think the library should be opened longer hours and on Sundays, even if you don't need to use the books. Some people like to come here to study or work on projects because home is not always as quiet."

So Perky Susie, who pays no taxes, wants property owners to pay for her convenience. You know what? I don't blame her. But what does that have to do with anything, except like in the school district case, we must pass the levy *for the children*. I don't know what Perky Susie wants to do professionally in her life, but she is getting a great lesson in the art of mooching.

The KBA PAC made a NEUTRAL recommendation on the library levy, and only mildly critiqued the request. But it didn't sit well with the library levy campaign leadership. The PAC received an e-mail from a library levy committee chair person that tried to take us to the woodshed. Most of the e-mail was normal levy propaganda but is a great example of when logic fails the argument always gets around to class warfare. The sender had to mention that one reason why we have libraries is to "... level the playing field between the *haves and have nots ...*" [emphasis mine].

One of my fondest memories of my childhood is going to the Miles Park Branch Library in Cleveland, Ohio. The Miles Park Library was located at Miles Park and East 93rd. It was built in the old world or Roman style of government buildings. It was a multi-floor structure made of stone or stone-like material with pillars in the front. Upon entering you had to choose between a small flight of stairs to the basement where rooms were available for special events or climbing a very wide set of wooden stairs that led to the main rotunda of the upstairs library. The stairs were dark and creaking with age (the library was built in 1906 and closed in 1987). When you entered the front door, you instinctively knew you were in a special place and needed to keep quiet just like church.

Upon entering the upstairs rotunda you came upon a circular checkout desk lit by a massive round overhead stained glass window. The main book rooms were off to the sides of the rotunda like stokes of a wheel. The library smelled like a library.

In 1962 and 1964 I joined the Summer Reading Club. Here are the books I read those two summers.

1962
I want to be a baseball player
At the airport
At the post office
Firemen
Always Ready

Danny and the dinosaur
Yertle the Turtle
No fighting, no biting
Sam the firefly
Mike Mulligan

1964
Molecules and atoms
A pony called Lighting
Stone Soup
Six-legged neighbors
Gus was a friendly Ghost
White buffalo and Tah-tank-ka
Lion
Magnets
What is an insect?
What is space?

The reason why I know this list is because I still have my Summer Reading Club Certificates of Completion complete with American Flag ribbons attached. (I can now disclose the fact that I read books called *Gus was a Friendly Ghost* and *Yertle the Turtle* because I have no issues with my manhood—okay some, but not major ones. However, reading books on molecules, atoms, magnets, insects and space has geek written all over it.)

The point of all this is that libraries do have a legitimate role in a free society and libraries do serve the common good. But given that like many other government services, only a limited number of taxpayers pay for those services, libraries must respect the fact that they have a limited mission. And catering to the whims of users that are not necessarily payers, like ensuring Perky Susie can continue to shake her pom-poms after school and not have to worry about getting to the library on time to do research for her Oceanography paper, *Gentle Giants: A look at the life of Florida Manatees*, or providing copies of film art classics like Rocky V does not necessarily fit that mission.

There is one more issue with libraries that they and taxpayers must address. With the rise of the internet and with all of human knowledge accessible literally at your fingertips, what is the future role of public libraries in the 21st century beyond the current transition period? Aren't society's information needs rapidly being met by private enterprises in a way and method far more efficient than public libraries?

Even though we may all have fond memories of our childhood libraries, most of us, and in the near future all of us, will have access to all of mankind's knowledge with a few clicks of a mouse. That includes everything from Yertle the Turtle to Einstein's General Theory of Relativity.

I can think of several services that libraries can still provide even in an internet world, but let's see if this government agency will adapt or flounder. (Of course a cynic would argue that as a government agency they don't have to adapt.)

My fear is that governments will try to control the internet; unfortunately that fear is beginning to be realized. As we speak the U.N. is considering getting a foothold in global internet control through attempts to enact a United Nations Working Group on Internet Governance, which is a euphemism for the United Nations Working Group on Information Control. Guess who one of the biggest backers of this effort is? Yup, our enlightened friends of the European Union: you know, the ones that Liberals would love for America to emulate.

PART V
United States of Flatland

Now patient reader, it is time to look into the future, but alas, sometimes the future is better left unseen.

25

My Genes Made Me Do It!

The devil made me do it!

—Flip Wilson as Geraldine

The comedian Flip Wilson often played a character named Geraldine who sought forgiveness for her questionable behavior by saying "The devil made me do it." Blaming the devil, or evil spirits in general, has been a common ploy people have used since the dawn of time for avoiding or taking the blame for lapses in personal judgment, to explain strange or undesirable behavior in others, or as a catch-all to explain the unexplainable.

As science progressed we have slowly pushed the devil aside and substituted both legitimate and dubious theories to explain or justify unique, misunderstood, or undesirable behaviors. Psychosocial-babblers do this very well, especially creating questionable excuses like Intermittent Explosive Disorder discussed earlier.

Think of the application of these excuses in a court of law. Someone gets mad in a traffic situation and decides to cut someone off resulting in a traffic accident and even possibly death. In court his Legal Unprofessional argues his client had Intermittent Explosive Disorder and even calls in a Psychosocial-babbler to testify. The person is not the master of his domain, but rather just an unfortunate soul who was a victim of a temporary emotional disorder. Of course excuses such as this are being used every day in our courts, often with the results of excusing bad and even evil behavior. In many cases juries have little or no options but to consider the bad science in their deliberations.

Advancements in genetics add a new wrinkle to the mix, and it is becoming customary to *excuse* or *justify*, as the case may be, selected problems or behaviors, on "your genes." The idea being that if the cause of an effect is genetic, then the effect has to be permissible or the punishment greatly reduced. Are we in danger of simply replacing the devil with the double helix?

Basically the argument that many would like to use to justify their behavior can summed up as follows: Given a particular behavioral trait X,

If X is genetic, then X is not a choice.
If X is not a choice, then X must be accepted by society

Because I'm trying to solve the problems of the world in a few hundred pages, for the sake of brevity we need to use some common sense and look at the big picture. By "accepted by society" I mean in macroscopic *legal or societal* terms, which implies that society has agreed to modify how it accepts X or overlook the proportional direct and indirect costs or consequences, if any, of accommodating X. Of course this means that some individuals or groups may not readily accept the outcome in some controversial cases. There is no simple solution for this conflict, and the argument needs to be looked at issue by issue, but in general this goes back to compromises we make in order to live in a free society. (Understanding the intent of this chapter requires understanding what I just said in this paragraph.)

But the two line argument above is too simplistic. Any behavior, whether genetic or not, must be measured by its impact to others or society in general. What is missing from the argument is a conditional statement covering the extent that the particular behavior impacts or harms others. One way we can modify the argument is thusly:

If X is genetic, then X is not a choice.
But whether X is or is not a choice, we must still determine X's impact
If X does not negatively impact others, then X must be accepted by society

The second argument gets to the core of the struggle between individual liberties and societal responsibilities. Keep in mind that "does not negatively impact others" could mean many things, but for our purposes here is more than just ruffled feathers. The impact we are talking about includes bodily harm, damage or loss of property, or other more direct and indirect costs or potentially major consequences that may not be immediately apparent. Our approach to this issue can't be formulated lightly, because the answer has profound moral, legal, and practical consequences.

This topic is so important that the U.S. Department of Energy's Human Genome Program specifically addresses ethical, legal, and social issues pertaining to its genetic research programs. As stated on the website:

> What social consequences would genetic diagnoses of such traits as intelligence, criminality, or homosexuality have on society? What effect would the discovery of a behavioral trait associated with increased criminal activity have on our legal system? If we find a "gay gene," will it mean greater or lesser tolerance? Will it lead to proposals that those affected by the "disorder" should undergo treatment to be "cured" and that measures should be taken to prevent the birth of other individuals so afflicted?

How do these arguments apply to a trait such as overeating and the physical condition of obesity? When does overeating transition from a mostly genetic condition to a mostly behavioral issue controlled by personal choices? Are people fat because "their genes made them do it?" The short answer for some (many?) is probably yes to some degree or another. But if this is true, then why fight it? Keep in mind the fat course at the University of Wisconsin spoken about earlier.

Is there a type of obesity that may have appeared in the butt and thighs of every female member of your family since great great grandma Betty, but is controllable through behavior modification such as dieting and exercising? Or another type that may also be traced genetically, but is recognized as an extreme, mostly uncontrollable, medical condition.

To what extent must society accept obesity in its various forms, including the case of people who are exercising their rights to just overeat, and what are society's obligations toward an obese person's civil rights regarding their obesity? Do obese people have any responsibility toward their obesity, or only if they wish to? What "reasonable accommodations" must be given to obese people and what inherent costs must society absorb? Do these costs include just the hidden price of increased health care or also special double seats on airplanes at no additional charge? Can you legally charge obese people for two airline seats if it is determined that obesity is a protected condition of birth? These are important questions that have become applicable because of how our legal system has evolved.

I picked obesity as an example because I would think (and I'm not expert) that it is a relatively sound candidate for supporting some sort of linkage between genes and behavior, more so than other more complex behaviors such as many criminal activities. And there are of course various "cures" for obesity with varying degrees of success.

What about criminal behavior? If you argue that criminal behavior is not genetic, you would be overlooking the fact that brains are physical objects and currently unknown genetically induced development might be the cause of certain types of criminal activity such as pathological homicidal behavior. But should we accept homicidal behavior if science could prove that the behavior is at least partially due to brain physiology which in turn could be shown to be genetically based? Of course not since it definitely negatively impacts others!

We use many descriptors in defining who we are including, heritage, race, sex, education, religion, and even silly ones like favorite sport teams. But before we as individuals knew anything about religion or sports all we had were our genes.

There are arguments within distinct groups such as people with autism, that the condition defines who they are and any attempt to treat it medically is unethical. There have even been reports in the news on how some parents with disabilities have refused treatment for their children with similar disabilities and are very upset over even approaching the subject of genetically preventing blindness or deafness. For many people this is hard to understand. But for the affected folks the condition defines who they are. One Wyoming deaf mother in 2002 fought the state over placing implants in her deaf sons. Here is what she said: "But I want them to grow up with a strong self-esteem, not trying to be something they are not. I want them part of the deaf culture."

What would happen if we were able to identify "blindness genes" and had the ability to correct the condition in the developing infant, but the parents insisted that blindness defines who they are and they wish their children to be left alone? Is this abuse?

Another controversial example is sexual orientation. Many proponents of homosexuality argue that sexual orientation is a condition of genetics and often use the first argument form as support for the societal normalization of homosexual behavior. (I recognize there is a distinction between orientation and behavior.)

The problem is that at our current state of knowledge, the linkage between genetics and complex behavior patterns such as sexual orientation has not been established in regards to all other potential variables. As also stated on the Human Genome website [emphasis mine]:

> There are several scientific obstacles to correlating genotype (an individual's genetic endowment) and behavior. One problem is in defining a specific endpoint that characterizes a condition, be it schizophrenia or intelligence. Another problem is in identifying and excluding other possible causes of the condition, thereby permitting a determination of the significance of a sup-

posed correlation. Much current research on genes and behavior also engenders very strong feelings because of the potential social and political consequences of accepting these supposed truths. *Thus, more than any other aspect of genetics, discoveries in behavioral genetics should not be viewed as irrefutable until there has been substantial scientific corroboration.*

This is a very important statement because it says that we just don't know enough to support general statements that link genes and behavior aside from some limited known cases. Some of us may wish a linkage to be true, but that doesn't make it true. But this doesn't rule out logical or legal arguments to allow or disallow these same behaviors: it just eliminates the genetic argument as support—at least for the time being. In a sense, using the genetic argument as a justification for most complex behaviors considering our current state of knowledge is at a minimum disingenuous. *Thus whether genetic or not, behaviors still must be measured against their impact to society.*

Although acceptance of varying degrees of homosexual behavior has waxed and waned throughout history, it has been generally considered unacceptable in most cultures for some time. Why? Before answering that, we have to also acknowledge that acceptance of various heterosexual behaviors has also waxed and waned over time. Why? You will see why I ask this question in a few paragraphs.

Opponents of more liberal attitudes on sex generally cite religious reasons as well as potential impacts to the male-female pair bond and ultimately to the institution of the traditional family, including marriage, because these are seen as the foundations of an orderly society. In other words, promiscuous sexuality in any form leads to a breakdown of society. Proponents of more openness such as acceptance of homosexual behavior, premarital sex, etc., are left to prove why the behavior in question is not harmful to society, although more often than not, it just happens.

One fall back position is that what consenting adults do in the privacy of their homes is no business of others, including the law, because those actions do not negatively impact others. Even if some Busy-bodies think that those private actions do negatively impact others, one can make strong legal arguments that trump even the second argument form because any proof they may provide at best can only be anecdotal or extremely weak. Which again is the cost of living in a free society.

I have no problem with the "consenting adults—privacy of their homes" argument, and I believe most people would agree. But once you step outside the private, your actions become part of the public, and societies have always reserved the right to define permissible public behavior within some general cultural framework. Sometimes this is an easy task; other times it is not.

It is in the public domain where issues such as sexual behavior really become controversial. And just when you think you heard it all comes a February 27, 2007, news story from Germany of a brother and sister (raised apart) who have four children together that are calling for the country's incest laws to be abolished so that they can continue their sexual relationship. Two of their children have some sort of disabilities but reasons for the disabilities are unknown. They want Germany to follow the example of countries such as *France, Belgium and the Netherlands where incest is no longer punishable.* Is our privacy statement all inclusive so that *any* two or more adults have the right to private sexual association, even siblings? And let's not forget that even the inbreeding problem might be fixable in the future. I don't know about you, but this discussion is getting creepy.

Nearly all forms of heterosexual behavior have increasingly become public, so why are we surprised when homosexuals want the same privileges? The problem is not that homosexuals exist or what they do in the bedroom, but rather society's blatant disregard for proper *public* sexual conduct. In the true story *MIG Pilot: The Final Escape of Lt. Belenko*, by John Barren, the Soviet defector Lt. Belenko describes his first experience viewing western porn as like watching people go to the bathroom. We let Elvis wiggle his hips, but we didn't know where to stop. I'm not a prude, but hopefully you get my point: too much of a good thing is a bad thing.

Issues like Gay marriage raise these discussions another notch. In America, any number of people can enter into a wide range of contracts without regard to race, creed, sex, sexual orientation etc., but by definition only one man and one woman can enter a marriage contract.

In my opinion Gay marriage proponents who argue that their rights are violated under the Equal Protection Clause are wrong for three reasons: (1) the Equal Protection Clause once again is being used outside of its original intent; (2) marriage is defined as between a man and a woman, not between one heterosexual man and one heterosexual woman and thus there is no discrimination; and (3) there is no constitutional right to marry. Adding that the ban on homosexual marriage is similar to the ban on mixed race marriages is also invalid since marriage was never defined as being restricted to a man and woman of the same race.

Will Gay marriage destroy the institution? Before you answer that, think about the current state of marriage today and who is responsible for its condition. Marriage as an institution has already been greatly weakened by the bimbos and himbos of Hollywood, along with every other middle class American that has taken his or her vows *lightly* and *often* (everybody makes a mistake once in a while, and sometimes divorce is the only effective answer). The institution, and thus society, has also been weakened by those that have determined that marriage is sooooo 19th century, but decide to play house anyway. It is important to note that all of these behaviors have been heterosexual in nature.

Gay marriage will not damage the institution in those respects. Instead, Gay marriage will redefine what it is.

Before we go on, here's a homework assignment for you. Take a few minutes and seriously try to write down a definition of marriage. After you're finished, put the paper down, think about what you wrote then go back a while later.

How did you do? Did you consider all possible variables? Did you include items that weren't necessary? Are you happy with the definition? Is it spiritual or dictionary-like? Did you include mushy stuff like love? How about kids? Did you consider the institution's historic relationship and role in society? Based on your definition, can society exist without marriage, or better yet, what type of society is needed if marriage is done away with? Who will be the nanny? Is your definition based on a classical pre-modern model, or does it take into consideration modern realities such as wide-spread divorce? What's the difference between your definition and just a legal contract? If you defined it as between one man and one woman, is your definition logically consistent if you changed it to read between any two or more people?

The exercise above was meant to get you really thinking about what marriage is versus just saying the word as many of us do discussing this topic. When many of us define marriage we do so only considering the relationship between the man and woman and we may throw in children for good measure. But the key to defining marriage is including its relationship and function to society. If we did away with the basic father/mother family unit as the primary institution for the rearing of children and for the caring of family and extended family members, then the alternative is a large socialist state. If this were not the case, would we be having this discussion at all?

Defining marriage between a man and a woman has a historic sociobiological basis with near universal application, even if in individual cases couples cannot, or elect not to, exercise certain presumed clauses of the contract, i.e., have and raise children or stay together until death do they part. Families may indeed take on many forms, but it must be recognized that the optimal family unit is the married father-mother with biological children.

Defining marriage between any two persons is arbitrary. As an arbitrary definition it will not, and should not, be allowed to stand under legal scrutiny. Why not three or more persons? Why not between a man and his dog? Why not between siblings? If marriage cannot be defined, then it cannot be defended.

◆   ◆   ◆

If a behavior is "genetic" then you would be able to tag some group of carbon, nitrogen, oxygen and other elements in some predefined arrangement to give rise to some desired macroscopic *deterministic* behavior pattern. I believe in certain cases we will find this to be true. However, if this were true to the extent implied then parents could one day redesign their children's genes, which even concerns homosexual advocates because parents can then change the sexual orientation of their children. But doesn't this in turn raise a whole bunch of interesting questions like if a fetus does not have a right to life, why should a fetus have a right to a natural prearranged set of genes?

Our judiciary system is already creating too many arbitrary laws from the bench based on situational justice and this process is undermining our legal and social systems. Here's a story from the same Human Genome website of how the general population gets bad science news and how it may affect legal and policy decisions:

> For example, a study published in 1999 claimed that overexpression of a particular gene in mice led to enhanced learning capacity. The popular press referred to this gene as "the learning gene" or the "smart gene." What the press didn't mention was that the learning enhancements observed in this study were short-term, lasting only a few hours to a few days in some cases.

> Dubbing a gene as a "smart gene" gives the public a false impression of how much scientists really know about the genetics of a complex trait like intelligence. Once news of the "smart gene" reaches the public, suddenly there is talk about designer babies and the potential of genetically engineering embryos to have intelligence and other desirable traits, when in reality the path from genes to proteins to development of a particular trait is still a mystery.

In terms of genetics, how we approach determining the behavior/gene linkage is extremely important not just in sexual orientation issues, but how we legality approach the whole nature versus nurture argument across all facets of society, including the concept of free will and personal responsibility. Let's also take note that justifying behaviors on genetics is a double edge sword for society. It was only a generation ago that we linked intelligence, laziness, trustworthiness and other traits and behaviors on race or heritage.

But talking about personal responsibility is not necessarily all about genes. Recently, some citizens testified before congress on how it was their credit card company's fault for their overspending because the contract was too complicated or even using the excuse that the fonts were too small to read. Could they be right about the contract? Sure, but where is the rule of thumb that says don't spend more than you can afford or pay back? *Its not that this is the first time people have made excuses for bad behavior. The problem is that our government is legitimizing the excuses for bad behavior across the whole spectrum of society.*

The Government Class is always willing to seize on any scrapes of information to justify making new laws. But the law must be based on time tested science, not on whims or personal desires. We must approach the genetics/behavior issue very cautiously. *If we haphazardly replace "The devil made me do it," with "My genes made me do it," or even "The credit card companies made me do it," then we are destroying the entire concept of personal responsibility and opening up a portal into legal, social, and moral quagmires that I don't think we can survive.*

That is probably the most important message in this book!

26

War, What is it good for?

Well, for starters, it kills your enemy before your enemy kills you.

—Me

I mentioned earlier that I thought the culture war is pretty much over. I believe what we are seeing now in the few sporadic conservative victories are remnants of the remaining conservative units that either haven't gotten the message or will die before surrendering. It's worth spending a few pages on why I think this is so.

There are a set of rules that military officers are taught called the Principles of War. The set of principles are a culmination of thousands of years of studying warfare going way back to *The Art of War* by Sun Tzu (c. 544–496 BC). But in their modern form are often attributed to Carl Philip Gottfried von Clausewitz (1780-1831), a Prussian soldier and military historian who wrote *On War*, a sort-of updated detailed version of Sun Tzu's work. The number of principles varies depending on country and author, but generally the modern list includes 9-10 rules (Sun Tzu's book had 13 chapters each covering a military tactic).

You can do your own research if you want to know more about them, but let me condense them down to the following three more fundamental principles, which the experts at the Pentagon may or may not agree with:

1. Kill as many of the enemy as you need to, but no more than you have to.

2. Destroy the enemy's ability to wage war.

3. Occupy your enemy's territory with sufficient boots on the ground to send a clear message on who won and who lost.

You can also apply the three principles above to a culture war by making a few appropriate changes in words. What is remarkable is that for a political ideology that is synonymous with peace and love, the Left has learned and applied the three principles very well.

The Left's ability to redefine word meanings and engage in emotional arguments is legendary. An example is the term "illegal alien." If you look up those two words you will find the phase is entirely accurate in describing people who enter a country unlawfully. Yet the Left pushes the term "undocumented workers" and demonstrators hold up signs with the phrase "No human is illegal." Try arguing immigration policy with a Liberal and soon you will find yourself spending most of the time defending yourself against the charge of xenophobia, including possibly explaining to your HR department why you shouldn't be written up for insensitivity or even hate speech. Another example that may or may not take hold is from the environmental movement, where an attempt is being made to equate global warming deniers with Holocaust deniers.

These tactics are used across all political issues and in some cases individuals have lost their jobs and reputations for no reason other than voicing their political opinions—some benign and some stupid—but political opinions nevertheless. Although there are conservative talking heads on TV and radio, from the water cooler, to the classroom, to the streets, the Left has left the Right speechless.

If you want proof of how well the Left conducts strategic warfare look at the two issues of abortion and Gay marriage. The former was fought and won at the federal level because the Left knew that statehouse-to-statehouse fighting would be disastrous. On the other hand, the Left knows that Gay marriage is dead at the federal level, which is why they are fighting the issue at the state level, choosing the first states very carefully hoping that once a few victories occur, people will become desensitized and the other states will either fall in line or the federal government will eventually be forced to act in support of the initiative.

If you want one more example of the Left's superb strategic thinking capability, watch the arguments over the coming years over enforcing "fairness" in media, which is liberal-speak for destroying talk radio. In this regard I have to give credit to Neal Boortz for calling this one. Boortz claims he financially contributed to the liberal radio station *Air America* because he wanted it to be successful. His reasoning was that he knew that if it went belly up, and it did, the Democrats would begin to go after talk radio which is predominately conservative. In January 2007, permanent presidential candidate Dennis Kucinich (D-OH), announced he will chair a new committee to look into "media reform."

The government looking into media reform? Hmmm, nothing good can come from that. As Yul Brynner said in *The Ten Commandments*, "So it shall be written, so it shall be done!" But let's remember that if this plan works, it was because the Democrats won in 2006, and they won in 2006 because Republicans screwed up the conduct of the Iraq War as well as on a host of domestic issues.

On the other hand, Conservatives have no team strategy to put the country right (ahem). The only issue that Conservatives sometimes use effectively is questioning the Left's patriotism, and even then we tend to back down when confronted with "How dare you question my patriotism?"

For the most part the conservative plan is just to conduct skirmishes when applicable. A big reason for this is what I mentioned earlier on the differences in how Conservatives and Liberals view government activism. But that excuse lets Conservatives too easily off the hook. One of the biggest reasons for this organizational failure is that *there is no Conservative political party in America willing to define the proper limited role of government and work toward that end.* Remember what I offered earlier as the motto for the Republican Party: "Republicans, we're a lot like Democrats, but just not as committed."

◆   ◆   ◆

The reach of the Left's cultural and political victories is also seen over how we conduct real war; the kind that kills people and destroys things. Here we need to be more careful and split the Left into the loony Left and the misinformed Left. The difference between the two factions are that the loony Left will never allow America to defend itself, whereas the misinformed Left puts so many restrictions on our war fighting actions that the outcome basically, intentional or not, greatly increases the chances of an American defeat and thus becomes a self-fulfilling prophesy.

These restrictions manifest themselves in how they influence presidents to fight wars tactically and strategically. To be clear, you can think of tactical objectives as taking out an enemy squad or maybe a fort. In general, strategic targets tend to be associated with the second condensed rule above, i.e., destroying the enemy's ability to wage war. For World War II movie buffs, that would include B-17 bombing missions to destroy German ball bearing factories.

When America now enters a war it does so without the second condensed rule, because destroying your enemy's ability to wage war means everything from using propaganda, enforcing naval blockades, shutting down borders, destroying communication and transportation infrastructures, and might possibly even include killing *legitimate* civilians and civilian targets. (It's important to note that the definition of what constitutes legitimate civilians or civilian targets has changed since World War II.) But let's assume for the moment that the direct killing of civilians should be avoided even when special situations warrant otherwise. Since using propaganda means lying, and naval blockades and destroying infrastructures always leads to civilian suffering and possibly civilian deaths, these tools are also off limits. And many on the Left chomp at the bit waiting for each and every American mistake. You can't win a war this way. You might as well not even try.

We have forgotten as a nation that evil exists in the world, and our leaders are almost ashamed to acknowledge that evil exists. In effect, we can no longer bring the war home to the enemy, nor allowed to kill civilians that are producing the weapons used to kill our soldiers or used to kill us as we go to work, go to school, or shop for groceries. Remember, those German ball bearing factories weren't manned by the SS, they were manned by regular guys and gals who had little girls with cute braided hair and little boys sporting lederhosen waiting for them at home.

In Iraq, the early phases of the war were seemingly handled according to text book. We attacked both the enemy military and civilian leadership by bringing the war to them. But we fell back to making the common modern warfare mistake of restricting our operations and our targets and constraining our troops. We made legitimate targets off limits, stood by as warlords grew in power, and allowed Iran and Syria to help equip and build-up the insurgency, while domestic opposition at home mounted. In early 2007, the Bush administration seemed to start allowing some limited attacks on Iranian and warlord operations in Iraq along with stronger border security. This is after nearly 4 years of ignoring the principles of war.

Another major failure of the Bush administration was mostly relying on justifying the war based on weapons of mass destruction (WMD). I think WMDs did exist, and maybe the administration stressed WMDs because the concept is tangible and thus an easier sell. However, the real justification for the war was the strategic goal of beginning the long arduous transformation of the Middle East into a democratic region—Iraq possibly being recognized as the soft underbelly and the easiest to justify. Although that concept was a harder sell, it should have been made more forcefully.

Another reason for our involvement in the Middle East is oil. Yes oil. It's not a dirty word. And preserving a supply of oil is in the strategic interests of the United States. No less than a village fighting for water if they lived downstream from their enemies who built a dam, used it as a weapon, and refused to discuss equitable water rights. It's too bad that our leaders are too ashamed to admit that oil is a legitimate national interest and too incompetent to implement programs using national resources to satisfy our energy requirements such as off shore drilling, alternate fuels, and wind, solar, and nuclear power. Wasn't that the reason for creating the Department of Energy?

The attacks on 9/11 were aimed at the American strategic targets: financial (Twin Towers), governing (White House/Capitol Building), and war planning (Pentagon). Except for a few at the pentagon, the people who died on 9/11 were civilians that the enemy saw as legitimate strategic targets. The cost in dollars and time to our infrastructures because of past and potential terrorist acts is tremendous; for example just ask the airline industry. So America's enemies understand and apply this principle and by using these tactics, including propaganda, the enemy has brought the war home to us. In the mean time, we pretend we can still win a war without bringing the war home to them. Even discussing this topic raises eyebrows because it is associated with "collateral damages." But how many truly innocent civilians have died in Iraq and died in Vietnam because we didn't bring those wars to a quick and decisive close?

So let me end this with the fact that in order to defeat your enemy you have to bring the war to their home turf, but presidents who now decide to conduct a war do so hoping that mostly using rule 1 and maybe a little of rule 3 will suffice to bring about victory. But by using that method you won't be able to defeat an enemy that is willing to exist on a daily ration of one bowl of rice, a clip of bullets, and a pound of explosives. It didn't work in Vietnam and it looks like it's not working in Iraq. But I hope I'm wrong about Iraq.

On January 31, 2007, President Bush gave a speech that included the topic of high executive compensation in the private sector, thereby delving into areas he has no official business in. If President Bush was publicly asked his views about excessive executive salaries, here's what he should have answered: "This is a matter for the free market to resolve. In the mean time, if you would excuse me, I have taxes to lower, a government to shrink, borders to protect, and a war to win."

The fact that the Iraq war drags on with mounting losses, along with the Bush administration's inability to properly communicate to the American people what the cost of losing would mean to America, emboldened the Left to victory in 2006 and ensured another wave of Liberal policies that will affect America for years to come. That's another lesson from Vietnam we failed to learn. And once a liberal law is in place....

In terms of understanding and executing cultural and political wars, the peaceniks on the Left have carried out their war plans brilliantly.

27

Death by a 1000 Boots

Lingchi is a form of execution used in China before being outlawed in 1905. Although there are historical inconsistencies in how the executions took place, some accounts describe the executions as consisting of cuts to the arms, legs, and chest, followed by decapitation or a stab to the heart. In the West the method came to be known as death by a thousand cuts.

—Wikipedia.com

Thomas Friedman is a New York Times columnist who wrote the 2005 best seller *The World is Flat*. Now, some of you that may have been fortunate enough to graduate from a government school that actually taught you the world was round may be confused right now: it is indeed round, so don't panic. And for those of you that are looking for every chance to beat up the New York Times, hold your horses on this one, even a New York Times columnist knows the world is actually round.

Friedman's basic conjuncture is that the new era of globalization and competition made possible by advancements in technology and accompanying social change has flattened the international competitive playing field. Certainly some part of Friedman's thesis must be correct; after all, when someone in the furthest reaches of Siberia can call his cousin in Iowa via a cell phone, something must be going on.

The old global play book relied on the classical model that a handful of super-powers such as Egypt, Persia, Greece, Rome, Spain, France, England, Soviet Union, or America, controlled the ball at any one time. If the world is going flat, a new playbook is needed to deal with competition from countries that never were or could ever be in the same league as the big guns.

Upon reading Friedman's book, I was reminded of a wonderful little book written in 1884 by Edwin A. Abbott called *Flatland: A Romance of Many Dimensions*. On the surface the only thing the two books have in common is the word "flat" in their titles. Whereas Friedman's book speaks figuratively of a flattened competitive world, Abbott's book deals with a flattened geometric world. A world where the two dimensional creatures take the shapes of lines (women), triangles (lower class serfs), polygons (men; the more sides the higher the social order), and the perfect shape, the circle, is reserved for priests (ha ha).

Abbott was a Shakespearean scholar that dabbled in mathematics. The worlds he created have been studied for both their satire of Victorian England, but also by mathematicians and scientists interested in understanding higher dimensional analysis, a subject critical in many areas of modern mathematics and physics.

Abbott uses a square as the main narrator with the name A. Square. Square takes the reader in a guided tour of his two dimensional world explaining everything from the physical designs of buildings to political and social structures. We learn that Square in a dream once tried to explain to the king of the creatures that lived in the one dimensional world, Lineland, what life was like in two dimensions. Of course the King of Lineland could not conceive of any dimension more than one. Since the king existed only at one point in his line kingdom, he only knew of left and right (or front and back) and could never directly interact with anyone or anything except the two points immediately next to him, which holds for all of his subjects in his kingdom. Interactions were transmitted from one point to another along the line.

Square viewed these creatures as fairly ignorant. Then one day a three dimensional sphere stopped by and tried to explain to our narrator his three dimensional world. Square heard the Sphere's voice but could not see the Sphere because the Sphere existed "above" his world. Think of Flatland as a sheet of paper. Square lived on the surface of the paper, but the sphere lived "above" the paper. As the King of Lineland couldn't conceive of a two dimensional world, our Mr. Square couldn't conceive of our three dimensional world. Mr. Square knew of left and right, and what he considered "up and down," but could not conceive of that dimension that we see as sticking out of the plane of the paper.

People too often have myopic visions of the times that they live in. As the world is going flat, America is being attacked by friends and foes alike. Our foes wish to defeat us; our "friends" claim it's nothing personal, just business. All the while, we are experiencing tremendous and uncontrolled migrations of people, cultures, and economies unparalleled in history that is fundamentally changing the global and American landscapes; yet most Americans do not see or refuse to see what is happening in an historic perspective, i.e., from "above" the paper.

Do you remember those maps you may have seen in history classes that depicted mass movements of tribes, populations, or barbarian armies from one area to another? The Goths, Vandals, Visigoths, Huns, Mongols, Jutes, Angles, Saxons, Normans, Reconquistas, Moors, Vikings and so on. These clashs of civilizations are often depicted as causing the end of a particular dynasty or empire. But often the subsequent conquests were not so much the result of the overwhelming superiority of the conquerors, but more often than not, the conquests could be attributed to the internal weaknesses of the conquered, just as the fall of Rome is often attributed to corruption, orgies, even lead pipes; take your pick. Like a pack of hyenas eyeing a wounded gazette waiting for the right time to pounce; our enemies and "friends" are waiting for the right time to strike us.

In the mean time, America is literally being internally trampled flat by the Government Class, its supporters, and in some cases, a poorly informed public. So instead of a death by a thousand cuts, America is being trampled to death by a thousand boots.

What would a map of "historical arrows" look like hundreds of years from now for students studying history of a country once called the United States of America just before its collapse? Where will the arrows originate from? But more importantly, what internal forces would the changes be attributed to?

There are many that will paint the points discussed here as racist, xenophobic, homophobic blah blah blah. But my intent is to present these issues as concepts of right and wrong not as a diatribe against peoples. Therefore, let us look, not in any particular order, at the 1000 boots that will trample America into Flatland, then into Lineland, then into Pointland and eventually into the has-beens of history.

1. Bilingualism and the Balkanization of America

2. Multiculturalism and the destruction of western values

3. Pathological Feminism

4. Destruction of the father/mother married pair as the preferred family unit and the isolation of fathers, or males in general, from child rearing responsibilities

5. At-whim divorce, at-whim marriage, and accepted widespread out-of-wedlock births

6. A distracted and politically inactive population

7. Acceptance and widespread adaptation of Hollywood pop culture as a substitute for fundamental social ethics

8. Government welfare as a right and government solutions as the norm

9. Corrupt, antiquated or unfair tax systems that reward indolence and punish achievement

10. Intelligentsia generated self-loathing, especially in higher education and in the media, in enough quantity to provide aid and comfort to our enemies

11. Inability to control borders, establish orderly immigration processes, enforce common sense laws in such basic but important processes as voting

12. A hyperactive judiciary and dysfunctional legislative bodies

13. A chaotic, self-serving, and failing education system

14. No minimally enforceable or accepted public standards of conduct

15. Inability to distinguish or acknowledge a minimum set of rights and wrongs

16. Inability to discuss problems in rational open dialogue; sometimes often due to coercive or intimidating laws or policies

17. Inability to identify and frame arguments against foreign enemies

18. Political inability to wage winning foreign wars

19. Inability to limit government growth and power at the national, state and local levels

20. Failure to right legitimate social grievances without regard to creating new ones

Notice there are no lead pipes in the list. Now I know a lot of you are saying "Wait just one minute. You said you were going to list 1000 boots. I may have gone to a government school, but I know the difference between 20 and 1000." Well multiply 20 by the 50 states and you'll get your 1000 boots.

28

In the year 2525,
if Man is still alive

Cyborg Host: Welcome back everyone; let's see how our contestants responded to the jackpot question in our final All-or-Nothing round: "What was the cause for the fall of the United States of America?" Let's see what our contestants have put down.

Cyborg 314159265358: Invasions from northern barbarians.

Cyborg Host: Sorry, Canadians suffered from many of the same aliments that were seen in the United States, and fell just before the United States collapsed into anarchy; eh. You leave here with nothing.

Cyborg 271828182845: The Dennis Kucinich presidency, in particular his Department of Peace.

Cyborg Host: Well a lot of humans who lived in that time period might have thought that, but sorry that's not what we were looking for. You also leave here with nothing.

Cyborg 161803398874: Toxic trans fat.

Cyborg Host: Oh, I'm sorry, that's incorrect also. Look's like all three of our contestants will leave today with nothing.

As we have seen these past 30-40 years, there has been a culture war in America that has forever changed and weakened the country. Much of the change was built on hatred of America and Western culture in general. And to the victor belongs the spoils.

Although the 20 items listed in the last chapter fall under societal, cultural, personal, or governmental failures, together they all represent national failures. These failures were achieved incrementally through the actions of a gigantic ratchet. They cannot be reversed by incremental corrections, so claiming victory if the Republicans roll back the upper marginal tax rate from 35% to 33% is being somewhat overly optimistic.

I have some friends that could be labeled as members of the Religious Right. A basic tenant of the Religious Right is that America is great because the Founders acknowledged God and they put that belief in writing and practice. I'd like to add to those attributes the following pragmatic ones:

1. They employed the concept of a "republic."

2. They fostered the development of an open capitalistic economic system.

3. They based the establishment of the nation on a western philosophical system deeply rooted in individual freedom and individual responsibility.

4. They established a legal and political system that, when executed properly, respected the rule of law.

I believe what we have today are mere remnants of what our Founders' built. As P.J. O'Rourke observed in the *Parliament of Whores*, authority has always attracted scum that has terrorized mankind since the dawn of time. These "prostitutes" would do anything to achieve and maintain power. However, as O'Rourke so eloquently concludes: "Every government is a parliament of whores. The trouble is, in a democracy the whores are us."

So is the future decline of America inevitable? I think history supports the following postulates:

•   All nations are fragile.

•   All nations die.

•   America is more than just a great nation, it's a great civilization.

As with all great civilizations, America has many foreign enemies. But our foreign enemies are incapable of destroying us without help from ourselves. I end these musings from the conservative next door with the last postulate courtesy of British historian Arnold J. Toynbee:

•   Civilizations die from suicide, not murder.

Many of us would like to think that God intercedes in historic clashes between right and wrong. He may have been there to ensure our victories at Valley Forge, the Battle of New Orleans, the Alamo, Gettysburg, the Meuse-Argonne Offensive, the Normandy Invasion, Inchon, the Tet Offensive, and on both roads to

Baghdad. He may have also been there when our founding fathers pledged their lives, fortunes and sacred honor, when Lincoln issued the *Emancipation Proclamation*, when the 19th Amendment was passed, in the chambers of the U.S. Supreme Court deciding *Brown v. Board of Education of Topeka,* or when Martin Luther King made his "I have a dream" speech.

There is something about the human spirit that fights on even when all odds are against it. So is America going to break the mold of the rise and fall of great civilizations? I don't know. I hope my vision is one of events that might occur as opposed to a set of events that will occur. But a necessary condition to turn the tide is breaking the destructive clutches of the Government Class.

What this country needs is a revolution. Not a bloody one, but one led by people willing to figuratively lose a foot, like Calamity Jane in Beavercreek. Because if we don't give the Government Class the boot, I do not believe that the Divine Providence of our Founding Fathers intercedes in suicides.

Epilogue

It's time to take a look at the quote at the very beginning of the book. It reads: *Papà, la luna che splende sull' l'Italia è la stessa luna che splende sugli Stati Uniti.* The message is to my deceased father. The translation is: *Dad, the moon that shines on Italy is the same moon that shines on the United States.*

The statement is a slight modification of a running joke my father had with my brothers and me. It comes from a story he first told me after I graduated with my Bachelor of Science degree in 1976.

Here is the story, translated from Italian as best as I can remember:

> A poor uneducated farmer worked all his life to save enough money to send his son to the university in the nearby capital. After four years and many sacrifices, the father, beaten down by years of toiling in the fields, proudly rode his only donkey to the capital to pick-up his son on the day of his son's graduation. Upon greeting his son, the father encountered a different young man than the one he left four years earlier. The young man standing in front of him was arrogant and consumed with his own presence. Nevertheless, although old and tired, the father told the son that he (the father) was not worthy to ride the donkey home and in honor of his son's achievement that his son should have the honors. The now arrogant son, agreeing that he was far too important to walk, jumped on the donkey.
>
> As the miles went by and darkness fell, the moon came over the horizon. The son noticed the moon and looking at his tired old father asked: "Dad, is the moon over the capital the same moon over our town?"

As I mentioned before, my parents had no formal education, but they were far smarter than I will ever be, because they had smarts not learned in school or acquired in a pampered environment. They understood the real American dream: that people of all races, religions, and cultures could make it here. Sure, it would take hard work, but they knew that America was a great country.

They came to America at a time when you were forced to learn English and going on welfare was not an option. But they knew that America was a great country.

They came to America at a time when discrimination was rampant to them and to others. But they knew that America was a great country.

They came to America at a time when they could not afford the luxury to consider themselves as victims, even as they were laid off from one job to another. But they knew that America was a great country.

They knew America was a great country because they had something worse to compare it to: Fascist Italy.

Like my parents and prior generations of immigrants, today's immigrants also know that America is a great country, because they too have a basis of comparison. It's ironic that our Intelligentsia can't seem to grasp this simple concept. But the American Intelligentsia is much like the son in my father's story: arrogant, self-centered, and consumed with their own self-interests, always confusing book learning with common sense and true intelligence.

My parents had a goal of all three sons graduating from high school, the idea that all three would eventually graduate from college went beyond their wildest dreams. But, my dad often told all three of his sons that no matter what we learned in school or achieved in life, he was still our father. As I got older, I began to understand exactly what he meant.

I have learned my lesson. It doesn't take a village to raise children; it takes a set of parents. Thanks mom and dad.